GILBERTA has written a strong portrayal of the sacrifices and support of the fighter pilot's wife. I'm glad that this story has been told.
—Leo K. Thorsness, Col. USAF, (Ret.), Medal of Honor, POW of Vietnam War

THIS is the story of young wives and husbands embarking on military careers, leading to travels and challenges they could never have imagined, and at the same time sharing, supporting, and being supported by close friends in the difficult times of war and separation. Guth tells it like it was and is today.
—Evelyn S. Garrison, wife of Larry Garrison, Maj. Gen. USAF, (Ret.)

GILBERTA Guth uses her God-given talent to share forty-five years of memories as the wife of fighter pilot Joe Guth. Laugh and cry with Guth through the births of their children, the humor of moving a refrigerator into a French home, and the ever-present danger of piloting fighter planes.
—William (Bill) H. Talley, Col. USAF, (Ret.), former Vietnam POW

A true love story, filled with intensity and excitement. The amazing collection of letters between the author and her fighter pilot husband describe their emotions and adventures while fighting a war and raising a family. Exceptionally well-written.
—Clare Gardner, widow of Larry Gardner, Col. USAF, three war veteran

GILBERTA Guth has penned a magnificent book of enormous power. *The Fighter Pilot's Wife* should be required reading for all Americans, especially for those who seek an insider's view of Air Force life.
—Tom Yarborough, Col. USAF, (Ret.), author of *Danang Diary*

GIL'S memoir captures the essence of life for all fighter pilots' wives—the pride and delights and fears of being married to unusual men who went forth every day, steely-eyed and confident, to soar in a dangerous heaven while we and their children remained firmly grounded on earth and waited anxiously for their return.
—Louise I. Duquette, wife of Norman Duquette, Lt. Col. USAF, (Ret.)

THE story of a remarkable husband and wife, deeply in love, sharing military life with all of the good and the bad: the upheavals of moving; the excitement of foreign lands; the military community of support and lifetime friends.
—Larry Garrison, Maj. Gen. USAF, (Ret.), Korea and Vietnam

With her usual grace, Gil has reached into her heart to share her memories as wife of an Air Force fighter pilot. In close formation with Joe, she successfully overcame the many hurdles of an Air Force career.
—Norman E. Duquette, Lt. Col. USAF, (Ret.), WW II, Korea POW, Vietnam

The Fighter Pilot's Wife brought back so many memories of that special time in my life. The innocence, loyalty, fears, and sense of duty were all touched on with great honesty.
—Patricia Davey, wife of Thomas Davey, Lt. Col. USAF, (Ret.)

THE

Fighter Pilot's Wife

A Military Family's Story

Gilberta Guth

CS

CALL SIGN PRESS

The Fighter Pilot's Wife: A Military Family's Story
By Gilberta Guth

Published by:
Call Sign Press
145 Oak Shade Lane
Novato, CA 94945
www.fighterpilotswife.com
707 939 9212

Publisher's Cataloging-in-Publication
(Provided by Quality Books, Inc.)
      Guth, Gilberta.
       The fighter pilot's wife : a military family's story
/ by Gilberta Guth. -- 1st ed.
     p. cm.
     LCCN 2005927774
     ISBN 0-9768678-0-X

     1. Guth, Gilberta. 2. Air Force spouses--United States--Biography. 3. United States. Air Force--Military life. 4. Guth, Joe, 1924-1998. 5. Families of military personnel--United States--Biography.
I. Title.

UG626.2.G88A3 2005   358.4'0092
                 QBI05-600099

DEDICATION

For Joe

TABLE OF CONTENTS

* * * *

1951-1953
Preflight Walkaround: Go-No-Go

1953-1969
Airborne: A Global Flight

1969–1998

Touchdown:
There is Life After the Air Force

* * * *

FOREWORD

* * * *

When we would learn what war does to the human heart, we must look to what women write. That has been so in every American war—every war everywhere—when women who could not go to the killing fields themselves, have sent their husbands, sons, brothers, and lovers. Such women live constantly on the edge of anguish, fear, hope, and agony, their hearts in their throats with news of every battle, every musket shot and cannon's thunder—or in Gilberta Guth's case, every take off and landing. Needing desperately to deal with this almost unbearable tension in some way, women in every war have written their deepest feelings and emotions into diaries, letters, journals, and memoirs. And some of what they have written has scaled the heights of living literature.

It has been my privilege in my own writing and research to read many such works by women in the Civil War. It is a heart-wrenching, but stirring experience, to listen to the power of their passion, the depth of their love.

That passion and power sings through every page of this memoir by Gilberta Guth. She is dealing with an entirely different world and different kind of fighting than her sisters in the Civil War could imagine, one more instantly lethal. As she believes, and many agree, there are few professions more dangerous than being a fighter pilot. But her fear, passion, and emotions are the very same that all such women, from the beginning of wars, have shared.

Her husband, Joe Guth, was a fighter pilot with the reputation of a Top Gun. All around him dear friends and fellow pilots were going on missions and not returning, dying in flaming crashes. And on so many of those tragedies Joe's wife, in tears herself, rushed to the side of the shocked, bereaved, inconsolable young wife, so suddenly left a husband-less widow with children. Shadowing her spirit always was the intense fear that she might be the next young wife facing this unbearable thing, needing this kind of love and support.

It never happened. Joe Guth was one of the lucky ones who lived to die many years later, in his seventies, long after his fighter pilot days and his long career in the Air Force had ended. He and Gilberta, the fighter pilot's wife, saw four children grown to accomplished adulthood. And now, after he has gone, she has written in his memory this lovely book, leaving for us, as so many women in other wars have, a loving, vibrant, telling account of all they hoped and feared and endured in a lifetime together. She takes us through it all, from the moment she met Joe Guth in the 1950s, fell in love with him, married him, and committed herself to sharing his danger-filled life. Here in this memoir she shares with us the fear, the tears, the anguish, but also the love and romance and final fulfillment, of their unique partnership.

It is a special kind of terror these women have endured when their men have gone to war. And it is a luminous legacy they have left for us in their writings. Gilberta Guth has done it again here, wrenchingly, elo-quently, and passionately—and in that same tradition of excellence. She has given us a loving and moving memoir from her heart to ours.

—John C. Waugh
Author of *Surviving the Confederacy: Rebellion, Ruin, and Recovery—Roger and Sara Pryor during the Civil War*

PROLOGUE

* * * *

Iawoke to see brilliant slivers of daylight beginning to filter in between the slats of the blinds. It was going to be another searingly hot, parched desert day. But I had been born and raised in Tucson, Arizona, so I was used to those scorching summers.

However, this day would be different. Fresh out of the University of Arizona, Class of 1951, I was starting my first teaching job today.

I had hoped to get a job in Phoenix. It would be a way to get out of Tucson, but still be close enough for visits to my family and the town where I had grown up. I was offered, instead, a teaching job at an Air Force pilot training base in the middle of the Arizona desert. This had been a big disappointment to me. I envisioned a barren, dusty existence in tents, with barracks and a Quonset hut schoolhouse. Not a very choice first teaching job. But my best friend, Joan, liked the sound of the opportunity and applied as well. She was offered a position teaching at the same school, so we both decided to take the jobs and be roommates.

It was a surprise to see that the base looked just like a small town. There were apartment buildings, a movie theater, bank, gas station, post office, commissary, and base exchange. There were clubs for officers, cadets, and enlisted men, complete with restaurants, dance floors, and banquet rooms. The school was a complex of temporary buildings, but a new, modern, campus-style school was under construction and would be opening the following year. The base was well landscaped, with residential streets and neat, well-kept homes for families. Not at all like I had imagined it.

So now here it was, Monday, the first day of school. I was lying in bed, drifting between sleep and wakefulness.

And then I heard it. Breaking into my reverie, it began as a low rumble. The rumble grew louder, becoming a roar, getting louder and louder. The blinds began to tremble, and the room seemed to quiver. Was it an earthquake? Leaning over to the window next to my bed, I peered out between the blinds in time to see a silvery streak of airplane, taking off into a steep arc, climbing into what seemed a straight upward path. The roar turned into an echoing sound as the mighty engine lifted the jet until it leveled off and disappeared from sight, leaving its sinuous trail of heat waves behind it, making everything in its path look wavy and distorted.

At that moment, a naive twenty-one-year-old, I didn't know that those sounds and those sights would be backdrops to my life for decades to come, decades marked by happiness, joy, fear, courage, tragedy, triumph… and love.

*   *   *   *

PREFLIGHT WALKAROUND:

GO-NO-GO

1951–1953

* * * *

Chapter One

WILLY

Six blue stars hung in the window of the rambling old house near the University of Arizona in Tucson. I had grown up here, in my grandparents' house.

World War II broke out when I was eleven years old, and I watched as one by one, six of my seven uncles enlisted and left for military service. The two youngest, Bill and Philip, were just five and seven years older than I, and they left for the Army right out of high school. The two eldest of the six, Harry and Manny, enlisted in the Army even though they were over the draft age. Of the two middle brothers, George served as a Navy Seabee, and Frank became an officer and made the Army his career. The eldest in the family, Calvin, who lived and worked in Guatemala as the chief civil engineer for the Central American Railway, was considered past the age for military service.

I was named after my father, Gilbert Cosulich. He was a lawyer, journalist, and writer, and could speak seven languages. I had lived with my grandparents since my parents' divorce shortly after my birth. Tucson was the same small desert city where my mother, Mary, and her two sisters, Carmel and Catherine, were born and raised, along with their seven brothers.

I saw my mother irregularly during my early years. She worked as a secretary in Washington, D.C., San Francisco, and Phoenix as well as Tucson, and later on in Paris. My father rarely visited as I was growing up. However, I always felt included in my grandparents' large family of ten children. I looked upon my aunts and uncles as my older brothers and sisters.

My grandfather, Harry Lesley, was a policeman, a quiet man who worked hard all his life to provide his large family with the necessities of life. My grandmother, Theresa Lesley, was the traditional homebody of that era. From her I learned the deep Catholic faith which was her source of strength throughout her life. That source of strength would become mine as well.

When the war started, the younger of my two aunts, Catherine, went to work in an aircraft assembly plant. She was one of the thousands of women in the wartime workforce who became known as "Rosie the Riveter." My other aunt, Carmel, remained behind to help fill the shortage of teachers as she waited for her fiancé to return from the war. My mother, Mary, the eldest of the three daughters, held secretarial jobs in crucial wartime government offices.

It was a family totally involved in the war effort, and although I was only in my early teens, I became sharply aware of the patriotism and spirit of sacrifice which were engulfing the nation during that time. I remember the ration books that everyone was required to have—coupons were carefully torn from each person's book for every purchase of food, shoes, and gas.

None of the blue stars in the window of the house were replaced with a red one, symbolizing "wounded in action" or, worst of all, a gold one, symbolizing "killed in action."

My grandmother and grandfather saw all six of their sons return safely at the end of the war. Their youngest daughter returned from her job at the airplane assembly plant to her profession as a hairdresser, and their second daughter married her intended upon his return from the war. As the wartime offices began to close, my mother returned to work in peacetime government offices throughout her secretarial career.

But the family suffered a heavy blow a year after the war ended. My grandmother died at the age of sixty-one. The entire family, including myself, was deeply grieved. She had been a mother to me, and losing her when I was sixteen years old was a loss that I would never forget. She had also been like a grandmother to many of my school friends, and at her church funeral two full rows of my classmates sat sharing their grief and supporting me in mine.

We all felt that the worry and stress of the war led to her illness and death at such an early age. I remember her silently saying her Rosary as she rested in the afternoon, or as she sat on the front porch in the cool desert evening. I have always believed that it was her prayers that brought her six sons home. I returned to that image of her with her Rosary throughout my life, and it was to become my inspiration through difficult times.

My Tucson High School class was the first since before the war to enjoy all three years of high school during peacetime. I was somewhat quiet and shy when I started high school, but was a good student. As opportunities for extracurricular activities and leadership evolved, I became more outgoing and confident. Like the majority of my class, I attended the University of Arizona, which was just six blocks from my home. I gradually developed into one of the campus leaders, writing on the school paper and participating in several other college activities. During my senior year I was president of the Delta Delta Delta sorority, and lived in the sorority house. Just before graduation I was elected, along with some of my classmates, and much to my surprise, to the national "Who's Who among Students in North American Universities and Colleges." When the congratulatory letter arrived, I almost threw it away, thinking it was just an ad to join some sort of graduating students' organization.

I had started to prepare for a journalism career. But at the urging of my family, I changed my major and earned a bachelor of arts degree in education and an Arizona teaching credential, so that I "would have something to fall back on." At that time the common view was that teaching and nursing were still among the more stable careers for women.

The Korean "Police Action," as it was called, was heating up during 1951, so most of the men in my college class left for the armed forces immediately after graduation.

A few days before graduation day the dean of the College of Education called me into his office. The superintendent of the Maricopa County School District, which included Phoenix, was coming to Tucson, and I was being recommended for an interview. My friend Joan was as excited as I was about the prospect of getting out of Tucson, so she asked the dean if she too could be interviewed by the superintendent.

Friends since we were seven years old, Joan Manes and I were very close. We were both tall, slender brunettes, so many people took us for sisters. We had gone through elementary school, junior high, high school, and college together, and both of us had joined the Tri Delta sorority. During our high school and college days, we had shared an interest in modern dance and frequently double dated. We both wanted to work in Phoenix, a bigger city. Instead, we both were offered jobs at Williams Air Force Base Elementary School. I would teach second grade, and Joan would have the first grade. Williams A.F.B. was a hundred miles northwest of Tucson, and about thirty miles from Phoenix.

Joan and I shared our disappointment about our job offers. But in talking it over, we reasoned that if we took the jobs at the base, we stood a chance of getting to Phoenix the following year. Our starting salary would be $2,750 per year. It seemed like a lot of money to us.

One big question was where we would live. After fruitless searches in nearby Chandler and Mesa, we asked Superintendent Barry for help. The first of September was fast approaching, and we still didn't have a place to live. With just a week left before school was to start, we were offered base housing, thanks to his efforts. Our apartment would be in the officers' family housing area, and our rent would be very low.

We pooled our resources and bought a black 1946 Dodge coupe. We pillaged our families' homes of furniture, bedding, lamps, and dishes. From my family's home, we took a dozen pairs of pink and green tropical-flowered drapes from the closed-in porch at the back of the house that had served as my room. Very early on the Friday before school was to start, we packed everything into a rented trailer, first from Joan's house and then from mine. My family stood on the front porch to wave us off, including Judy, my eight-year-old red cocker spaniel, who sat on the porch looking as if her heart was breaking.

"My God," said my Uncle George, looking down at the dog, "look at her face."

I turned to Joan, who said resignedly, "Okay. Let's take her with us." Joan was not a dog lover as I was, and her favorite pets were cats.

But I knew she would learn to like Judy, a well-behaved, devoted dog. A couple of strong classmates of ours followed us in their car on the two-hour drive to Williams Air Force Base. At the entrance to the base there was a sign that read, *The Fighter School Williams Air Force Base Welcomes You.*

We had to tell the Air Police on duty at the entrance who we were and why we were there, and show our drivers' licenses before they waved us on through. Neither Joan nor I had ever been on a military base before, so this was all very strange and new to us.

We were filled with anticipation as we drove to our apartment near the flightline. When we walked in we were pleasantly surprised: it was a spacious, partially furnished, three-bedroom place on the second floor of a large, framed building. Our friends helped us carry our possessions up and into the rooms where they belonged, shared some sandwiches with us, and then departed.

With just the few furnishings that were there and our meager belongings to work with, the task of turning the huge space into a home appeared overwhelming at first glance. But, undaunted, we dug into the task. We built a bookcase out of boards and bricks to divide the living and dining rooms. We hung the flowered drapes in every room and polished the hardwood floors until they shone. We placed books, cushions and plants around, and when we were finished, we proudly surveyed our first bachelor girls' home.

"It looks pretty good!" Joan and I told each other.

We spent a few hours at the school that weekend, readying our classrooms with supplies, bright pictures, and alphabet letters. The school principal, Mrs. Lowers, held a meeting for all of the teachers. Most of us were, like Joan and me, single young women just out of college.

I was excited, but a little nervous about being in my very own classroom for the first time. I'd had a semester of practice teaching during my senior year, but this was the real thing. The first lesson I taught my students was how to pronounce my last name. Since all my second graders were not yet reading with ease, I had to carefully write each syllable on the board and slowly take them through the pronunciation of "Miss Co-su-lich... Miss Cosulich." I liked my little students, and I felt that they were going to like me.

As Joan and I settled into the routine of teaching school, we started getting acquainted with the parents of our students and the other residents of Williams Air Force Base, or "Willy," as it was called. Our students were the children of flying instructors, crews, and other personnel involved in the administration of the flight training base. We began to receive invitations from the parents to have dinner at their homes and to various functions at the Officers Club and the Cadet Club. I liked it when I was introduced by an instructor's wife as "my baby's teacher." We also started meeting many of the flying students.

Within a couple of weeks Joan, the other single teachers, and I were besieged with requests for dates. We began to realize that Willy wasn't a bad place to be after all. In fact, Joan and I agreed that it was going to be "more fun than college!"

We didn't spend a lot of time in the kitchen of our apartment. We subsisted on fruit juice, milk, cereal, toast, peanut butter, instant coffee, and a dish we named "teacherfurters." It consisted of a split hotdog with a piece of cheese crammed down the center, topped with a slice of tomato, and broiled in the oven. Our rent was a real bargain, and we didn't need to buy much gas. So the rest of our salary was spent, of course, on clothes. The biweekly paycheck of $110 slipped through our fingers rapidly, and payday found us eagerly collecting our checks and rushing to the bank to cash them.

We shopped in Phoenix for the feminine, full-skirted styles of the day: dresses and skirts, some with stiff petticoats underneath, and tailored blouses and soft sweaters to give us a neat, polished look for teaching school. For evenings we bought dressier full skirts and dresses, frilly tops, and high-heeled shoes.

One month we were so low on cash that Joan and I, heads hanging with embarrassment, had to ask the principal to advance us $20 so we could buy enough food to last until the next payday.

There were several different groups of flying students at Willy. The cadets were young men who had degrees or some college but no previous military experience. They would be commissioned as second lieutenants when they finished their flight training. The commissioned officers, called student officers, had previous military experience and were

FLIGHT SUIT-CLAD GILBERTA AND JOAN "LOOK INTO THE WILD BLUE YONDER."

at Willy solely to learn to become jet pilots. There were also French, Belgian, and Dutch cadets, sent by their governments to learn to fly, and then return to serve in their respective air forces. All of these student pilots had completed the basic six months of flight training at other U.S. bases, and were at Willy for the second six months of advanced training. Following this, both the cadets and the student officers would graduate from Willy and receive their pilot's wings.

Joan and I soon put up a chart, which we called "The List," on the inside of the coat closet door. We listed the names of the young men we were going out with and charted their looks, behavior, and personalities. We made entries such as "Good-looking but has hands like an octopus. Beware!" The two single teachers who lived in the apartment across the hall would come over and refer to "The List" if they were going out with anyone whose name was on the chart.

We thrived on the attention we received from these exciting young men. It was quite a leap from our dating experiences in high school and college, which were mostly with classmates we'd known for years.

One Saturday, Joan and I decided to go play tennis. The tennis courts were strategically located next to the bachelor officers' quarters, or BOQ, as they were called. Several of the student officers were hanging out their windows, calling to Joan and me as we awkwardly batted the tennis ball back and forth: "Thatta girl! Good serve! Way to go!"

Suddenly, on the ground in front of me lay one of my falsies. Mortified, I picked it up and said to Joan, "Let's get out of here!" We never played tennis there again.

With our working hours and the early flight schedules of the student pilots, we didn't usually stay out late during the week. Most evenings we just had dinner at the Officers Club or in the nearby town of Chandler. On weekends, however, after dinner or a dance, we frequently ended up with our dates back at our apartment, talking and playing the popular records of the time, like "Sweet Caroline," "Moulin Rouge," the songs of Teresa Brewer, and music by the big bands.

One morning about a month after we arrived at Willy, the school principal called Joan, the two teachers from the neighboring apartment, and me into her office.

"The superintendent of schools, Mr. Barry, has called me," said Mrs. Louise Lowers. "He has received reports that you girls have been having men in your apartments until the wee hours of the morning."

We sat stunned as she continued, "He wants all four of you to go into Phoenix to meet with him."

All of us started to cry. We couldn't believe what we were hearing. Peggy Duane, one of the spunkier among us, spoke up.

"Mrs. Lowers," she said with a trembling voice. "You know all of us. Nothing untoward has ever happened in our apartments. These accusations just aren't true!"

Mrs. Lowers smiled kindly. "I know you are all fine girls. But you must go into Phoenix and meet with Superintendent Barry. You'll have to assure him that in the future you will not give any reason whatsoever for there to be questions about your conduct, and that you'll be very careful about your reputations here on the base."

None of us had a clue as to why anyone had made these complaints about us. The only thing we could figure out was that some of our downstairs neighbors in the building heard our music and voices when we invited our dates in after an evening out, and probably jumped to the wrong conclusions. It was the early fifties, a more innocent time when "reputations" could be questioned over even a slight infraction of behavioral rules.

The next day the four of us drove to the state capitol building in Phoenix. As we walked down the long dim corridor to the Maricopa County Superintendent of Schools' office, we felt like we were walking to our execution.

Mr. Barry stood up when we were ushered into his office, and began the meeting by saying, "I've had calls about late-night visitors in your apartments. This has got to stop. You were given base quarters as a privilege, and as teachers you are expected to maintain unquestionable behavior."

The tears started again as all four of us shook our heads in disbelief, still unable to comprehend how someone could have made such complaints about us.

Again Peggy stood up and, struggling to maintain her composure, said, "Mr. Barry, we are all fine women. We resent the suggestion that anything unseemly has ever occurred in our apartments. Who has made these accusations?"

He refused to answer, but continued, "Mrs. Lowers and I believe that you all deserve another chance to prove that your reputations are above reproach. I'll be in touch with her about this. In the future, remember that, as teachers, your behavior on the base is under close scrutiny."

We wiped our tears, assured him that we would be careful, thanked him and left.

The next day we met with Mrs. Lowers to tell her about the results of the meeting.

Her voice was kind as she said, "I'm sure that from now on all of you will be very cautious not to give the wrong impression of our teachers here on the base."

It was very embarrassing to learn that there had been complaints about us. But from then on, we were careful about keeping our voices and our music down when we had late-night visitors. And we made sure that visitors usually were gone by midnight. That was the last time we heard of any dissatisfaction with us.

It took a while to become accustomed to the shrill whine of the jets taxiing from the flightline onto the runway, and the deafening, rumbling, roaring sound they made as they took off. There was the smell of jet fuel in many areas of the base, and virtually every man in sight was either in uniform or in a flight suit. And no matter where we were on the base, we could hear the constant noise of the planes.

My second graders didn't seem to notice the noise of the jets at all, as though it was so much a part of their lives that they were used to it. They would continue their reading, coloring, and writing their numbers and ABC's without looking up, even when the rumbling made the blinds on the classroom windows quiver.

Then, one day we heard fire trucks. My students looked up at the sound. I went to the window, and saw a column of black smoke rising from the direction of the runway. The children jumped from their seats and crowded at the window, as though they recognized what that sound and that sight meant. It took great effort to get them back to their seats and calmed down. I was stunned to learn later that the father of one of the children in the school, an instructor pilot, had died, along with his student, in a crash just off the end of the runway. I learned to dread the sound of fire trucks, or crash trucks as they were called, and the sight of that column of black smoke.

We were hit hard the first time someone we knew was killed in a crash. Once again, sirens and black smoke signaled catastrophe. When we got home after school we learned that the new boyfriend of one of the teachers who lived across the hall from us had died in the crash. I had seen him just a few evenings before, picking up our neighbor for a date. Joan and I were both shocked. We didn't know what to say or what to do. I felt helpless and inadequate. The impact of this sudden loss deeply affected our neighbor, and she was unable to teach school for several days. A cloud of gloom was cast over the carefree lives we thought we were living.

A few weeks later I went to a dance at the Officers Club with a tall, handsome young student officer. I was wearing my favorite dress, a frosty pink organdy, with a full skirt, tiny waistline, and big, puffy sleeves, and high-heeled, white sandals. As I stood watching the band while my date went to get us drinks, there suddenly was a young, blond student officer next to me saying, "Hi, do you go out with people here on the base?"

"When I know them," was my cool reply.

Holding out his hand to shake mine, he said, "How do you do. I'm Joe Guth."

* * * *

Chapter Two

HELLO

I shook Joe Guth's hand, not quite knowing what to say. My date returned with our drinks, set them on a table, and said, "Let's dance."

He was promptly cut in on by the brash First Lieutenant Joe Guth.

"Hi, Joe," said my date. "Well, okay, you can have this dance with her, but I'll be waiting for you to bring her back."

As we started to dance, Joe Guth blurted out, "I like you! I like your manner and your manners!" He sounded as though he was surprised by his own words.

But I wasn't so sure that I liked him. I thought it was pretty nervy of him to cut in on my date. "Just who does he think he is, anyway?" I thought to myself.

Within a few days, he called and asked me out to dinner. It was kind of flattering that he seemed so persistent in spite of my rather cool reaction to him. When he arrived at the door to pick me up, Joan let him in and came to my room.

"Wait until you see his shoes!" she whispered with excitement. I went into the living room, and there he stood, not in uniform, but in an impeccably tailored light grey suit, white shirt and silk tie, and russet brown shoes that had been polished to a glossy sheen. I learned later that they were Threadneedles, British-made shoes which, at that time, were only available in St. Louis. They had caps on the heels and on the toes, which made confident, clicking sounds when he walked.

"He looks," I thought, "like an ad for expensive men's clothes." To my amazement, I found out later that he had, indeed, been in some newspaper photo ads for men's clothing in his hometown of St. Louis. That first evening, Joe Guth took me to an Italian restaurant in Chandler. I was impressed by how he could talk about anything, and seemed so... worldly.

Joe Guth had entered the Army Air Corps during World War II after one year at the University of Missouri, and was trained as a gunner on the B-24 bomber. He went to Officers' Candidate School, and after being commissioned as a second lieutenant, he qualified for flight training, to his great joy. However, he was disappointed to learn that the quota for pilots was filled at the time, so he trained as a navigator on the B-17. Stationed in Panama, his plane's mission was submarine patrol until the end of the war. He returned from overseas and completed a bachelor's degree in psychology at the University of Missouri. He remained in the Air Force Reserve and sold insurance until 1951. With the Korean War raging, he was recalled to active duty in the Air Force.

It was then that his lifelong dream of becoming a pilot was finally realized. He was at Willy for advanced jet pilot training, following six months of basic flight training at Greenville, Mississippi.

I wasn't sure about this Joe Guth. First, he was five and a half years older than I. As a twenty-one-year-old, twenty-seven seemed much older to me. He was from the big city of St. Louis, and appeared to me to be much too sophisticated—different from my college classmates or even the few young men I had met at Willy. He was blond and blue-eyed, not usually my preference. And, most importantly, he was under six feet tall, usually a cause for immediate disqualification by a girl who had reached her full, self-conscious height of five feet seven by the time she was fourteen, and who loved to wear high heels. Besides, this guy was so sure of himself, almost too much so.

There was something very unsettling about the way he seemed to know everything. When we went for evening walks under the resplendent Arizona sky, he would point out all the constellations by name. He had a highly competitive nature and was a success at everything he did, winning the base championships in both handball and golf. His confidence and self-assurance were unflappable, his energy and enthusiasm boundless. He had a wonderful sense of humor, and everyone seemed to know him. I was overwhelmed, but also very attracted.

One evening I had a date with someone else to go to the Baseline, a popular restaurant close to Willy. As we were entering, a group of others from the base were coming out, and one of them shouted, "Come on everybody! Joe Guth is having a party!"

"Joe Guth," I thought, "knows everybody, and everything."

Later, when I asked him about it, he told me that he and his buddy, Bill Pearce, had rented a motel suite and had thrown a very loud, wild party.

"You weren't invited," he said, "because you're my 'nice' girlfriend."

Somehow I was flattered by his remark, but there were also questions in my mind about just how wild this guy really was.

We talked about music, literature, the classics, philosophy, psychology, and about his passion for flying. He made me laugh more than anyone I'd ever known. He named our 1946 Dodge coupe "The Menace to the Highways." He won my dog Judy's heart by scratching her back with his foot. He won Joan's affection with his intelligence and his disarmingly mischievous sense of humor. And he was beginning to win mine with his very persistent, confident style of courtship. He persisted in his pursuit of me with the same self-assurance and self-confidence that he exhibited in everything else.

"How would you feel about the possibility of being married to a pilot?" he asked me one evening.

I didn't quite know how to answer his question, so I mumbled something about there probably being a lot of moving around in that situation.

"Do you want me to be a Catholic?" he asked. "I can be a Catholic."

There was an urgency to his courtship which was new to me, and a little overpowering. I had recently broken up with my college boyfriend, and I was unready for another serious relationship so soon.

He asked Joan out for a date, and, to my surprise, this disturbed me a little. However, when Joan came home she said, "All Joe did all evening was pump me about you, and how he could make progress with you. He told me, 'Competition has never bothered me. I'm used to getting what I want.'"

STUDENT OFFICER, JOE GUTH, IS GILBERTA'S DINNER GUEST AT WILLY.

I was surprised when she told me this. It seemed to me that it was very arrogant of him to talk to my friend this way. Now I was even more unsure about my feelings for him. I didn't even know if I liked him at all. But my uncertainty didn't seem to deter him.

The time was approaching when his flight training would be completed. He would be leaving Willy, and my school year would be ending at about the same time.

It was on one of our starlit walks that Joe Guth asked me to marry him. In a way, I hated to say no, but I couldn't say yes. It seemed to me that we had known each other such a short time. I was very cautious about the idea of marriage, probably because of the failure of my parents' marriage. A lifelong, happy marriage was an ideal very close to my heart. I just didn't feel that I knew him well enough to say yes, and then wait for a year for his return from combat duty in Korea.

The next evening, he told me, "You don't know how you hurt and disappointed me last night." He looked deeply wounded, and appeared incredulous that I could possibly have turned him down. His reaction only added to my confusion about how I really felt about him.

"Why can't he accept and respect my feelings?" I asked Joan in frustration.

"I don't know," she said. "But it's obvious that he really loves you, Gilberta."

As the time drew near for parting, he seemed to become more and more frustrated with my uncertainty and my refusal to make any promises to him. It looked as if this romance might be drawing to an end before it even had really begun.

* * * *

Chapter Three

GOODBYE

The end of the school year arrived soon after Joe asked me to marry him. He was about to finish pilot training at Willy, and I was preparing to leave for the summer, to stay in Guatemala with my uncle Calvin and his wife. The eldest of my seven uncles, Calvin was one of the American executives with the Central American Railway.

I encountered Joe at the Willy Base Exchange one day, and told him I would be leaving for Guatemala City in a few days.

"Oh, Guatemala City, eh?" he said. "I've been there. The city's not much, but you'll probably have a good time."

I was irritated by his comment, and thought, "This guy is such a know-it-all. Is there any place he hasn't been?"

Nothing had been resolved between us. He had finally taken my refusal of his proposal to heart, and appeared resigned that our relationship was probably not going anywhere.

On May 10, 1952, Joe received his coveted silver pilot's wings, along with the others in his 52-C, or 52-Charlie class. His was the third pilot class to graduate in 1952. Hence the "C," or "Charlie" designation using the third letter of the alphabet. We both left Willy at about the same time. I was headed for Guatemala, he for aerial gunnery training at Luke Air Force Base, Arizona, in preparation for a combat assignment in Korea. There was what was called a "pipeline" to Korea, which sent newly trained pilots directly into combat for a one-year tour.

There was no "understanding" between Joe and me when we parted. So we said goodbye, each of us not knowing if the other would even write. He asked me to write first, if I wanted to stay in touch with him from Guatemala.

Uncle Calvin's and Aunt Lupe's friends were mostly railroad executives, and they led an active social life. My uncle and aunt took me under their wing and included me in all of their social activities. We went to receptions at the U.S. Embassy, and parties and dinners at the homes of their friends. Many of the children of their colleagues were close to my age, so the summer was filled with sailing, picnicking, dances, and parties. I was having a wonderful time. But I was also thinking about Joe Guth, so I decided to write to him at Luke.

I wrote what I thought was a "friendly but not romantic" letter. He answered right away, and we continued writing each other throughout the summer. A lot. And I thought about him. A lot. I was having a great summer. But every day I would walk out to the mailbox to see if there was a letter from him waiting for me. If there wasn't one, I was very disappointed.

After three months of fun, it was time for me to return to Arizona to begin my second year of teaching. Joe had completed his aerial gunnery training at Luke and had gone on a thirty-day leave to St. Louis to visit his parents before leaving for Korea. A few days after I arrived back in Tucson from Guatemala this letter came from him:

```
                                    26 August 52

Hi Gilberta,

I suppose that, although you enjoyed your
travels, you're pleased to be home. You feel
like the wizened traveler who thinks to
himself when with lesser nomads, "poor
unfortunates, they know so little of the
world and life." Welcome.

If you can entertain me scrumptiously on a
coffee substitute, letting me scratch an
itchy dog, ride in a Menace to the Highways
at the fashionable Willy Air Patch for a few
```

days, run your Guatemalan soiled fingers
through my one inch curly locks I'd love it.

I have made reservations with TWA to fly,
yes, commercially, to Phoenix, arriving
there, at Sky Harbor Airport, at 4 p.m.
Friday, 5 Sept. I will leave Sunday or Monday
via TWA for Camp Stoneman, Calif., depending
on connections.

How does that sound? Do you think the Menace
can make it into Sky Harbor so that you can
meet me?

Affectionately, Joe

I was delighted. I wrote him immediately that yes, I would meet him in Phoenix in the Menace on September 5.

As Joan and I drove from Tucson back to Willy to prepare for our second year of teaching, all I could talk about was Joe Guth and how excited I was that I would be seeing him again. I didn't know what to expect from his brief, weekend visit on his way to Korea. I only knew I was very much looking forward to seeing him.

We opened up our apartment, which had been reserved for us over the summer, with all our furniture and belongings still there. The beautiful new school was waiting for us, and we happily prepared our classrooms for the new year.

September 5 arrived at last, and I was getting ready to drive to Sky Harbor Airport to meet Joe. I couldn't decide what to wear—it had to be something special, but also comfortable in the oppressive desert heat of September. I decided to wear the dress I was wearing the night Joe introduced himself to me and cut in as I was dancing with my date at the Officers Club: the pink dotted Swiss organdy, and my white, high-heeled sandals. I let my long dark hair fall in waves around my face, even though it was by no means the coolest way to wear it.

I took one last look in the full-length mirror, got an approving nod from Joan, and then I was on my way in the Menace to Sky Harbor Airport near Phoenix.

He stepped off the plane, tanned and fit in his crisp summer uniform, smiling a dazzling smile. The summer sun had bleached his blond hair lighter, and had brought high color to his skin, making his sky blue eyes look even more intensely blue. We ran to each other's arms, hugging, kissing, and just holding each other for a moment. I felt his strong, muscular body as he pulled me close to him. He stepped back, my hands held in his, his gaze moving slowly from the tip of my shoes to the top of my head, as if he were memorizing what he saw.

"Gee, you look good to me," he said softly.

He picked up his bag and we walked out to the Menace. We both started talking at once, interrupting each other, laughing, savoring those moments of reunion. It was as if, knowing that there would be so little time, we both wanted to say as much as we could, as fast as we could. He opened the passenger's door of the car for me, climbed into the driver's seat, and we started the thirty-mile drive back to Willy.

He talked about his visit with his folks, how his mother had become hysterical as he was leaving, refusing to come out of her bedroom, crying and screaming, "I'm not going to watch you go off to war again!" He and his father had tried in every way they could to comfort her, but she was beyond consolation. Giving her one last hug, and embracing his father, he had gotten into the waiting taxi and left for the St. Louis airport to catch his plane.

He described his mother's severe distress and depression when he had left for the service in World War II. He said, "She had a nervous breakdown, and the doctor insisted that she get some sort of little job to keep her busy. So she worked at a stationery store, stuffing wedding invitations, announcements, and that sort of thing." I could sense his deep concern for his mother, and I was touched by it.

He talked about seeing all his friends in St. Louis, his high school and college friends, his aunts and uncles, the neighbors. There had been golfing and several goodbye parties to send him off. And now we were facing our last time together before his departure to begin a year of combat in Korea.

As dictated by the mores of the time, as well as my strict Catholic upbringing, Joe stayed at the Bachelor Officers' Quarters not far from our apartment. But we tried to cram as much into those three days as we could... talking endlessly, going for moonlit walks, to dinner and dancing, kissing and hugging, and gazing into each other's eyes. He seemed very different than I remembered... more serious and sincere, and not at all arrogant.

We were falling in love.

We talked about how we'd write often, telling each other all about ourselves in our letters, what we were doing, what we were thinking, what we were feeling. The hours passed too quickly, and then Sunday evening came and it was time for me to drive him back to the airport. We tried to make small talk, to keep our conversation positive and encouraging. I was desperately trying to hide my fear and my dread of saying goodbye.

JOE, GILBERTA AND DOG JUDY ENJOY WEEKEND VISIT BEFORE JOE DEPARTS FOR KOREA.

Sitting in the airport lounge, we clasped each other's hands, trying to reassure each other. We heard his flight to San Francisco being announced, and we stood up, both attempting to smile, knowing that this was the final moment before the long and uncertain year began. Tears started streaming down my face. I tried to hold them back, but they just kept coming.

"You be good, Toots," he said, wiping the tears from my cheeks with his handkerchief, smiling gently. He had never called me that before. It was a term of endearment that I would hear again. And I liked it.

"You be good, too, Honey," I said through my tears.

"Bye, Gil. I love you." One last kiss and he started to step away.

I didn't want to let go of his hand as he turned to go. "I love you, Joe!" I cried. "I'll pray for you every day!"

He walked outside to the ramp and up the steps to the waiting airliner, turning to wave one last time before disappearing into the plane. I stood watching through the boarding lounge window as the huge plane taxied out to the runway. I heard its engines revving up, the sound accelerating until it started its roll down the runway. It lifted, rose, and roared out of sight.

I stood there straining to see the last glimpse of the plane, to hear its engines as it disappeared from view. Walking back to the car, I felt the tears welling up again, and as I opened the door and got in, I couldn't hold them back. On the drive back to Willy, I kept remembering the weekend, what we had said to each other, where we had gone, what we had done... the moonlit walks, the dancing, the candlelit dinners, the hand-holding and the kissing, and mostly, the talking. We had covered a lot of territory in those few days. We had learned more about each other than we had all those months he was at Willy. He had been sincere, intense, and expressive. I thought of the uncertainty of the year ahead, with him halfway around the world facing dangers I could only imagine.

Arriving back at the base, I trudged up the stairs to the apartment, walked into the empty living room and stood staring at the couch where Joe and I had sat, holding hands, talking, laughing, and cuddling, just a few hours earlier.

Joan had gone out for the evening. Only Judy was there to greet me, her tail wagging and her soft brown eyes looking up at me as if she could sense how alone and fearful I felt. Going into the kitchen, I opened the refrigerator and stood staring at its emptiness. I found a day-old teacher-furter, took one bite and threw it away. I went to my room, the tears starting once again. Throwing myself onto my bed, I cried myself to sleep.

* * * *

Chapter Four

LETTERS FROM KOREA

The new school year began the next day. All I could think of was Joe, our visit, and the uncertain year that stretched before us. I had great trouble concentrating on my work. I caught myself gazing out the window, plagued by thoughts that he soon would be flying combat in Korea. I wondered how we would get through the year. It was with great effort that I managed to weather that first week, until this postcard arrived from San Francisco:

> Sept. 10, 1952
>
> Dear Gil,
>
> Had an uneventful trip from Phoenix but am beginning an eventful evening here at the "Top of the Mark" with all the troops.
>
> Love, Joe

The "Top of the Mark" nightclub was the traditional partying spot for pilots and troops leaving for combat in the South Pacific and the Far East during World War II. It was now serving the same purpose during the Korean War. I learned later that it was also the spot from which wives and sweethearts watched the troopships leaving San Francisco Bay, sailing under the Golden Gate Bridge and out to sea. To this day the

"Weepers' Corner" of the nightclub, with windows on three sides, is a reminder of the heartaches of those wartime separations.

Joe was there celebrating one last big party with his fellow pilots. I imagined the bravado, the joking, the drinking, and the wisecracks as they used these moments of camaraderie to bolster each others' spirits.

JOE GUTH (TOP, SECOND FROM RIGHT) AND PALS CELEBRATE BEFORE LEAVING FOR KOREA.

He, like all the pilots in his 52-Charlie flying class, was now in that pipeline to Korea. They had earned their pilot's wings, gone through aerial gunnery training, and were now on their way to the combat zone.

They were being processed for departure at Camp Stoneman, near Pittsburgh, California. From Stoneman they were to be taken by bus to Travis Air Force Base, where they would board a large transport plane and be flown to the Far East. Camp Stoneman is gone now, but a memorial to the troops and pilots who processed there stands in a Pittsburgh park next to a children's playground. It's a modest spot, but there's a sense of history about it. A weathered arch stands near the waterfront which reads, *Through These Portals Have Passed the Best Fighting Men in the World.*

Joe wrote this letter from Camp Stoneman on September 12, 1952:

Dear Gil,

I wrote you a long letter the other day but didn't mail it. After reading it now I tore it up. It was corny, and sad, and too long. I wrote it during the mental depression of leaving you and having to come to this huge horrible place. It was very sad and melancholy and I don't want you to think of me that way.

Everything is much better now. We've been going to San Francisco every night and seeing the sights, Chinatown, Fisherman's Wharf, International Settlement, all the girlie shows, and all the bars in San Francisco.

During the story swappings I told all the troops that we would probably be married when I get back if things remained the same.

They were pleased but none believe that Uncle Joe, the perennial bachelor, will do the deed. I've arranged the situation as we wanted it, to get to know each other by mail. If it works out, fine. If not, well, we'll see.

Gil, I love you and still want you. I wish we
had had more time together and I miss you
already. As we both agreed, in a way it was
fortunate that we didn't have more time last
Sunday, and with the rapid developments in
such a short time, it's probably best, for
both of us, that we have to continue our
courtship by correspondence. When I think of
you, Wow, boy howdy! What would happen if we
had, say, two weeks together. (Stop thinking
boy.)

Honey, we should be leaving very soon. I
don't know what my overseas address will be
but as soon as I find out I'll write again.

Your Joey

As I read his letter I felt the tears welling up. His sincerity and tenderness filled my heart and made me long to see him again, even for just one more moment. I asked myself how I was going to make it through a whole year, if I missed him this much after just a few days.

He called me from San Francisco just before leaving the U.S., for one last goodbye. The connection was so clear it sounded like he was in the next room.

"We'll be leaving soon, Gil. I just wanted to hear your voice one more time," he said.

I was trying to sound brave as I said, "I'll be thinking of you. Take good care of yourself!"

"I will, and you be good, Toots!"

"You be good, too, Honey. I'll pray for you!"

One last goodbye, and the connection was broken. I stood holding the phone in my hand, staring at it. Just seconds before I had heard his voice. Now he was going to be on his way halfway around the world, to begin a perilous year of combat. I felt that surge of emptiness and fear again. It was a feeling that would become familiar during the next several months.

A few days later I received this postcard, picturing a Pan American Stratocruiser at Honolulu International Airport:

```
                            September 19, 1952

Gil,

A card and letter will follow from Tokyo. A
long but interesting trip. We don't have a
long layover, but I am all eyes. Until the
privacy of an envelope.


Joe
```

He wrote the following postcard and letter while in Japan, the last stop before Korea:

```
                            September 24, 1952

Dear Gil,

Looks like the US, but it isn't, believe me.
We are spending the day here in Tokyo. Some
place. YOHURADESTA... First thing I learned
in Japanese. Means "How much."


Your Joe
```

```
                            September 25, 1952

My Gil,

Stationery, pencil, time, and a hundred
things to say to you, a thousand fleeting
thoughts of Stoneman, the last stop, San
Francisco, the cab drivers, the girls at the
Nob Hill Officers Club dance, of you, of
love, a galaxy of thoughts.

I want to tell you everything, but to tell of
one thought would take pages and there are so
many I can't choose.

Most dominating of all was our talk Monday.
Two things you said have haunted me. I can
still hear you... "You be good, too." and
"Honey, I'll pray for you." The heart is a
strange thing. I know it actually isn't true
```

but I can feel a tugging and tightness when I think of you.

A mental impasse. I'll try later.

Later, September 25

The privacy of an envelope I promised in Hawaii. So many of my thoughts are of you I don't fear the future very much at all.

My Gil, I'm not used to it.

With a brain dulled by traveling, when its thoughts are settled I'll write a letter. We are flying to Tokyo, via Hawaii, Kwajalien, and Guam.

Later, same day

"The Air Force Way:"

Guth is the first (alphabetically) Lieutenant on the list. The list is cut. I leave all my friends behind. All new friends must be made again. Friendship in the service is an insecure affair.

Saw Pearl Harbor and reminisced ironically two seconds.

I'm going to the land of the people who killed our sailors and started it all 11 years ago.

Somewhere above I said I was going to write a letter.

This is a letter?

I'll try later.

Later, Same day

Just passed Iwo Jima. It's a tiny island, hardly worth fighting for... Strategic, I suppose.

Gil, sometimes I feel like opening my heart
and soul to you like on page 1, but other
times I clam up and can't say things that I
feel. Like you said we should both tell each
other everything, and I want to, but I'm not
used to it. Give me time.

These are not confessionals, but attempts to
tell everything, and I could do it much
easier if we were together.

Every time someone hurt me I got tougher so
that I wouldn't be so easy next time. After
my full number of experiences I'm real tough
with a hard shell. You are the only one that
has gotten past that shell in a long, long
time. You are the only one with whom I have
ever considered giving myself freely but even
now I'm holding back some I think (because of
habit only). I'm not trying to because I
trust you, more than anyone ever. It's not
because I'm positive things will work out as
we planned but if they don't I know you'll be
honest.

This is why I wanted you even before our last
visit. Much more now though. Gil, do you
understand what I'm trying to say. If not,
copy back the doubtful parts and I'll try
again.

We should be in Haenada, Japan, the Tokyo
Airport, in two hours. Almost there.

I'll write more from Japan and when I know my
address.

Later, Same day

A new investment, a Japanese pen. A bargain—
540 yen, $1.50 cold cash.

We got to Tokyo two nights ago, but after we
got settled in our quarters, which are tents,
and ate, we went right to the sack. Yesterday
we processed until noon and then were free.

We all, of course, went into Tokyo. We are now at Fuchu, about 30 miles from Tokyo.

My impression of Tokyo and the Orient—Eh, I don't know. It doesn't show me much. The first and most lasting impression is the smell, everything smells, the people, buildings, cabs, streets, everything. Sort of a musty smell. Every inch of Japanese soil is utilized. What doesn't have a building is farmed. They have no animals and poor soil, so they fertilize with human waste, called night soil. I guess that's why the whole island smells as it does.

With that knowledge you can see how it would dampen any favorable impressions. Everything is so small and tiny, the people—they actually stare at us as giants. The rooms in the houses we've seen are about 10 feet square.

We can eat no vegetables, fruits or anything unless canned from the U.S. because of dysentery from the night soil.

They do have many wonderful jewelry pieces, trinkets, silver, china and things like that. When I get my first R & R (rest and recuperation leave) after 6 weeks, I'll send you a goodie.

When we got back today our orders were in, and as I guessed I go to F-84G's. I tried every angle I knew to get out of 84's into 80's or 86's but no soap.

The F-86 Saberjets are the true fighter pilot, air to air combat jets. They are engaging enemy MIG's, and that's what I wanted. The F-80's and the F-84G's are both used for air to ground support of ground troops. The F-80 is well powered for the amount of ordinance it carries. But the F-84G is so loaded with ordinance it's not as good a performer as the F-80.

Tonight I go to Korea, the 58th Fighter
Bomber wing in Taegu. The base is known as
K-2.

They fly us over late at night in a C-47. I'm
kind of anxious to get there now and get it
over with. I'm a little scared, Gil, but I
suppose that is to be expected. I know
everyone else is.

Do something for me. Might be too
sentimental, but I want a picture of you, a
large one. Have a hundred or so made and send
me one.

Joe

Joe's vivid description of his surroundings and of his true feelings touched me. He had always exuded such confidence and invincibility, even a cockiness at times. And now he was expressing himself with complete vulnerability and honesty, even admitting that he was "a little scared." I felt very close to him.

A day later the following letter arrived:

Taegu, Korea

The traveling is over. We're here. Where
"here" is I don't exactly know. All I can say
is that it's a place.

The talk (after one day) says that we will be
here exactly one year less one month. Left
the U.S. 19 Sept. 52 and will leave here 19
August 53. Unless I can get in 100 missions
before then. But if we don't get more planes
we can't fly the missions.

I could go on for hours tonight but I'm so
hungry for a letter from you I've got to mail
this now. Mail is supposed to take about 7 or
8 days to the States—the same back—so a 2 to
3 week correspondence per subject.

So Joe had arrived in Korea to begin his one-year tour of combat. I relished these first cards and letters from him. But the emptiness I had felt that evening at the airport didn't go away. As more of his letters from Korea began arriving, I continued to be surprised and impressed by his graphic descriptions of life there:

```
                                        29 Sept. 52

Hi, Gilberta

At one glance you could tell there is a vast
difference between this place and any place
outside Korea. At first it would seem that it
is all physical but the big difference is in
the men themselves. Which is cause and which
is effect I don't know. Is it the physical
surrounding, so poor it dejects the mind or
is it the mental anguish of Korea that makes
a man's attitude, "to hell with everything, I
don't care what I look like, don't care what
I wear, eat, when I sleep, what I do, don't
care."

The reason, I'm sure, is because everyone has
too much free time and free time is time to
worry, worry about being killed, what is
happening in the States, what they will do
when they get back, their girls, wives,
families and all the other multitude of
anxieties one can imagine if he has too much
time to think.

My escape from time has begun, and will
succeed in literature, fiction and study.
Each book I read I'll describe to you and
will make recommendations.

I'm thinking of you. I can describe
everything perfectly—your kitchen, dining
room table, mirror, chairs, paper, coffee,
dog, living room, radio, couch, door, bath,
stairs, the base, everything. I feel nearer
to you because I can see it all.
```

To help you, here's a description of this
place:

The entire, everything, is a drab color, sort
of a brown or beige. All one story unpainted
wood buildings, long, narrow, tarpaper roofs,
with pot bellied oil stoves, and drafty
doors.

Scattered over the base, at random, are
outdoor "outhouses," (without the crescent
door). They're not dirty, they're just not
clean. My house of patronage is two blocks
away. Very inconvenient.

The inside of the B. O. Q. is the same color,
a splotchy drab. I have a corner area. The
major next to me has a series of wooden boxes
hammered together to make a closet and desk.
This also serves as a partition and affords
some privacy. The only furniture issued is a
wood and canvas cot which sags back-
breakingly. I have scrounged an old
ammunition box for a footlocker. With a
hammer, nails, old packing crates, and my two
little hands I have a desk and cabinet for
small pieces of junk, papers, books, mirror,
alarm clock, ink, pen, 1/5 Scotch, and
lighter fluid.

My next carpentry project is a bed. It must
be comfortable since I plan on spending all
my free time there reading.

This all must sound very depressing and it is
but it need not be if one looks at it in the
right way. I'm determined not to let myself
become depressed no matter what.

Most have stopped shaving but I made myself
promise myself to shave every day except my
mustache. Haven't shaved it since leaving the
States. It's over a quarter inch long now.
When I can twist the ends I'll send you a
picture so you can see if you want me to wear

it always. It's too blond to be seen clearly yet but it will be beautiful. Comments please.

I want to say things about us but without hearing from you as yet I'm still too confused.

It should take us about two or three weeks to correspond.

Have read four books, one on the plane and three here. Will tell you about them in the next letter.

They can't speed "Air Mail" letters I know but I sure wish your letter would come soon. I'm real anxious to hear from you.

I still love you. Joe
P. S. I'll continue to love you too.

Thus began the correspondence between a combat pilot in Korea and his girl back home. In spite of what sounded like a very Spartan environment, his letters were upbeat, and he wrote often of his determination not to let himself become depressed.

The whine and roar and rumbling of the jets at Willy were constant reminders to me that he was flying in hazardous combat. I often found myself staring out the classroom window, thinking of him and feeling an almost unbearable longing for him, wishing for time to pass. A year seemed like such a very long time. And Korea seemed so very far away.

Soon the phone started ringing again in our apartment. There were plenty of invitations for dates and social events at Willy. But for me a lot of the excitement I had felt that first year was missing. I spent many of my off-work hours writing to Joe. In response to his request to have my picture taken and to send him a "large one," I found one of the best photographers in Phoenix and made an appointment. The photographer asked me what the occasion was, and when I told him it was for my boyfriend in Korea, he held up a foamy net formal.

"This calls for something special," he said. So I changed into the formal, and he began to set up different poses.

"Now, in this one, look like you love him. This time, look like he has just asked you to marry him."

He took several shots, and when we got the proofs Joan and I pored over them and selected the one we thought was the best. I mailed it in plenty of time for Joe to get it before Christmas.

Joe wrote that he was going to Catholic Mass so he "could learn more about" my religion. We hadn't ever addressed the subject of my religion much, so this news astonished and pleased me.

I was stunned when I read of his going into the city of Taegu with six of his buddies, and what they encountered there:

```
Do you remember one night when you and Joan
and I were sitting at the dining room table
and I was expounding my verbosities on
communism and poverty and starving hordes in
China and India and the Orient in general?
Well, I saw it, real, alive, and horrible. To
explain it all would require a volume but one
scene nightmares me still. We were in an open
ammunitions truck and driving along a main
street where you could breathe and get away
from the choking stink. Passing U.S. 5th Army
Headquarters Compounds and, having to get
away, we went into one of the P. X.'s.
Adjacent to the P. X. was a barbed wire
enclosure around a local train station. A
pass was needed to get in or out. Inside were
hundreds of Korean refugees going from one
point to another. Crawling in and out of the
holes of the barbed wire were small children,
orphans, illegitimates and others without
parents, who were begging for food and rags
of clothing. Three of us had been in the P.X.
and were outside sitting in the truck looking
at the thing. Some of the kids had no
clothes, some with just shoes, some with
trousers.
```

All their bellies were swollen with hunger
and malnutrition. One of these kids was lying
there dead, or dying, four or five, an
orphan, I suppose, completely covered with
flies. We were eating popcorn from the P.X.
We stopped. One crumbled his bag and threw it
over the high fence. They fought for it like
wolves. I threw mine and went into to the
P.X. until we all left, never looking again.

Joe's depictions of these events shocked me. I shared the realities of these and other horrors of the war which he wrote about with Joan. The havoc of the war in Korea was being brought to us firsthand through his descriptive and sometimes graphic writings. He also wrote about the lighter side of life there:

All is not sad, however. In the officers'
mess (dining room) are Korean girls waiting
on tables. They are young things and are
very, very shy and gentle. The only English
they know is that of the mess vernacular;
knife, fork, spoon, coffee, chow, etc. and
the slang we teach them. They are all real
tiny with coal black hair. The older girls,
20, 21, 22 are not so shy but the real young
ones can hardly look at you without giggling.
Some of the girls wear their hair straight,
but the younger ones are distinguishable by
the braids or pigtails—these are the virgins.
A new one, with pigtails, started the other
day and was so shy she wouldn't wait on the
tables. She stood with her face against the
wall and peeked out.

For some reason it embarrasses the devil out
of them for you to look at their ankles. A
large table of us was sitting near the exit
near closing time. The shy one was clearing
the empty tables peeking at us and giggling
with an older girl, but still with pigtails,
and we started staring at the eldest's

ankles. The shy one ran screaming and
laughing from the mess. The older one ran to
the wall laughing and hiding her face. The
more we laughed the more she laughed and
jumped up and down. Finally she couldn't
stand it any more and dared to run past us
outside. We each of course think the other
race is crazy.

Barring gambling losses I should be able to
mass a huge amount of cash. I have lived for
the past week on six dollars.

My mustache is growing into a wild, golden
Zapata affair.

Honey, I sure wish I could hear from you
although it will be a week or more before the
mail has time to get here.

Until I do hear from you it's like a one-
sided conversation and living on a memory and
a hope.

Your Joe

It took a whole month for Joe to receive my first letter to him. He wrote immediately after its arrival:

15 Oct 52

You remember how anxious you were to hear
from me; you can imagine how anxious and
pleased I was to hear from you, not having
heard from you since we talked September 15.

The normal correspondence cycle, they said,
was about 15 days. Hoping it might be less I
started checking in about 12 days. No mail,
no mail. Then I found out no Air Mail had
been delivered in five days. No mail. Grrrr.
But yesterday it came, and I'll bet I've read
your letter five times.

Just got another letter from you. It almost
caught up with #1 because of the delay. Your

letters are wonderful, although it's the actual you that I want. I don't think you realize how much you mean to me.

There are so many things I want to talk to you of but can't until we know more of what we are going to do. One that I have to discuss however is this, something neither of us want to consider or think about, is that if something happens to me you will never know it. Temporarily, one of the fellows has your address, but I feel that you are much more deserving than a short note from a buddy in the event of an event. I wish you could become acquainted with my parents to cover that event and if We do work out you will want to know them anyway. Any suggestions?

I'm hesitant to suggest this but all barriers are down now.

The next morning:

After a very fretful night's sleep during which I thought of nothing but you I'm extremely melancholy.

I think of you too as I go to bed each night, sometimes of the future, sometimes of the past, and sometimes, without analysis or parallels, just emotion and desire, how it would be if it were Us instead of just me there and with my vivid imagination fully aroused sleep is impossible, and more than once I've had to get up and take a walk to keep from being a complete physical wreck.

My desires and imaginations embarrass me. Do you ever think of me like that?

Because of time zones and the International Date Line you are awakening at the same time I'm going to bed, on the same day. As I went to sleep last night at 10 PM Wednesday, you were just waking at 7 AM Wednesday morning.

```
As I go to sleep I think of myself being
there with you and waking you, seeing you,
holding you, kissing you.

These things are hard for me to say—do you
want to hear them—they are my thoughts.

I have to ferry a jet over to Itazuki, Japan,
so I'll be gone for a few days but I'll write
again as soon as I get back.


Your lover, El Mustachio
```

This letter, with its reference to the possibility of something happening to him, "in the event of an event," intensified the ache in my heart. I was moved to tears by the passion in his words of love. I knew with certainty now that I loved him, and that he loved me. I wrote him that, if he wanted me to, I would gladly write to his mother.

It was weeks before Joe's letters to me and mine to him began arriving with sufficient regularity for us to exchange any discussion by mail, even though we both were writing almost every day. I would drive to the post office during my lunch hour to check my P.O. Box, Number 267. When I saw an envelope with that familiar handwriting of his I couldn't wait to read it. Sometimes I tore the letter open while standing in the post office, and eagerly read it while I walked out to the car. I'd sit in the car with it until I had quickly scanned the entire letter, looking for those emotional words of love and longing.

The days passed, and the steady exchange of letters continued. It began to look as though we were making good progress in getting to know each other better, in spite of the mail delays. I was also learning more about him, and some of what he was revealing about himself surprised me.

His letters reflected his strong affection for his parents, aunts, and uncles. In one, he described in detail the Christmas gift he selected for each and every relative. I was beginning to understand that he had grown up in a very stable, loving home environment. In a way I was surprised by this, because my early impressions of him were that he was very much a worldly "loner," unlikely to make a serious commitment to anyone or anything. I was to learn that I was completely mistaken:.

20 Oct 52

First off, did you register to vote in the
coming elections? If not, you had better do
so and vote. Joan too.

Now about Itazuki. Since you're pinpointing the
places I've been, pin Itazuki and next to it the
large city of Fukuoka. These are on the Japanese
island of Kyushu. While in Fukuoka I did my
Christmas shopping. All the gifts are, of
necessity, with the Oriental touch but some are
very nice.

For Mother a set of earrings, bracelet and
necklace, of black onyx with a pearl in each
piece of onyx.

Some jewelry is extremely cheap compared to
Stateside prices, like onyx, jade, moonstone,
pearls, etc. For Dad a set of cuff links and
tie clasp of silver and jade. I like this so
much I was going to keep it for myself but
I'll send it and get another when I leave.

Aunt Frieda, blue moonstone earrings and
ring. Aunt Dorothy onyx earrings with pearls
and silver. Aunt Catherine and Uncle Rob a
set of bamboo beer mugs which, when lifted to
drink from, play "China Night." Uncle Herman
a set of bamboo mugs and tray. Aunt Lilly,
the whatnot collector, a set of the "Seven
Lucky Gods" of Japan carved in ivory. Uncle
Milton gets a Japanese "Pocket Lighter" which
when filled with fluid keeps your hands,
pocket, and feet warm while fishing or
hunting. Uncle Ed, brother Jack and Grandma
didn't get anything yet, but they will.

And for Gil, since I can't send myself, and
there are absolutely no decent substitutes, I
have, seriously, what I think is the finest
of its kind I've ever seen. I wanted to get
both you and Mother the same but that would
never do and the Mamasan (Japanese
Grandmother) said the gift I got Mother was

more apropos. You'll have a chance to judge
my taste. I'm also sending you two little
trinkets I got in Seoul. Don't judge my taste
from these, which you can open now but don't
you dare open the other gift until Christmas.
They will be marked appropriately so there'll
be no confusion.

Mother and the rest of the relatives keep
asking me if I need anything or want anything
for Christmas but my requests have been
extremely rare. Anchovies for our midnight
repasts. Flannel pajamas for the now freezing
cold and sweat socks which we can't buy. If I
were in the States I would need new golf
clubs, new civilian clothes, money, etc., but
here—nothing.

This last paragraph is to certify that I'm
not hinting for Christmas gifts. I get a real
kick getting things that I think you all will
like, more so than getting anything. The only
thing I would really like and want is you.
Boy, that would be the cat's meow, you in my
footlocker for Christmas. Not so. However,
there is another way you could please me
greatly!

In our hundred-foot-long barracks there are
three pot-bellied oil stoves and to match
there are three pot-bellied indigenous dogs,
"Put-Put," "Pierre" and "Clanky."

After being here for quite a while or after a
particularly scary mission, some pilots get
the shakes so badly they have to rest with
sedatives. These we call the CLANKS. We also
call Put-Put's daughter Clanky. At first,
(she is now six weeks old) when someone would
jump at her or scare her she would just stand
there and shake, losing all control over
herself. Now, however, she is fairly well
housebroken and is gaining courage. Reminds
me of Judy.

Just came back from Mess. It was the usual
mess. No cows over here. Consequently no
milk. Boy-howdy, what I wouldn't give for a
quart of cold milk.

We, of course, are on a seven-day week, and
the days blend into each other, none having
any significance. So on Sundays the chaplains
always post their sign on the mess hall door:

TODAY IS SUNDAY COURTESY CHAPLAINS, INC.

Father Powell, the Catholic priest, goes to
the flightline every time a mission takes off
and blesses each man and his plane. It gave
me the willies the first time I taxied out on
a training mission. It seems incongruent and
macabre for him to be out there. If we have a
successful mission we blow up and burn
hundreds of the enemy. If it is an
unsuccessful mission we blow up or get
killed.

El Mustachio is now a month old. A month! See
how the time flies—just 10 more months to go.

I wish there were someone to kiss, you,
mother, etc., to see the reactions to El
Mustachio. For reaction observations only.

It was obvious from his letters that he was doing everything in his power to remain upbeat and optimistic, but also as realistic as possible. Reading between the lines told me that it was a challenge for him. I tried to keep my letters positive and encouraging. I wrote him about ordinary events, such as funny things that happened in my classroom and on the base. But I was careful not to write too much about the social life on the base.

21 Oct 52

Hi Lover,

A short letter.

Yesterday I sent you the two little things I
picked up in Seoul. I wanted to get you
something nice but there aren't many nice
things here.

We have a houseboy for the barracks named
Kim. He's 22 years old, and married. He makes
the beds, sweeps the floor, fills the water
canteens, etc. I was mailing my big box of
Christmas goodies to the relatives and he
insisted on carrying it to the P. O. He is
very reserved, quiet, courteous, but always
smiling. Had never heard him laugh out loud.
While walking to the P. O. he asked me what
was in the box.

"Christmas presents."

"For whom?"

"Oh," I said, "Mother, Dad, brother, aunts
and uncles."

"No present for wife," he said.

"No wife," said I.

"No wife," said he. "How old you?"

"Twenty eight."

With that he started smiling, then giggled,
then roared laughter.

"Twenty eight—no wife!"

I had to take the box while he stumbled
alongside, laughing.

Don't know what's so funny. Seems as if he
thinks I should be a subject of Freud.

Will close, Ichibon (Number One).

Love, Joe

He continued to write very vivid and expressive letters. But the delayed arrivals of our letters to each other were beginning to cause confusion and, sometimes, misunderstandings between us:

```
                                            Taegu

                                       24 Oct 52

     Dear Gil,

     You stinker you. Evidently you're not going
     to write unless you receive a letter first. I
     was angry about it and with you for the last
     few days but there is nothing to be gained by
     getting upset about it. Since I have become
     El Mustachio I've become calm, cool, and
     collected. Magnanimously, all is forgiven.
```

His reference to me as a "stinker" gave us a term which we both used when there were long mail delays, or when one received a letter from the other which caused frustration or consternation.

I loved getting letters that told me interesting details about what his days were like. When he described the base, the planes, flying, and his reactions to things, it made him seem closer:

```
     I have not been flying with my own squadron
     as yet. Before flying with them we have to
     complete the training course which is 15
     hours in the F-84G. This is the newest and
     hottest of the F-84's. When we first got here
     there was a big push by the Reds and all the
     planes were used for combat. They needed
     pilots so badly however we started training
     in the T-33. I was made an instructor pilot
     because there were no instructors. They still
     need pilots badly so they decided to send us
     into combat with just a few hours in the
     F-84G. By the time you get this letter I
     should have flown my first mission against
     the enemy. Don't know the airplane real well
     yet but suppose I will learn.
```

You remember seeing pictures of olden days
when knights wore so much heavy equipment
they had to be hoisted onto their horses?
Well, we are now reverting back to the same
situation. In the practice gunnery missions
we wear full combat equipment in order to
learn how to fly with everything on. It takes
the crew chief and his plane assistant plus
all the strength I have to get into that iron
bird. I weigh 150 lbs. (lost about 10 lbs.)
and with all the equipment I go over 300 lbs.

Below is a list of the gear we have strapped,
tied and buttoned on. Shorts, T-shirt, long
underwear. Have you ever worn long johns? It
itches. Cotton socks, heavy wool ski socks,
an extra two pairs stuck in a pocket, heavy
combat jump boots, flying suit, flight
jacket, heavy winter fur-lined parka and
trousers, silk insert gloves, cotton gloves,
and leather gloves over all, and finally a
wool beanie. These are the clothes.

Now for the equipment. A small penknife, a
jack knife, and strapped to my leg on the
outside a bayonet knife. A .38 caliber pistol
with a full belt of ammunition and a .45
caliber pistol with three clips of ammo.
Between the long johns and the flight suit we
wear a corset-like G-suit which pressurizes
your legs and stomach to keep you from
blacking out. On the outside, again, over the
parka, a May West, to keep you afloat in
water when inflated. Between the May West, on
the back a 70-pound survival kit with too
many things to mention in it, on the bottom
of the parachute a 40-pound life raft with a
hundred more survival items. Inside again, a
vest with batteries and radio. Outside again,
and finally a parachute and helmet with
oxygen mask and visor. My guess is somewhere
around 180 pounds of gear and equipment. A
truck takes it out to the plane and the crew
chief and his plane assistant help us into it

JOE DOES A PREFLIGHT WALKAROUND. YOUNG CREW CHIEF LOOKS ON.

and into the plane. The only thing we can move when strapped in the plane is feet from ankles down, and arms from elbows down.

Don't know how we fly. Disbursed throughout are flares, shark repellant, vitamin pills, candy bars, halazone tablets, extra survival kits, extra ammunition.

Enough—could go on for pages.

As I mentioned, I am due to leave here August 19, 1953. Unless, however, I fly 100 combat missions before that date. The way they have been flying missions I should finish in 8, 9, or 10 months, maybe, not probable, 6. How does my getting back to you in June or July fit into our schedule?

Am thinking of you a great, great deal.

28 October

Hi Sweets,

I'm sorry, you're not a stinker. Got your
letter yesterday saying you hadn't heard from
me in quite a while. Guess there was quite a
space between some letters. Won't let it
happen again.

If there is dirt all over this letter don't
mind, or think I'm intentionally dirty, but I
am dirty. So is everyone here. No water. We
haven't had any for two days. Our water
supply was poisoned, by guerrillas it's
suspected. They boil and ration out a little
for teeth brushing but none to bathe with or
drink. Plenty beer to drink however and wine
with our meals but would like some water.
There's some sort of adage or cliché about
water and well running dry or something-
anyhow—!

Bert, our adjutant, is on a five-day leave to
Tokyo and he's going to bring back some oils
and canvas. To painting once again, Lover.
For four days I have been sketching my first
scene, the area in which I live, a very
simple scene, floor, wall, two windows,
footlocker, bed, and desk. Have all the
details worked out except the lighting and
colors which Bert should bring back. I'll
send it to you when it's finished.

Four of us went on a reconnaissance mission
up to front lines last night. Night formation
flying with weather all around is as
dangerous as flying can get without having
the enemy throw up flack at you, but when I
saw the firing on the front line I realized I
should have no complaints. There was a push
on to recapture one of the key hills and it
was like a Fourth of July exhibition.
Everything was being thrown, from pistol and
small arms to heavy arrtilery. Some show.

Gil I suppose my letters sound as if I'm a little bitter or that the life here is completely humorless but it's not.

This story was funny to us, so much so that La Rue laughed so hard he fell down and sprained his ankle.

We were at the bar having a beer before dinner when we had an air raid. The lights went out and we all started scurrying for revetments (bomb shelters). Ray Kelly (remember him, 52-Charlie class at Willy), had just gotten here and didn't know where to go. I grabbed him and we stumbled to our hole. After the all clear we started back to the bar. Sneaking its way through the

Base is a river, or creek, or sewer or something that stinks horribly and has big hunks of green blob in it. Really an awful thing. We affectionately call it the Nile. As Kelly and I were walking back talking, Kelly disappeared. There he was, and then he was gone. He had fallen into the Nile. He came up the bank crawling, and sputtering, "Get me out of here!" No one wanted to help him for fear the green stuff would eat their clothes off or their hands. After a scalding hot shower and burning his clothes "Nile Kelly" came back thoroughly initiated to K-2.

Put-Put, Pierre, and Clanky say hello. Think of you most at night before going to sleep. It would be easier without my imagination.

Your Joe

Joan and I laughed when I read her this letter. We had met Joe's friend Ray Kelly at Willy.

At times Joe wrote as though he was almost desperate for reassurance that I would marry him immediately upon his return from Korea. I, on the other hand, was still desperately needing to know him better and to feel more certain that ours would be a lasting commitment:

K-2

Oct 31 52

Dear Gil,

This is the most difficult letter I have ever
written and rewritten and rewritten.

First off, I want to assure you that this is
not an ultimatum and that I do not want to
stop writing, that my feelings and love for
you have not changed. But it is my attitude
toward you which seems to be altering a
little.

I'm afraid you might think this too severe,
but these are some thoughts that have
bothered and disturbed me.

It's not an altering toward a specific issue
nor has it occurred in an instant. It's also
a very slight altering growing during the
long time between your letters of Oct. 8 and
22.

I think that I'm, in a word, disappointed.

It's not primarily what you wrote but what
you didn't write. I had always imagined that
when I finally chose someone and confessed my
love and she loved me, she too would do the
same, coming to me and telling me of her love
and desire for me, and we would be as one,
all arising spontaneously, not having to be
coaxed and primed. I'm enough of an egotist
to want that because you see I too need to be
wanted and loved. It seems that I have been
making all the decisive declarations and I've
been waiting for you for such a long time
Gil.

I can see you now, as you read this rearing
back and saying, "It isn't so," and, now, on
the defensive, preparing your retorts which
might develop into a literary script. Don't
please, because I'm not trying to be
argumentative or accusative.

We should be as one, Gil, and I don't feel as
if we are. We were, I thought, and could be,
and we're very close but not as one.

The reason we have to be as one, and the
reason it's so imminent is due to the
circumstance of Korea. I'm sure everything
would have worked out if we had been in this
same relationship six months ago or if I
could be there now, but it can't be.

Gil, I am literally fighting for my life
every day and I need every ounce of courage
and strength for that fight and not for the
fight against worry, frustration, and anxiety
because of you. I've got to be strong. In the
past I made myself be strong, the pillar, the
island, the shell, defying all and
everything. With you with me, as one, I can
do it, but if not as one, I am going to do
it.

It isn't the missions themselves that taxes
one's reasoning so much as the fears after a
mission and before the next one. The day
before my first combat mission we lost two
fine pilots. Captain Bateman, who was on his
93rd mission and Dan McKinney. Dan was a very
good friend of mine. You remember him, I'm
sure. We double dated with him once or twice.
He was the tall, dark, good looking, loud boy
with the Oldsmobile 88. They both were hit
while carrying napalm and went down before
they knew what happened. That shook us up a
bit, especially those who were close to them.
That afternoon I got your letter hoping for
the things I wanted to hear. I was not in a
good mental attitude for my first combat
mission with these two things on my mind. I
wasn't sharp and I missed the little things,
which was evident in my flying. I told you
often that when flying there can be nothing
but thoughts of flying and from now on that's
all there will be.

Gil, please don't misunderstand and let me
know if you see my circumstance.

This letter, so far, has taken me two days
and after reading it I can see that perhaps I
was a little more upset about McKinney than I
should have been but that is how I felt then.

Now I feel much better and the rest of this
letter will be in a lighter vein.

That letter carried an impact. I was shaken to think that, somehow, worries about me had the potential to distract Joe from his flying. Joan and I both remembered Dan McKinney. This was the first time Joe had written about losing a close friend in Korea. There would be many more.

I continued trying to keep my letters as encouraging as possible, without actually agreeing to marry as soon as he returned to the States. I began writing him more questions about himself, his likes and dislikes, since we'd had so little time to learn much about each other:

You suggested that I was high-strung. Yes, I
am at times, but can you think of any man
under the sun who flies jets and who is
associated with death as frequently as it
occurs who wouldn't be a little tight and
taut?

Spoiled—yes, I haven't noticed it, but
everyone says I am so I must be. However I'm
not above menial tasks nor am I a duty
shirker. I think I can understand your
question, having seen nothing of me but as an
officer at Willy. But I believe that
basically I'm a worker and a doer. When I
maneuver out of a task I do it more for the
sport of out-thinking someone than shirking
the duty. This is where people think I'm
spoiled, I think.

One question I asked him was if he liked children. Another was how he felt about the difference in our ages:

> As for caring for a little Joey, I've never been put to the test, but I feel certain that I could do as well as anyone else.
>
> Chronological age has never entered my mind, and of course I talk to you as someone of equivalent age. If you were a mental juvenile or idiot I would hardly have anything intimate to do with you.
>
> To discuss one of the variables now, others later. I think it's good for you to have a reserved nature to balance my decisive one, but do you have to be so extremely cautious? Do you ever say, "to hell with it," and do a baddie, something you shouldn't do? Try it. It's fun once in a while. I'm now being flippant and sarcastic.

I knew that my "extremely cautious" approach had to do with my strong desire for a stable, lifelong marriage. I hadn't ever talked with Joe about this other than to say that I hoped we could learn more about each other by mail, and that I looked forward to his return so that we could continue our romance in person.

> Later, same day
>
> I'm sending also a goodie box for you and Joan for Christmas. So you don't get confused, it's a wooden box 6"x5"x3 1/2" and plainly marked "DO NOT OPEN TILL CHRISTMAS." I sent Jo something so that she wouldn't feel she didn't have something from the Orient.
>
> Don't you dare, either one of you, open it until Christmas Eve, do you hear? Just 98 more missions to go.
>
> Love, Joe
> P.S. Notice the workmanship on the box, although it was just a menial task.

This last remark was in response to one of my questions to him about how much he enjoyed the menial tasks around a home. I was to learn that he was actually a very talented carpenter. Although he often wrote of his frustration about Us, some of his letters were upbeat and reassuring.

K-2

6 Nov 52

Dear Gilberta,

Me love, I'm in no condition to write, physically, but I just got two letters from you and was very pleased, especially since I must seem like such a stinker after my last letter.

I don't feel anything like I did in the last letter. One part of your letter asked if I feel I know you, which I'll answer later, but do you know me? Having a somewhat explosive, moody and sensitive nature, you will have to take me with a grain of salt when I'm in these extreme moods.

Forgiven?

This writing is little better than chicken scratching but who could do better standing up. One of the reasons I haven't written in the last few days is that I have been unwell. I have a virus infection of the nerves which has manifested itself in an itching, painful rash on my seat, my left seat only. Doc said it is the shingles and I am now taking vitamin pills, penicillin pills, A. P. C. pills, aspirin pills and cocaine pills. Actually with all this dope in me it isn't too painful but it still feels like I have a hundred toothaches in my left seat. Everyone thinks it is very funny since it is in such an awkward and uncomfortable place, and I have been the butt (awk) of numerous poor jokes.

Pleased to hear you voted. Did your man win? Mine did.

Here Joe is referring to the election of President Dwight Eisenhower. I responded that I had voted for the first time in my life, and that yes, my man had won.

You said you are somewhat stubborn. Now that
I think of it you are stubborn, aren't you! I
think that perhaps this is the trait which is
holding the progress of Us up.

Lover, I'm going to the Club and ease my
hundred throbbing toothaches with liquor
while standing at the bar. I want this to get
in the first mail tomorrow, so I'll close.
Tomorrow I'll write again on some important
subjects. Gil dear, I do love and miss you so
much. I want you to love me, too. I'm trying
so hard to make you. I want Us more than I've
ever wanted anything in life.

Your Joe

I was deeply moved when his letters contained such emotional words. I missed him terribly, and wished I was ready to say what he so wanted to hear.

                                            7 Nov 52
Hi, Toots,

Excuse the pencil but I'm writing this in
class and have no pen here. It's a very
boring class on jet engines and I promised a
letter today.

My seat is much better today and I'm sitting
again, very cautiously, however.

Gil, I don't know if I told you about my
Mother and the caution I have to use with her
so I'll go into the details. Mother is
extremely nervous and had a nervous breakdown
some years ago. When I was sent overseas in
the last war she almost had another one. When
I left home again in September, remember how I

told you that she almost went berserk, knowing
I was coming to a combat area. I told all
sorts of soothing and easing lies about flying
and Korea to try to put her at ease. Since I
have been here I wrote and told her that I
would probably never see combat. I said that
before we could be sent into combat we had to
have more training and there were very few
planes, so few that we were three classes
behind and that we would probably not get into
a training flight until January or February.
She has never mentioned it so I think she
half believes and has mentally suspended the
issue. I know it isn't right not to tell her
the truth, but I know that she would die a
thousand deaths by worry and anxiousness if I
wrote of the grim tales that happen. I hope
to be able to finish in 6, 7, or 8 months
before she really begins to suspicion.

This all leads to what I should and should
not write to you. Do you want to hear what is
happening or prefer that I leave these
stories out.

In answer to Joe's question, I wrote that I was glad when he described daily happenings in his letters, and that I was honored when he shared his feelings about events, both good and bad. And I was deeply impressed by his concern for his mother.

Our whole life here is concerned about flying
and pilots and when one of them goes down
there is just something missing and so
concerning that I have to write you about it.
The 69th has had some hard luck lately. Four
days ago the spell of "52 Charlie Class" was
broken. We had never lost a man until he went
into his dive and never pulled out. Vido
Mitchell... did you know him? Yesterday
Burton, also of the 69th, was shot down over
Sininju. Enough of this.

Although I was glad that Joe shared so much with me, I sometimes found it difficult to comment when he wrote about these sad events. It was especially hard when he wrote about losing a friend whom I had met.

I was beginning to see more and more that, in spite of the "hard shell" he had built around himself, he had a very tender heart, not only for me, but also for others that he cared deeply about:

```
                                           K-2

                                     8 Nov 52

This is a fairly coherent letter, to my
surprise. If we can get it straightened out
about you corresponding with my folks, Mother
will write. Don't expect to hear from my
Father because I have only received two
letters from him in my life. Say to Mother as
little as possible about my being in combat
here. Please don't tell her I actually am
flying combat missions.

Am off flying status for a few days because
of my seat but I have three missions, just 97
more to go. Speaking of the letter of
introduction, I'm at a loss as to what the
content should be.

'Dear Mother and Dad,

This is to introduce Gil Cosulich, a girl
whom I'm interested in but she can't make up
her mind.'

'Dear Mother and Dad,

Introducing Gilberta Cosulich, a girl that I
feel you must know because of her A's in
creative writing.'

'Dear Mother and Dad,

Meet Gil, a nice little tomato I dined and
danced while at Willy.'

Seriously, I would like to tell them of our
intentions, but I don't know what your
intentions are. Honorable, Madam? Some
suggestions please.
```

I replied that I would be glad to write his mother, after he let her know she'd be hearing from me. I suggested that he tell her that we were writing steadily, that we were quite serious about each other, and that we were going to continue seeing each other when he returned to the States.

In some of my letters to him I enclosed funny photos, cartoons, and clippings. I cut the label out of one of my sweaters which read "100% Virgin Wool," and snipped the word "Wool" off. I then glued the label to one of my letters under my signature. It got this reaction from him:

```
                                       9 Nov 52

I thought your little token was wonderful. I
got such a boot out of it everyone insisted
on seeing it. (In the wool scarves we have
are: packer's number, manufacturer's name,
etc. Also the certification of 100% Virgin
Wool). Many are now making the same little
tokens for their girls.

Roger

100% VIRGIN

Warren

It's spreading like wild fire... a terrific
idea. See what you started?

From the 27th of November to the 1st of
December I'm runway control officer in
Itazuki, Japan. I will have some pictures of
El Mustachio made. Am using Mustache Wax to
keep the ends curled now. Send some of those
thoughts of yours and I might not need the
wax.

Love, Joe
```

```
                                            10 Nov 52
Dear Gil—and Judy,

And Judy—so her feelings won't be hurt.

Tonight I was fortunate enough to draw
Airdrome Officer and am sitting on my duff
until tomorrow at 0800.
```

He explained that as Airdrome Officer he would be responsible for the overall activity and security of the base. This duty, he said, rotated daily between all operationally qualified pilots.

```
I'm glad the Post Offices and their free
loading employees have such a wonderful
attitude about getting the mail to the
service man overseas because if they didn't
the lousy system and service might be close
to the point that I would forget how to read
before mail got here. Some 4 or 5 days since
the last Air Force heroes zoomed in on their
C-47 to bring enveloped messages of glad
tidings and cheer.

Am now sitting with relative ease on my left
rash thatched rump (That's hard to say). It
was nothing really. (That island again.)
```

He described how he was working on a painting as a diversion from the demanding routine of flying combat and all of the concerns that went with it. His words showed his internal struggle to keep his spirits and his courage up so that he could face the dangers another day:

```
After I assembled my sketches, oils,
canvasses and brushes I then danced to the
tune of guffaws, quips, titles of the
"Artiste," "Rembrandt," "Van Gogh," "Da
Vinci," "Heavens to Betsy, where's my beret,"
etc. I then began.

My first scene (sound like James S.
Fitzpatrick) is of my general living area.
```

Most, at first, thought I was of the Cubist
school, but I proved I'm of the Primitive
class. Most of the lines are, so far,
angular, because the objects are angular—bed,
desk, footlocker, etc.

Seriously for a moment. My first colors were
disappointing in that with the limited colors
available everything was turning out bright
and colorful and I'm trying to capture the
drabness and unorderliness. My big problem
was the wooden colors for the bed, desk,
clothes closet, and windows and to blend the
G. I. blankets, beige walls and dirty brown
floor. The wood has turned out acceptable and
the blankets and sheets extremely well. Floor
and walls haven't been captured yet.

To Joe's surprise, and pleasure, some of the other pilots, upon seeing how he was using painting as a diversion, began to show an interest in taking it up themselves:

Since my immersion into paint the Major next
to me has started sketching in charcoal and
is doing an excellent reproduction of my
Marilyn Monroe nude calendar which Woody is
going to do over in oil on canvas. Bert is
going to begin since he has now found a
subject, and Schellhouse is sheepishly
querying as to prices on oils, canvas, talent
requirements, etc. Moral conquest at least,
if not a masterpiece.

Although some of his letters described the lighter side of his life in Korea, other parts of the same letter might contain more serious details about his routine there:

Different organizations and individuals are called different and sometimes funny names. One that I get a boot out of is the nickname for intelligence. After each mission we are thoroughly interrogated and asked a million seemingly unimportant questions. Consequently the name we always use: "THE HEAD SHRINKERS." The motto is "NO HEAD IS TOO BIG FOR US."

Tomorrow your glorious hero gets two opportunities, as we say, to swipe, as we call it, "Bust You're A— Hill." "Bust Your" is a 100 foot cliff right off the end of Runway N which gives you plenty of opportunity to Bust Your.

Gil, I'm not meaning to be vulgar when repeating these things, but with no restrictions things are apt to become risqué and I hesitated repeating it but I said "What the Hell."

I imagine you spend numerous hours pouring over these letters—not for content but to try to decipher them. I thought of closing when I should have but I'm in a jovial mood and what the hell!

Four missions down and after tomorrow I'll be considered a combat veteran.

To bed since tomorrow I go to devastate the enemy.

Your glorious hero.

Joe
P. S. I love you.

By mid-November Joe started to express an even more intense need to know that I would be planning to marry him immediately upon his return. In the following letter his frustration and disappointment are clearly evident:

K-2

16 Nov 52

Dear Gil,

Our letters seem to be following the cycles.
Two or three small talk ones followed by the
slightly tragic exchange of pursuit and
doubt, certainty and uncertainty.

In one of your letters you asked if I knew
you. Gil, I know you to the extent that I
predicted your answers to my letters.
Ordinarily a love letter of the type you sent
would drive anyone frantic, but you answered
with the same doubt, uncertainty and
confusion I expected and left me with the
same emptiness. Another hope unfulfilled.

These disappointments are not unusual,
however, since it happened many times at
Willy. After Willy I had given Us up with
full intentions of forgetting you, and
maneuvered the situation to the place where I
wouldn't have to do anything about it by
insisting that you write me first, fully
expecting never to hear from you again and
ending it all. You did write from Guatemala,
however, the first of two times you have
surprised me.

Since you did write to me at Luke I was
forced to conclude that We might not be a
wholly fruitless pursuit after all and
decided to try it again.

I came to you at Willy, however, expecting to
find the same Gil, so unimpressed with me she
wouldn't kiss me and so conservative she
wouldn't say anything but "I don't know."

Then the second time you surprised me.

You could tell and know how pleased I was
during our visit and how wonderful it was for
both of us.

The altering I speak of is the regression from the assured feeling of Us to the same feeling of wondering.

Gil, I can feel the same toward you and love you with the same intensity and still alter a little. I was sure everything would turn out all right and never had an alien thought after the last time we were together, but now instead of thinking, "I'm sure everything will turn out fine and we will be able to make plans and think about the future" I think, I'm sure everything will turn out fine—or will it?"

Gil, I'm not angry with you because you can't make up your mind and don't think any less of you because of your indecision.

All I can do is wait and honey I can't promise how long I will wait. I don't know myself. I have no suggestions other than wait and if you do make up your mind and I haven't changed mine—we'll see.

I've thought, "Am I such a miserable catch she can't make up her mind!" or after drinking at a party with lots of singing and laughter, when I'm feeling cocky and sure of myself, "If she doesn't come to me soon the devil with her. I'll not wait any longer. I've gotten over her before. I can do it again." Then come the thoughts of you that eat at my heart and my whole mood changes with just a few thoughts.

One little word or thought can do so much.

Honey the whole picture isn't black. Just a few dark clouds scattered intermittently, which is not unique among lovers I've heard.

The affair about McKinney caused a thunderstorm and it's been raining for three days so this is probably in a heavy mood. But please don't feel sad or blue.

Be happy and smile for me.

Joe's expressions of love and his struggle to stay optimistic invoked many conflicting emotions in me. I wanted him to feel reassured, but I was still plagued by my need to know him well enough to predict a lasting marriage. I hoped we could continue our courtship for a while when he returned, rather than plan on an immediate wedding. I also knew I wasn't expressing the promises that he longed to hear. And I could tell that he was trying very hard to be accepting of my uncertainty:

```
                                              22 Nov 52

My Little Darlin,

Something new has been added as you can see.
I'm now a typist. Having nothing to do with my
money and needing a sound type investment this
$49 bargain of a Smith Corona fitted the bill.

Don't remember telling you of my typing
experience, which is very little. But during
my last tour my secondary duty was as library
officer. I was doing right well with my self-
teaching until some ass showed me that I had
my fingers in the wrong place. I corrected
with catastrophic results as you can see.

Received your very nice letter the other day
and agree wholeheartedly about the stinker
letters. Until I received it I had prepared
for the worst thinking our avid correspondence
might take a bad turn but fortunately if we
both take each other with a grain of salt
everything will probably be smoother.

Honey, it's 10 o'clock on Saturday Night and
I'm so tired I can't press the keys.
Honestly, I started this letter three times
and haven't had enough time to finish because
we've been flying so much. Had a few beers at
the club and left early to write you but my
eyes are drooping. As I close tonight I want
you to know that I have been thinking about
you, in a very nice, but sometimes naughty
way, since your last letter.

Gilberta, I do love you. Until tomorrow.
```

23 Nov 52

Sunday and I'm still as busy as I was but I
think I can finish this time.

If you and Joan are going to have your own
private Christmas party and will not see each
other during the holidays you can open my
gift to you early. I think I'm as anxious to
hear how you liked the gifts as you are to
open them. One thing I insist on is that you
be in a happy and party mood when you peek in
the box. Perhaps you each had better have a
couple of beers before opening it.

I've rolled up 10 missions this month so far.
If this keeps up, I'll be home long before
August.

Do you remember Charlie Harris in Baker
class? He went in the other day, straight
down on his bomb run.

You do remember Quintus Fuller I'm sure. He
was in my flight at Willy. Five of us had the
same instructor. Fuller was on his first
mission and was hit by flack on his bomb run.
He pulled off the target and his right wing
came off so he ejected immediately. While
coming down in his parachute they were
shooting at him and a .50 caliber machinegun
bullet creased the back of his head. (This is
a funny story because he is OK now.)

His wound didn't slow him down a bit when he
hit the ground. He landed in a rice paddy
freshly fertilized with night soil and he,
with his blazing 45 and the three planes in
his formation strafing, held off the Gooks
until a helicopter came in to pick him up.
When the 'copter lowered the seat for him to
be pulled up he was so excited and covered
with night soil he missed it and as it went
by he lunged and caught it with one hand. The
next thing he knew he was 500 feet in the air
hanging by one hand with a hundred pounds of

equipment on. A young medic, risking his own
life, grabbed him by the jacket and hung onto
him as the 'copter flew out of range of
intense enemy fire.

Then, using every ounce of strength he could
muster, the kid pulled Quentis and his
hundred-plus pounds of equipment up and into
the 'copter. Since Quentis was picked up in
enemy territory he cannot fly combat anymore—
that's one of the regulations here. But he
refuses to get into an airplane anyway. He
insists on going home by boat. Fuller is a
Southern extremist from Alabama and his
classic remark was "Korea is just like the
States. The farther north you go the
unfriendlier folks get." Fuller's fortunate
in that he got the Air Medal and a Purple
Heart and flew only one-half a combat
mission, then goes home. A fat deal.

Quintus did return to combat in Korea, completed 100 missions, and was awarded the Distinguished Flying Cross. Years later he told us, "I've tried to find that nineteen-year-old kid all these years. I'd like to thank him for saving my life."

The rest of the story is that on November 13, 2003, fifty-one years after that daring rescue, the paramedic, Elmer Leroy Davis, gave Quintus a surprise phone call. He had finally been located with the help of the Helicopter Pilots Association. Quintus was in attendance in February 2005 when Davis, who had also served in Vietnam as an Army paratrooper, was awarded the Distinguished Flying Cross for his role in the rescue of Quintus Fuller. This high honor, given for "heroic airmanship," was presented to Elmer Leroy Davis by General John Handy, Commander of U.S. Transportation Command.

Joe's letters were filled with these amazing tales, as well as very tender expressions of love. Sometimes the things he told me made my heart ache for him and left me with the helpless feeling that there wasn't much I could do to console him other than continue to write understanding, encouraging words to him.

In the following letter I learned something else new about him. He had a real love and appreciation for dogs:

I wasn't going to tell you about this but I can't keep it a secret forever. Several days ago we lost our dogs. A month ago there was a loose dog on the runway and a plane while taking off ran over it. The dog disintegrated of course, but the nose wheel of the plane was sheered off. The pilot did a good job and landed with a minimum of damage. After that an order came out to shoot all loose dogs. We built a big pen for our dogs but they couldn't be kept there all the time. The other day the A. P.'s shot all three of them, Put-Put, Pierre, and Clanky. Everyone is mighty perturbed and unhappy. I agree that dogs shouldn't jeopardize a pilot's life and a quarter million dollars of airplane, but there must be some middle road between that and killing the only pets we had. The barracks is lonesome.

I have prepared myself for your picture. I'm sure I shall like it however. Mentioned to Mother that when I had time I would write you a letter of introduction and you would probably write her.

Ichibon means "Number One."

And so Ichibon Girl I'll close and write when I have another free ten minutes.

Love, Joe

23 Nov 52

Hi, Lover,

Since you have been sending me such nice tokens I thought you would be completely deserving of the token I have enclosed for you.

I am sure I gave you a set of navigators' wings while at Willie, but you don't have a set of pilots' wings. These are the small ones that you can wear if you need a pin or something.

Had planned on sending this token a day after the letter I wrote earlier today, but I'm scheduled to fly for six hours tomorrow and doubt if I'll have the chance.

Last week on returning from my eighth combat mission everyone was late and, after dark this field is really a tough one to get into because of the mountains. We were all short of fuel, which made the situation worse. One of the troops panicked, drove his plane into the runway, blowing the tires and sheering off the gear. We had to circle, waiting for them to try to clear the crash, running shorter on fuel all the time. I got in shortly after with an eyedropper of fuel left. Just after I landed another got all excited and burned out his brakes, catching fire. It was quite a show, but the outcome of it was an accelerated training program for five days, without combat missions, to improve our efficiency so as to cut down on the accidents. Train, train, train, fly, fly, fly. Bah.

Hope you like and wear the wings. I'm earning them.

The training program is to last for three days more only, at which time you'll get a long nice letter.

Until then, Your Hero, Joe

Descriptions of flying incidents like these were dramatic reminders of how extremely dangerous his occupation was. But I wanted to hear these details. They brought him closer, and gave me a way to respond in my letters with interest and appropriate concern for him.

It wasn't until years later that Bill Talley, a close flying buddy of Joe's in the early 1960s, told me about a serious plane malfunction that Joe had in Korea. Joe was to take a test flight and was faced with what could have ended in tragedy.

The maintenance people had mistakenly connected the elevator control linkage in reverse. The pilot expects the aircraft to climb when he pulls back on the stick, which is connected to the elevator. This reversal of the linkage caused the nose of the aircraft to go down when Joe expected to climb, and to climb when he expected to descend.

Joe flew the aircraft around the pattern several times to burn off fuel so that the plane became lighter in weight. He then approached the runway and was able to land the plane safely.

"Only Joe's experience and skill enabled him to realize the problem and handle the flight successfully," Bill told me.

Receiving his wings from Korea touched me deeply, and helped me feel really connected to him. I frequently wore them on my sweater or on my collar.

```
27 Nov 52

My Dear Ichibon,


You may weep a glad tear in your can of beer
for the passing of El Mustachio. However,
before passing we preserved for posterity the
devil himself. These two classic photos,
enclosed, are to be entered under the GREATS
section of your "People I Must Remember"
book. I wanted to be sure that I had a
picture I like with a mustache before the
razor did its job. I think I look much better
with a mustache but it was getting too long
and bothersome. It took two months for the
complete growth, so two months before I come
```

home I'll start another one.

(Photo #1) "Guth, you already have flown
10,000 combat missions but we need you
desperately to lead the Fifth Air Force for
another 10,000. 'Click,' went the shutter of
the now famous camera, and I replied, "Oh,
very well."

(Photo #2) The rakish MGM production was
filmed as I thought, "just one more martini
and she'll be ripe and I'll take her outside
and I'll put her in the car and I'll drive
her off and I'll and I'll—Gilberta, how about
just one more martini!" (Thinking of when I
get back to the States.)

The third is a filming of my canvas which
isn't finished and I didn't want photoed, but
the cameramen were running around the
barracks playing Scoop and insisted on the
canvas pose, too. Just a few things and a
frame and it will be complete. You can see
the picture of us you sent me on the wall in
the photograph, also in the painting, above
the bed.

Don't laugh. The Far Eastern Air Force is
having an art contest and since I have
completed the canvas I may as well enter it. I
realize it isn't very good but it is an
accomplishment, however little. The entries
have to be in by the first of January so you
won't be able to hang it in your attic until
my revolutionary masterwork wins. I'll probably
win an art scholarship to Budapest or
someplace. To all the scoffs and jeers and
ungentlemanly remarks and comments as, "It
doesn't have the right perspective," or, "It
doesn't look right," I have the answer. With a
"Yes, I paint" leer I say, "I paint it as I
see it."

Today the good cooks prepared us a supposedly
delicious Thanksgiving meal. All I can say is

that they tried and meant well, but as to
approaching anything like mother (or Gil)
could prepare, they failed miserably.

We're building a bar in the end of the
barracks and since I've been painting, the
committee decided to commission me to do
numerous murals on the walls. They don't know
it yet but I'm going to paint Mr. McGoo's all
over the place.

Glorious here still has ten missions and we
are still training so I doubt if I will get
any more this month.

Remember Tom Tudor? He went to the same
University as you. He went through Willy and
is now here in the 69th. He's a good friend
of mine and I thought perhaps you would still
remember him.

Tonight we celebrate the opening of our bar,
"The Bamboo Room." We were just sitting
around doing nothing yesterday and someone
said, "Why don't we partition off a room and
build a private bar?" Everyone went apish and
started immediately. I'm glad they didn't say
let's build a hotel. As in all newly
undertaken fiascoes millions of ideas are
expounded and the newest, which Bert has been
sent to Taegu after, is some dancing Josans,
Korean girls, for our gala opening. If
they're smart they won't be here.

Darlin, I, like you, think about you all the
time. I don't think the hour goes by that I
don't think of you.

The ex-El Mustachio sends his love.

El Greco, Joe
P. S. Comments on the photos, please.

JOE CLIMBS INTO HIS F-84G FOR A COMBAT MISSION IN KOREA (PHOTO #1).

"EL MUSTACHIO" RESTS IN HIS BARRACKS AREA IN KOREA (PHOTO #2).

I could tell that Joe was going to great lengths to stay constructively occupied when he wasn't flying. He seemed to be falling into a routine which was helping to keep his spirits up.

Then his letter of December 2, 1952 arrived:

```
                                    2 Dec 52

Dear Gil

I should have written days ago and have been
meaning to but so much has happened in the
last week that I just couldn't bring myself
to write about it. Don't know how come I'm so
deserving of these lousy deals or why they
chose me out of the thousands of pilots here
but it seems that I've been given the El
Shafto again.

Several days ago I was told to report to the
commanding officer and after reporting he
told me I was not to fly any more combat. I
am to leave the base here and go to a new
base, PCS, permanent change of station, on a
Top Secret project.

The services have several classifications of
material, the lowest being Restricted, then
Classified, then Secret, and the last, Top
Secret, which is reserved for things like the
Atom Bomb and the Yalta Conferences.

Being a Top Secret affair, no one knows
anything about it, so I can tell you very
little about it myself. It seems the orders
came from Washington and they put the people
on the list specifically by name.

There are a number of people on it but I'm
the only pilot from the 69th.

Gil I think the reason I'm so angry is a
matter of personal pride. I've always wanted
to be a fighter pilot and complete a tour of
combat and I had the chance until this thing
came along. Now it seems that I will continue
```

to be a Stateside commando.

That is not the most important matter, however. Here in Korea we get three points a month toward rotation. Thirty six points are needed to leave the Far East. In Japan you get only one point a month and the normal tour there is thirty-six months.

No one has the slightest idea where it is going or what is to be accomplished, but the rumors have us going on an intensive training program in Japan flying the new F-84F or the new F-86D. If this is the case, which I'm praying that it is, we will train for some months, and then come back here and finish up. Another alternative is that even if it is not a deal where we will come back here we may not have to stay in Japan the full tour.

Gil, Honey, I seriously don't know what I'll do if I have to be away from you and the States for another two and a half years. It seems the weight of the world has been thrown on my shoulders, having to face an assignment like that.

While at Fifth Air Force I found out that a Colonel I knew while at Luke is to be the CO of the affair, named Operation Snowshoe, and as I was leaving the building I saw him and asked him if I could get off the list, but since we were fairly good friends at Luke I doubt if he'll let me off.

Darlin, I really don't feel like answering your stinker letter, but when I do I promise it won't be a stinker. I'm tired and don't feel like writing any more.

It's times like these that I really need you. I need you so much, Gil.

You're in my mind always.
Your Joe

I read and reread this letter, trying to comprehend what it meant to the future of my relationship with Joe. He would be leaving Korea, and would be sent to Japan, possibly for another two and a half years, on a yet unknown assignment. I felt like all my hopes that we could have a future together might be dashed. I was deeply disappointed and confused, and so upset that I didn't feel like writing him. Next day the following letter from him arrived:

3 Dec 52

Hi Baby:

I'm sorry about that letter I wrote yesterday. As I recall it you probably think I decided to dive into the Nile and give it all up. Am in much better spirits today and things don't seem so bad.

Suppose it is adopting the philosophy of making the best of anything no matter how bad it seems and employ the old-womanish rationalization that everything always turns out for the best.

This manly attitude was fed by something as you can guess and that is the strong and seemingly authoritative rumor that although it is an assignment in Japan it will not affect the MOT, Month of Tenure. So that at the longest, if true, I should be home at the latest, next August.

Several other rumors about the same subject that seem to make it more bearable but enough for that subject, at least until something is definite and I really have something to cry about.

Have been put back on combat status and got #12 today. It was a scary one in that all my fuel was siphoning overboard and no one noticed it until we were over the target. By that time it was too late to make it back to the base, having just an eyedropper left, so I decided to try to make K-13. Crossed the

front lines with 30 gallons and touched down
on the runway with 10 gallons. Refueled up
and came back. No sweat!

Haven't much to say in answer to your
"stinker letter" in that I'm not going to
write another stinker myself. Much would be
reiteration anyway and we both know what the
situation is so let's be nice and see what
comes of it. Haven't gotten around to writing
that letter of introduction to my parents for
you but will as soon as things quiet down
here.

Honey, the beer at our new bar was just
replenished and I'm late so I'll close for
now, but tomorrow you'll get another
masterpiece of sarcasm, wit, funny tales,
ironical bits of satirical humor from the
FIGMO as they now call me. F— I Got My
Orders, or as some call me OMGIF, which means
in kittenish Korean, Oh My Gosh I'm F_____.

The Top Secret Kid,
Joe

He was obviously trying to maintain control of his emotions until
he found out more about this new assignment. I, however, was thrown
into a state of anxiety, having no idea of what was going to happen.
Would he be gone an additional two and a half years? Would I ever see
him again?

8 Dec 52

Dear Gil,

Everything here is so secret that I feel like
I'm living behind the Iron Curtain. People
walk around saying nothing because they can't
say anything. For four days all persons were
frozen in their places and no one was allowed
to come to this base or leave the base or go
into or out of Japan. We all assumed it was

because Ike was coming here. We waited patiently and then yesterday we found out he had been here and gone. During this incommunicado mail came in but none went out so the letters of pathos I wrote you probably didn't leave here until yesterday.

About my new assignment, I can't say anything, mostly because I don't know much more than I did but what more I have found out is secret so you will be in the dark for a while yet. It may be a month or so before I can tell you where I am stationed or what I am doing.

Yesterday evening during one of our regularly scheduled impromptu parties I put on a show. Swiped a black blanket and put a dagger with it to fill the role of a cloak and dagger act, symbolizing my new secret assignment. The troops were receptive.

I'm not flying anymore here, so I can party all night long and sleep all day since I've been relieved of all my secondary duties. As a result of this newly acquired freedom I've gone berserk.

Our new CO was coming from business in Taegu last night and found a little waif lying in the road and the little fellow touched his heart so he brought him home. He's now our mascot. We call him George and anything that comes to our minds but George seems to be sticking. George is here now watching me type. He seems to be fascinated by the typewriter. I have some classical records on the record player and while the player was giving out with the Toreador's Song he was humming it. He's only about six but is into everything. Can't imagine where he learned the Toreador's Song. He woke McGee up by pushing a loaded 45 pistol in his face. Don't know who he belongs to but he's probably an orphan. Kim asked him where his Mamasan and

Papasan were and he gesticulated and answered with a "Boom." Guess they were killed.

Painted another picture. The other one, of my area, took about two weeks to do, but I whipped this one out in one day. This is of the Surrealist and Symbolic schools. The ideas of several things are combined into a broad general theme of an attitude on life. It was bright flashing colors all through it and no one quite understands it but all of the laymen seem very impressed with the color and like it much more than the first one. Bert insists that I enter this one in the Art Contest too. As soon as I get settled in my new home I'll do one especially for you. If the ideas keep coming through to me and I keep throwing on the oil you'll have enough paintings to cover your walls completely.

Received a letter from my Mother today and I'll quote a paragraph: "Joe I think that is very nice of you to want Gil and me to write to each other, only Joe—if she is a school teacher—and, Oh, me, you know the letters I write." She is referring to her grammar and spelling. I know you'll be as lenient with her as you are with my grammar and spelling. Please be.

This has been a beautiful Fall so far, Korean style, but the weather is changing abruptly, down to ten above zero today. After rolling out of the sack the other day at 0530 for duty as runway control officer and shaving in cold water, I decided on another investment, an electric razor. Never did like them but the idea of shaving in the sack before going out into the cold intrigued me. Got one and don't like it but don't like shaving with cold water, either.

George refuses to sit at the bar with the boys. He doesn't like sardines, but loves cheese. OOOPS. He dropped a record and is crying.

And so to the strains of the "Moonlight
Sonata" and the wailing of George I'll close.

I'd better not sign my name to this letter,
being a top secret person, so I'll close as

Lover

I didn't write him for several days after learning that he might be overseas for another two and a half years. I honestly didn't know what to write. I thought that he might be getting additional information about his assignment, so I decided to wait until I heard more from him. My delay caused him considerable concern, as expressed in the following letters:

14 Dec 52

OFFICIAL REPRIMAND

SUBJECT: Failure to write letters

TO: Miss Gilberta Cosulich
Civilian Box 267
WAFB
Chandler, Arizona

On November 26, 1952, I received a letter
from you, a very nice and wanted letter. Not
expecting another for a few days I didn't
concern myself about not getting one.
Anxiously hoping for one after four or five
days I trudged twice daily to the cubical of
despair and happiness, my mail box. Six days.
Seven days, a week.

Now there was cause for concern but with
necessary rationalization I reasoned that I
had no reason to worry because it was
probably due to our free loading friends of
the post office. Eight days, nine days, and
then ten. All sorts of wild ideas flirted
with my imagination. Surely the masterly
malicious mailmen couldn't have been so
idiotic as to lose a letter. Having changed

squadrons and groups I spent half a day
checking through all their old mail thinking
that perhaps some inane a— had sent it there.
No mail from you. Had been receiving mail
from Mother and other people so I excused the
post office employees.

Tomorrow will be two weeks and something must
have happened. No reason to get excited
because there is nothing to do until I get
word on the situation. Keep cool and calm.
Now it occurred to me that perhaps you just
didn't write.

Black black black black black black black
black

Then it came.

Grey grey grey grey grey grey grey grey

and then two days later another came and all
is fine again.

Bright bright bright bright bright bright
bright bright

The reason for the delay, and I quote, "I
wanted to hear from you again before I
wrote."

This reprimand will be as paragraph 3 as an
endorsement and will be answered immediately
and mandatorily.

Dear Gil:

As a general rule I can take the good with
the bad and not complain too much and few
people ever know how concerned I am about
things. I was not going to write to you and
ever mention the long delay but since we
agreed to tell all, I did. I was very angry
with you, and still am to a certain degree.
However, as of the moment all is forgiven.

Have to finish this in a hurry and then pack,
for tomorrow I'm to leave for my secret

assignment. Sounds like a movie. We had a
briefing the other day and found out where we
were going and when. Can't say where we will
be stationed until we get there. Don't know
as yet what we will be doing, but if it is
what I suspect I doubt if I'll ever be able
to tell you what we are doing until I get
back to the US. Everyone here is dying to
find out where we are going and what we will
be doing. They have all made guesses and some
are correct as to where but none have the
slightest idea of what. I don't know what my
new address will be but Bert will forward all
my mail so until you get my next letter with
my new address keep sending them to this
place.

Enclosed, as you have seen, is my letter of
introduction for you to my parents. Hope it's
O. K. I know Mother will be pleased to hear
from you as she has said several times that
she would like to.

My mind is roving and I can't concentrate
because of my concern about tomorrow and how
all this new stuff will end. Excuse, please.

George has completely captured the barracks.
I guess we really needed a pet or something
to take our minds off flying and the
situation here. Don't know what fatal
attraction I have for children but I'm
George's favorite. He wakes me up every
morning and spends the whole day with me.
Taught him to play hide and seek with a
basketball, and he squeals with delight when
I can't find it. He caught me cheating,
peeking through my fingers, and now makes me
hide my face in the pillow. The troops have
taught him to play solitaire, dice, to palm
money, all sorts of words and funny sayings.
He's really a card, and smart. Our boy is one
of the smartest kids I've ever seen. Not just
because he's our boy, of course, but he shows

real talent. He won't come near me now,
because I'm leaving, I guess. He saw me
packing a few things and asked Kim what I was
doing and when Kim told him I was leaving he
ran out and I haven't seen him since.

In a way I'm sorry to be leaving. All my
friends are here and I wish I could spend
Christmas here with them. This will be a
lonely and sad Christmas and New Year's Eve.

Received your most welcome gift of olives and
anchovies and was pleased with your mother's
antipasto, too. Haven't used them yet because
we have no gin and no ice for our martinis
but will think of you when I have a chance to
use them. Tell your Mother that I did get
them and I thank her.

Going to close. Will write from my new
station.

Am thinking of you all the time and will
reserve my thoughts and mind for you on New
Years Eve.

Later

Have finished packing, including my
typewriter, and am about to go to our bar for
a last drink with the boys.

Honey my thoughts of you and knowing you are
thinking of me helps a great deal, but I wish
you could be with me to help me face the
difficulties and hardships ahead of me.

Thinking of you, Love, Joe

I sensed Joe's loneliness and regret at leaving his fellow combat pilots. He left Korea the day after writing this letter, still not knowing fully what was involved in the new Top Secret assignment. He only knew that it could mean his remaining overseas an additional two and a half years.

* * * *

Chapter Five

LETTERS FROM JAPAN

It was December 15, 1952 when Joe and his thirty-two fellow pilots flew their planes from Korea to Komaki Air Base, Japan. He wrote of a sharp contrast between their Spartan life in Korea and what they found upon their arrival in Japan:

16 Dec 52

Dear Gil,

Am here, my new station, Komaki Air Base, Nagoya, Japan. Yesterday we flew our F-84's from K-2, Korea here and there was quite a reception committee to greet us, a General, numerous Colonels, and hoards of lesser officers. We seem to be something special. Can't say what we are going to be doing here because I don't know myself as yet but I can't even tell you of my suspicions. All you are allowed to know is that I am here permanently and the duty I am to perform is Japanese Air Defense. Air defense is what we are to say we are doing, so that's it.

The base itself is a typical Air Force base like you would find in the States but to us it seems like the Astor Hotel after living like ghouls in Korea. These things wouldn't seem strange to you but we are like prisoners

reprieved, a tile shower, our own rooms, the
little fact that the shower and latrine are
in the same building makes it seem like a
different world.

I suppose we looked very funny to the
reception committee, grizzled, hardened,
dirty, and they just smiled when they saw us
gape at the quarters.

There are only thirty-three of us but they
had a party for us at the club and had
invited all the nurses at the hospital nearby
and the civilian girls who work for the Air
Force and the consulate. Never seen so many
white girls at one time. When we found out
about the party we did our best to spruce up
but after living like a caveman for three
months it was a hopeless task. Hadn't combed
my hair for that time and when I tried it
looked worse than it did before. Didn't have
any uniforms—just flight suits—and we looked
like scraggly scarecrows. We tried to dance
but with the big combat boots and jump boots
and not having danced in three months we
didn't do so good.

Had a wonderful time and all I can say is
that it's great to be a human being again.

We haven't been briefed by the general as yet
so I don't know much more than I did before.

During the weeks at K-2 when I didn't have
anything to do I had the beginnings of an
idea about us which seems more probable now
and although it's still in its embryo stage
it might be the thing to do. I don't want to
say anything about it now because I don't
know how long I'm going to be here. The only
reason I mention it is that I want you to
know that I've given it considerable thought
and that when I do tell you of it you won't
think that it's an unconsidered decision.

Don't mean to keep dwelling on this subject

but I can't get over this place. My room is really something. Harry Archuleta is my roommate... he went through Willy with me, an old time navigator and we have a lot in common. His home is in Casa Grande, Arizona, and I think you met him while we were at Willy. He's married and has three youngsters.

Speaking of people you remember, do you remember Jack Helms, a cadet in Charlie class? I'm sure you met him because he was one of my best friends. He was killed the other day, went straight in on the target. I'm going to write his parents, but these are really tough letters to write. He was one of my best and dearest friends.

Have to close now Darlin. We are all going in to the five-story Base Exchange and buy some respectable clothes.

Love, Joe
My new address:
1st/Lt. J. R. Guth
9th Fighter Bomber Squadron
APO 710, c/o PM
San Francisco, Calif.

I could tell from Joe's letter that he was trying hard to make the best of this sudden change in his flying assignment. My thoughts were filled with unanswered questions. It occurred to me that perhaps he would be in less danger in Japan than he had been in Korea. But I knew that he wasn't able to share any new information.

The Christmas holidays were approaching, and Joan and I decided to give a party in our apartment for some of the friends we'd made at Willy. I saw this as a good distraction from my constant concern and anxiety about my relationship with Joe. We invited our fellow teachers, the parents of some of our students, and a few of the flight instructors and their wives, plus some of the student officers we knew. We decorated the apartment with garlands, candles, and a Christmas tree. There were plenty of beverages and finger food, music, and holiday cheer. We sent Joe some of the pictures from the party, since he knew many of the people who came.

20 Dec 52

Dearest Gil:

I'm stupid and I know it. While lying here daydreaming of you it suddenly occurred to me that you won't get the last letter I wrote to you until after the holidays after you get back to Willy from Tucson. I was going to call you long distance during the holidays and wish you a Merry Christmas and a Happy New Year, but I don't know your telephone number in Tucson. AWK, I don't even know your address.

"What are you going to do now Joe?" "Duh—well—er—ah—I don't know, George." Unless you have told the post office there to forward your mail you won't hear from me until you get back to Willy from the season's festivities. Not getting my last letter you won't be able to write me at my new address until then, which means I don't hear from you for a long time. I sure hope you told the post office at Willy to send you your mail to Tucson over the holidays and used a little more foresight than I. I could have taken your address off the packages you sent me but I'm not that clever.

As usual I acquired more junk in three months in Korea than most people acquire in three years and when it came time to pack I couldn't get all the stuff into my bags. Had several Christmas presents that I had to open, one from the Salvation Army in St. Louis. Don't know why they sent me one and before I opened it I thought it was a joke, but they sent several newspapers from St. Louis, a Coronet magazine, a pocket book, Mickey Spillane, a can of peanuts, can of hard candy, soap, salve and several other

things. Most of the things weren't of much
value but the thought was extremely nice and
I'm going to write them a nice thank you
note. The other was a package from my mother
that I thought was a Christmas package, but
it was a package she had sent a long time ago
with pajamas and all sorts of eating goodies.
I'm glad I opened them because it removed a
lot of the bulk. I really didn't open any of
the presents that I wasn't supposed to open.

In cleaning out my desk I threw out all the
old letters that had accumulated except yours
which I wanted to keep. Have them all tied up
in a neat package.

I'm really sorry you don't like the mustache,
it added something, quite a bit, I think.
Mother liked it and so did Dad, and most
others too. You, however, will have your way.

Today is Dec. 20 here, and although it's
about ten o'clock the 19th there I'm
pretending it's the 20th and you and Joan are
opening your presents from me. I sure hope
you like it. Joan, too. Don't I wish I could
be there and see first hand the expressions
on your faces. Hope you're not disappointed.

I'm real anxious to see the picture of you
that you're sending. Have a nice place to put
it now that I'm living in a room and have
some decent furniture.

Speaking of the mysterious box the present to
you came in, I made it myself and I remember
when I made it I was thinking over the letter
you wrote asking about my domestic abilities,
and I thought to myself, "She should see some
of my woodworking handicrafts." That is why
it is such a good box. So there!

My letters sound like obituaries I suppose
but I think you do want to hear of the people
you might have known at Willy. One of the
seven people to come to Willy from Greenville

basic pilot school with me was John Corbett.
I'm sure you recall him. I had been with John
for almost two years, and knew him for as
long a time as anyone I've known this tour.
He was killed the other day. Got hit by flack
on a dive bomb mission and didn't bail out.
They say his plane exploded behind enemy
lines. John told me over and over again in
the States that he was sure he was never
coming back from Korea. I told him over and
over to get out of flying if he didn't think
he was going to come back but he stayed with
it and he isn't coming back. Believe me if I
ever have the feeling that I'm not coming
back I've taken my last airplane ride. I
don't think there's enough rank in the Air
Force nor enough money to get me into the
plane when I didn't have the utmost
confidence.

Gil, some of these things must sound like
they are happening in another world to you.
To me they are gruesome but it's all the life
there is here. The world I'm in is Japan and
Korea and flying and a completely new life. I
suppose it's just because I've gotten only a
few letters from you recently and because of
the messed up mail situation it will be quite
a while before I'll hear from you again but
you seem to me to be in a different world.
During the days, and months now, all I think
about is flying, this new secret project, the
new people I'm with, my new life in Japan,
the obscure future, and all the other
concerning subjects. The only contact with
the world over there is through your letters,
and Mother's, but sometimes it seems that you
are just a dream and I've caught myself
wondering if you're really real or if I've
been imagining the whole thing. I know you're
real but you seem so far away and the future
so dim that I have to make myself believe it
isn't a dream. Honey, I wish there were

something we could do about it.

Christmas is but four days off but the spirit of Christmas has completely missed the Air Base of Komaki, Japan. I wish to hell I had your phone number so I could call you and bring us both back to reality.

I think I know the reason all seems so hopeless now. In Korea we all looked on the situation as something to endure until we got back in a short time, but now with the possibility of staying here years, the future seems to have faded into the mist of uncertainty. It probably sounds like I'm completely depressed, but I'm not depressed, just confused. For one of the few times in my life I'm unable to sift all the facts and desires and come up with a workable solution. I don't know where I stand, where I'm going, or what to do.

I'm sure this is a temporary state and soon I'll be able to straighten it all out. Until then I'll remain confused but still loving you and although in a dream you are the only thing that means anything to me. The New Year of 1953 will be ushered in, in my thoughts, by Miss Gilberta Cosulich, Teacher Extraordinary.

And so, from Mr. and Mrs. Guth's best looking son, Joe, all my love for 1953 and thereafter.

Love, Joe

The disappointment, loneliness, and heartache Joe expressed in this letter tore at my emotions. He was struggling to cope with the total change in his hopes and plans forced upon him by this new assignment. Facing what seemed like a bleak Christmas, he was finding the struggle even more difficult.

I tried to write cheerful, funny letters, and mailed him festive Christmas packages, but I knew that mail delivery would be slow and sporadic as usual. My heart ached.

Joan and I exchanged Christmas gifts before we left Willy for the Christmas vacation. She was going to be visiting relatives, and we wouldn't be seeing much of each other in Tucson over the holidays.

So the night before leaving Willy, we sat in our living room, took Joe's suggestion, and opened a bottle of beer. I took the small wooden box we'd received from him with our names printed neatly on it, and the words DO NOT OPEN TILL CHRISTMAS underlined in red. He had constructed the box so strongly it took some effort to get it open. Inside were two little packages, wrapped in brightly colored paper. First, Joan opened the one with her name on it. It was a beautiful silver ring mounted with a large moonstone.

"Oh, how beautiful!" Joan exclaimed. "Thank you, Joe Guth!"

Then I opened mine. Inside was a bracelet, inlaid with jade and pearls. It was gorgeous.

"Oh, Joe," I said softly. "It's so lovely. Thank you." I wore it proudly for many years, and I still have it.

During the two holiday weeks in Tucson, there were a few get-togethers of old friends and classmates, and a couple of parties. But I thought of Joe constantly, and was very glad to see this letter from him when it arrived at my family home:

```
                           St. Nick's Night

                              25 Dec 52

Dear Gilberta,

It's Christmas Eve and I've become slightly
loaded while sitting in the Club in solitude.
All the troops went to town for a gala
celebration but I have to fly tomorrow, so
just a small party for me. Hooray!

I wish all the mailings to me would come as
swiftly as your Mother's. Your portable tree
came, which I finally assembled after
employing much Yankee ingenuity, and it is
```

now decorating the room of Lt.'s Archuleta and Guth. Thank you. Unfortunately my other friends and relatives don't have as much influence as your Mama because nothing else has gotten here for Xmas. The good fortune, however, is that she sent your address in Tucson, so I can tell you of the news.

The news, the whole subject of this letter can be told in one sentence. I will be stationed here in Japan for at least two years. TWO YEARS Gil. It didn't come as an awful shock because I've suspicioned it all along. I know what my duties will be and there is no question of their importance, tremendous, to the Air Force and the country, but this is no consolation to my broken plans and aching heart. Like all subservients of the military however I will be a good soldier and perform my duty.

It is not of paramount importance how long I will be here, not my duties, nor my attitude, but its effect on us is most important. Please write immediately, but after careful consideration, and tell me what this means to you in regards to us.

This has taken quite a while and I'm nearing oblivion, so I'll go beddie bye.

Your Joe

I read and reread Joe's letter. It was no longer a surprise that he would be gone another two years, but this confirmed it and made it official. Now that it was for sure, I didn't know what was going to happen next. How could I agree to wait for him for two years? Becoming engaged by mail seemed to be so full of risk and uncertainty. Where did our courtship stand now? What would be the outcome? I didn't know what to do.

29 December 52

Dearest Gil:

Had the second letter from my brother, the first in 1945 while overseas. Actually there isn't much point in us writing since Mother relays all the news, but once in a while it's nice. Don't remember how much I told you about him, but his name is Jack, age 24, 6' tall, not quite as good looking, equally as good an athlete. He's going to get married the 10th of January. He's a graduate engineer from the Rolla School of Mines, U. of Missouri, and is with the US Geodetic Survey. All this briefing because he may be by to visit with you in January or February. After they get married they are going on a honeymoon and then visit with my folks for a couple of weeks in St. Louis during which time he is going to get a new car and then drive to Washington State. He suggested that he may be going through Arizona and wanted to know if we're serious enough to have him visit you. I know you would like to have him stop by and say hello.

In a way I wish you hadn't sent me your picture. It's sitting on my dresser and you're looking at me with that look that would get you, and myself, into serious trouble with the church and all the social and moral laws in the land. Each night and each morning you'll be looking at me like that and it's downright teasing, but I love it and I'm very pleased to have it. An excellent picture, didn't remember the dimple, and there is only one thing I'd rather have, the real thing!

I think I'm more anxious to find out how you and Joan and all the relatives liked your gifts than I was to get mine. I do so much hope you really like them. I'm more eagerly awaiting the mail to find out.

A very simple closing, as we both close our
letters. All I'm thinking about is you all
the time. Maybe we can do something about it.

This was a short letter to you. I'll write
tomorrow or very soon about all the other
things but for now, I love you.

Joe

I was still thrown by the news about his extended overseas tour, but I was glad to see that his morale was improving. However, the long delays between our letters continued to cause frequent uncertainty and frustration between us:

6 Jan 53

My Dear Gilberta,

Came into my room this afternoon and looked
on my bed and screamed, tossed my cap on the
floor and stomped on it, beat the wall,
hollered, raved, ranted, kicked the wall,
pouted, cursed the world, the military, the
Japanese, the Koreans, the masses and
multitudes, gnashed my teeth, pulled my hair,
fell on the floor and writhed, foamed at the
mouth and when the tantrum ended there was
still no letter from you. The bed, except for
the blanket, was bare.

Now don't misunderstand Miss because I'm not
accusing you of not writing again, but I hate
the world, all the people in it pick on me,
even the teachers in school used to pick on me.

If I've ever said anything nice about the
people of the US mails I take it all back.
They're vindictive, nauseous, heinous,
monsters, masters at the art of mental
torture, and would make the sadistic oriental
mind look like a tale from the Vienna Woods
lyrics.

I did get a letter from my Mother yesterday which was written on the 30th of December, just seven days old, but her previous letter was the 19th. That leaves several letters out and those two letters sound like the beginning and ending of a book with the middle left out. None of it makes sense without the middle.

At present I'm debating how to end it all and I've almost decided the best way would be to lose myself in the streets of Nagoya. If I didn't mark the trail it would take years to find me and I doubt if any normal American could find his own way out.

I wasn't going to write until I heard from you, but I know you are writing and I see no reason for punishing you or me for the evils of the system. Hope you will forgive me for not having written sooner. Will write again in the next few days. As you know, letters are hard to write when there are no reference letters. Have a lot of small news which I'll relate next time I write.

The most remarkable thing about your picture is that you look so fresh and clean, and the most descriptive word, kissable. Spend a lot of time staring at it.

Love, Joe

The long periods of time with no letters were interspersed with the arrival of several at once. In between times, however, we were both struggling to keep an optimistic outlook.

I had sent Joe's parents a Christmas card and letter as the holidays approached. A letter from his mother arrived early in January. It verified how very close his family was:

Tuesday, Jan 6, 1953

St. Louis, Mo.

Dear Gil,

We received your most welcome letter. Joe had
written and told us he sent a letter to you
as an introduction, so I was really looking
forward to hearing from you.

You wrote such a lovely letter. I am almost
afraid to answer, as I am a very poor letter
writer. But I'll try. Joe had talked many
times of you Gil when he was home on leave,
and wrote many times about you in his
letters. So I feel I know you quite well.

Joe sent home such lovely Christmas presents
to everyone. His brother Jack also sent home
Christmas presents for everyone. I think Dad
and I are such lucky parents to have two such
thoughtful boys.

We did have a nice Christmas but a lonely
one. This was the first year that neither Joe
nor Jack was home with us for Christmas. We
also got a very definite order saying Do Not
Open Before Christmas. I also received a
beautiful set of earrings and bracelet. I
just love it.

One of our best Christmas presents was a
letter from Joe saying he has a new
assignment and was leaving Korea. His last
letter came from Japan (as I guess you know.)
No matter where he is sent, we feel it is
better than being in Korea. We can understand
how Joe feels about wanting to stay in Korea
and getting three points a month, so he can
come home in a year. Being sent somewhere
else he only gets one point a month. We would
rather have him safe even if it does take a
little longer.

Gil I thought my heart would break the day we
got his first letter telling us he was in

Korea (That's between us.) I always try and
write cheerful letters to him.

That is one reason why Mr. Guth started
getting me interested in building a new home.
It did help because it kept me too busy to
think.

We are living in our new home four weeks now
and just love it. We like the neighborhood
and shopping is close by. I haven't had much
time as yet to shop because of moving, but I
know I'll love it.

Yes Gil, St. Louis is quite a city. I only
say that because I have never lived anywhere
else, although we have traveled quite a bit.
Yes, we have been in the Southwest, just
passing through. We spent a month in San
Francisco and California. We loved California
and Dad would like to live there, but me I
guess I still like my hometown best. There is
an old saying about St. Louis, "If you can
live in St. Louis you can live anywhere." We
have very hot weather in summer, and very
cold weather in winter, lots of snow.

I don't know if Joe told you his brother Jack
is getting married the 10th of January (next
Saturday). Jack is stationed in Seattle
Washington and is marrying a very lovely girl
from near there, named Joan Hayes. We visited
Jack in Seattle and met Joanie, and we both
liked her very much. We are not going to the
wedding because they are having a very small
one. They are leaving on a honeymoon right
after the wedding, then they are coming to
St. Louis to stay with us for a week or so.

We are having a small wedding party for them
on the 17th. Jack always wanted Joe to be his
best man at his wedding, but Uncle Sam has
his way.

We haven't had a letter from Joe for almost a

week. We just wonder if he will stay in Japan
or be sent somewhere else.

Yes, Joe does write interesting letters (of
course that's my boy).

You know I could go on for hours about my
boys, but I better close for now.

A Happy New Year to you, Gil

Sincerely, Mrs. J. Guth

The sincerity and warmth of her letter touched me, and made me feel even more connected to Joe. She and Joe's dad were obviously very proud of and close to their sons, and Joe had made it apparent that he loved his family very much.

There were more long periods of time with no mail, interrupted by the arrival of many letters all at once. When we did receive several of each other's letters at a time, we both wrote about how glad we were, and how eagerly we had been waiting. In between times, however, it was evident that both our spirits were sagging.

Even though Joe was now in Japan, out of the combat areas of Korea, he continued to lose good friends in the war. Most of them had been at Willy with him, and I had met many of them. It shocked and saddened me greatly when he wrote me of losing someone whom I knew.:

10 Jan 53

My Dearest Gil,

The mail finally came yesterday, a whole
boatload of it and I'm once again only a week
behind in the news of the US. Your most
wonderful and welcome letters of Dec. 26 and
Jan. 2 were there too. When I get a whole
pile of mail from a lot of different people I
start to read theirs first and save yours
until last, but invariably I can't wait and
end up by reading yours first, once, twice,
maybe three times and then give some time to

the less important people.

The picture of you with Joan and Instructor O'Hara at your Christmas party is real good, but with the one of you on the balcony I've gotten as close as a quarter inch and even with my 20-20 plus I can't make you out too good. Send me the others when you get them. I'm covering the wall with them. A pin-up yet!

Honey, I'm so pleased that you, and Joan, liked the gifts I sent you. I had never seen much jade until I got here and I was very impressed with it. There seems to be a lot of it here. Much of their work is in jade. The relation of how you and Joan opened the box was a treat to read. I'm real glad you liked them.

A little bad news about some of my friends. Enclosed is an article about Tom Tudor. Haven't been able to find out which hospital he's in, but I hope the article is right when they say he's OK.

The Phoenix Gazette

'Blinded' State Jet Pilot Lands Safely

SEOUL, Jan. 8 (AP)—An Arizona jet pilot, blinded by Red ground fire over North Korea, was "talked in" to a safe landing by a fellow pilot yesterday, the U. S. Fifth Air Force reported.

An air spokesman said 2nd Lt. Joel T. Tudor of Yuma suffered no permanent injury to his eyes and was "resting comfortably" in an American hospital in South Korea tonight.

Lt. James E. Larue Jr., of 2408 Pelham, Houston, Tex., was credited with "talking" Tudor back to a safe landing at an advance allied air base.

TUDOR, A GRADUATE of Williams Air Force Base jet school in Chandler, Ariz., had just dropped his bombs on a rail line near Sariwon, in northwest Korea, Wednesday afternoon when Red antiaircraft fire shattered the canopy of his F-84. Pieces of jagged plexiglass hit him in the face, temporarily blinding him completely in the left eye and almost completely in the right.

"Tudor radioed me he had been hit and couldn't see his instruments or distinguish anything," said Larue, the flight leader. "I pulled up near him and started telling him which way to go and

LT. JOEL TUDOR

when to go up or down or use more or less power."

Larue said Tudor remained "cool and collected" throughout the ordeal.

TUDOR SAID making the blind landing was the toughest part, "but Larue talked me in all the way."

It took three passes at the field before Larue got Tudor talked in to position at the far end of the runway. Then, said Larue, Tudor was going too fast and "I told him to pull his gear and belly in."

Col. Victor E. Warford, Chickasha, Okla., wing commander, commended Larue for very good judgment in telling Tudor to belly in.

PHOENIX GAZETTE RUNS AN ARTICLE ABOUT NEAR-FATAL CRASH OF JOEL "TOM" TUDOR.

Years later Tom personally told us of his amazing crash landing and ground ejection. Flying a combat mission in North Korea, his aircraft was hit by ground fire and he was blinded. His wingman, Jim La Rue, led him to the runway of a U.S. base and talked him down over their radio frequency. The ensuing uncontrolled landing resulted in Tom's aircraft catching fire and finally stopping in the runway overrun. Tom realized he must evacuate the burning aircraft immediately. In his panic, and because he was blinded, he inadvertently activated the ejection seat. When the ejection seat fired into the air, he tumbled several times, and the parachute did not deploy. He struck the ground on the upper back and shoulder of his young, strong body. He sustained extensive injuries and endured months of hospitalization and treatment. Miraculously, his sight returned and he was healed of his injuries.

```
Another of my friends didn't fare so well,
however. Al Rase was another of those who
came from Greenville to Willy with me. While
at Greenville I was in charge of a flight of
12 student officers. Of the 12, seven came to
Willie: Myself, Grady Hinson, Billie Graham,
Bill Walker, Jack Denton, John Corbett and Al
Rase. Walker got anoxia and has a permanent
brain injury, John Corbett went in a short
time ago and now Al Rase. To go in like John
isn't so bad, but to go like Al is a horrible
way to die. He was on a night mission and got
slightly lost. He radioed in and asked for a
steer back to the base, which they gave him,
but he was out over the ocean. He ran short
of fuel and didn't make land because of the
terrific headwinds he was bucking and had to
bail out. He didn't wear his Mae West, a sort
of water wings which keeps you afloat in the
water, and although he was only 23 miles from
land we assume he drowned. While coming from
Greenville to Willy he and his wife drove out
with me and I knew them both well. He had a
baby boy just before he went to Korea. The
whole thing is so tragic.
```

Judging from your letters and mine we both
spend most of our time, except while
concentrating on our work, thinking about
each other. I too spend a lot of thought
saying, I wonder what the little darling
would think of that, or I wish you could see
this or that, or hear that funny story. Oh
Gil there are so many things I want to share
with you and say to you and do for you that
letters don't quite get across.

Honey, with some of the small talk down I
feel that I must say something about the idea
I had. When I mentioned it I wasn't sure of
my length of stay here in Japan but merely
had a strong suspicion. Now it's true. I will
be here for a long time. The thought nucleus
I had was in the event I did have to stay
here a long time and I've been working on it
all the time.

There is something, however, which keeps me
from telling you about it, and that is your
uncertainty about Us. I want to give you all
the chance I can to decide something. But
this change of stations and length of tours
calls for new thinkings.

Joe at this point was only hinting at what his ideas about our getting together were, but I sensed that what he had in mind was for me to go to Japan to visit him, and possibly to marry him over there. I still felt too uncertain to agree to such a plan. So we continued to correspond with no immediate plan being discussed.

Today, Saturday, we had a 16 ship show
formation over the city of Nagoya and over a
number of the bases here in Japan to show them
what a real fighter bomber outfit looks like.
We roared across the places with the tip tanks
interlocked at about a hundred feet going over
550 mph. The phone calls have been coming ever
since we landed complaining about the broken

windows from our jet blast and the waking of
babies and all sorts of things. It was really
fun though. Even the crew chiefs said they had
never seen anything like it. It was like 16
Acrojets instead of four.

Have been at the club a number of times and
after a few beers all I can think about is
you. I seem to get so sentimental about you
that I've considered giving up beer. The
other night, while trying to get a good glow
on, because of no mail from you, so that I
could go right to sleep without lying there
thinking about you all night, the radio
played Kay Starr's "Wheel of Fortune." As you
remember, that was popular when I was at
Willy and it used to play every morning at
the mess hall and I could remember those
mornings as happy ones after an evening, a
nice one, with you. That ended the beer
drinking and I came back to the barracks and
flopped in the sack like I had been smoking
marijuana.

My Christmas was very bare as I wrote, and
New Year's Eve was worse. Four of us decided
to go to Kyoto instead of staying here 'cause
nothing was doing anyway. Herb Meyer, our
flight commander, has more money than he
knows what to do with, and he bought an old
1946 Buick convertible. In that we went to
Kyoto. It's just 85 miles away, and we went
on the national highway of Japan, which we
assumed was a good road. We left at five in
the evening, expecting to have a good dinner
and ring in the New Year properly. We didn't
reckon on the Japanese highway, however, or
the condition of the car, because we had two
flat tires and the road was so full of bumps
and holes we didn't make but 20 miles an
hour. As '52 went out and '53 came in we were
still 20 miles from Kyoto and hungry, and
cold, and worse still, cold sober. We

stopped, got out, and toasted to each other
and all the loved ones back home with raw
whiskey. Happy New Year. You, however, were
in my thoughts as much as if you had been
there.

I told Mother and Dad about my being in
combat, not much, just that I had flown 12
missions. I, of course, didn't say anything
about the people who had been killed, but you
can be vigilant about that subject.

Must close, and do so with all my love. You,
too, please keep the letters coming often.

Today, Jan. 10, my little brother is getting
married. I do feel like Uncle Joe today.

Your Joe

It was sad to read that his Christmas and New Year's had been so bare, as he called it. It was apparent that he was still striving to accept this sudden change in his assignment and with it the extension in his overseas time. I, too, was trying to accept the change of events, and to comprehend what it all meant to our future.

Early in January I enrolled in a creative writing class at the nearby college to help the time pass and also to accumulate some of the units required to keep my teaching credential current. I learned that Joe, too, had an interest in writing. He sent me some of his short stories, and asked me to send some of mine to him.

Another thing I was learning about him was that he could put away enormous amounts of food without ever gaining a pound. He told me that flying took huge amounts of energy, and he needed to stay "refueled."

12 Jan 53

Dearest Gil:

Didn't get to write yesterday as I said I
would 'cause we flew all day again. Sunday
yet! Last night they had their usual banquet
at the Kanko Officers Club in Nagoya. It is a
buffet dinner for a dollar and it is the most
fabulous thing you have ever seen for one
buck. I had three helpings, the first time
everything, the second time just more steak,
another dozen fried shrimp, two more lobster
thermadors, spaghetti, enchiladas, covered
with salad and Roquefort dressing. The third
time I just had the lobster, spaghetti,
enchiladas and Roquefort. Then I had two
double drambouies and a pot of coffee. I
could have died happily and almost did. I
still felt stuffed this morning.

All day I've been retyping the short story
and "The Perfect Squelch," which I've
enclosed. The next time you have to hand in a
story for your class in creative writing,
hand this one in, if it won't upset anything.
I would like to have your instructor's
unbiased, professional opinion on it. Maybe
she can tell why none of my stuff has never
gone over. Tell her to please not spare the
criticism.

The other is a real true story, and I think
it's the kind the Post likes. Would you
please edit this one and send it off. I'm
anxious to see if this one draws any
response.

Yesterday I got your letter of the 4th so it
appears that it's just taking the normal time
again. Also heard from mother saying she and
Dad received your letter. She said that you
write a wonderful letter and was real pleased
to get it. Dad was especially pleased since
he would be able to read your letters but

wouldn't have to do any corresponding. He doesn't write very often as I told you.

The local movie house, which also doubles for the chapel on Sundays, plays only three movies a week, all of which I've seen, so time is beginning to hang heavily again. Think I'll go to the library and get a good book for tonight.

A good friend of mine, Howard Pierson, is stationed here in Japan, too. He was in basic flying school at Greenville, Miss. with me. I talked to him on the phone last week and he is in B-29's out of Yokota, near Tokyo, flying combat missions in Korea. I'm going to try to ferry a plane to Yokota, this coming weekend and visit him. If I can, there will be a big party in Yokota this weekend.

Don't think I mentioned that I got Joan's letter and was very pleased to get it. Jo, I do agree with you on the things you said about Gil and I do have the confidence.

(Secrets, Gil!?)

Honey, I miss you and want you very much.

With love, Joe

Of course my curiosity was aroused by his reference to my friend Joan's letter to him. When I asked her about it she told me that she had written to thank him for the Christmas present. She also wrote him about how cautious I was about relationships. She said she encouraged him to be patient, and to stay confident that things would work out okay for us. Joan liked Joe very much, and I knew that she hoped we would find a way to be together.

18 Jan 53

My Dearest Gil,

It's 0445 in the morning and I'm very very
sleepy. I want to go back to bed so bad, but
up and at em! I wanted to jot this off to you
because I probably won't have time during the
rest of the day and I haven't written for a
long time.

Was in Yokota for three days, weathered in,
and have been so busy I really haven't had
time to write. Didn't know they could get so
much work out of me.

Even this early on a Sunday morning, as all
other mornings, my first thoughts are of you.

Will write soon.

All my love, Joe

20 Jan 53

Dear Gil:

Don't know how long this letter will be cause
I'm about ready to flake out. Dropped you
that short note Sunday and then flew all day.
Yesterday, Monday, we started classes. We go
10 hours a day, and after the second day I'm
ready to drop. My feeble little brain won't
take much more. When we first came on this
deal I looked on it with a wink and my tongue
in my cheek but now even I am awed. I'm
beginning to think I'm a very important
person. They made it plain to us that the
penalty for divulging any information to any
unauthorized persons was HANGING, so that's
enough.

Last Tuesday I got weathered in at Yokota AB
for three days, coincidentally where my buddy
Howard Pierson is stationed, and we had a big
ball for two nights.

G. C. wrote, "I'm waiting for a letter from you—I want one,"

J. R. G. wrote, "I'm waiting for a letter from you—I want one."

SOLUTION: LET'S WRITE MORE OFTEN.

On my behalf I say this, I've been trying to wait a little while and try to write a long, real interesting letter, but if you are like me, and I'm sure you are from what your letters say, you would rather hear little pieces more often than one letter occasionally. So, I'm going to drop you a note at least, very often even if I don't have too much to say, at the sacrifice of these long masterpieces. Masterpieces? Right!

From your last letter it sounds like my story will get there too late for you to hand it in for your class. Your stories must really be good. Will you please send more soon, Miss Cosulich, so that I can read them first hand, and maybe you'll autograph one for me. Can I have one for my very, very own after you become famous?

I'm thinking of you. Getting a little sleepy, so I'll close for now, but promise to write very soon.

With all my love, Your Joe

22 Jan 53

Hi, Honey:

School, school, school, school, school, bah humbug. I would think that any normally bright person would be able to learn almost all there is to know in almost a quarter of a century of school, and I am beginning to think I do know almost everything but as our instructor said today,

"Don't think that because you guys know a lot you know it all, because you are merely pimples on the ass of progress."

That brought a lot of laughs and guffaws, but it also made me realize how much I don't know.

Our correspondence was filled with small talk over the next few weeks. At times it appeared that we were making good progress in understanding each other. My letters continued to be upbeat, but Joe could see that I was still non-committal about the future of our relationship.

25 Jan 53

Honey, I too waited and waited for your letter and I don't know what to say. I've read it over and over again and I am still at a loss as to what to say. Nothing I guess.

Oh Gil, honey please excuse this miserable letter, but I haven't been able to think about Us much lately with school and all so my thoughts are completely jumbled and uncertain. I think a critical time between us is nearing and if you are unable to decide I will have to do something one way or the other.

I'm eating my heart out for you Gil.

Love, Joe

"THERE I WAS..."

Those words brought tears to my eyes. He was getting more discouraged about my continuing uncertainty, and it sounded like he was almost ready to "do something one way or another." I liked his attentiveness and his expressions of love, but I also felt like he was really pushing me, rather than allowing my feelings to unfold gradually. It bothered me that he seemed so desperate for a firm commitment before I was ready to make one.

I was becoming more interested in finding respite from these concerns in the social life at Willy. There were plenty of phone calls, dates, parties, and dances. The attention was comforting and fun. I developed a crush on an extremely handsome student officer. He was so handsome that one evening, on one of my dates with him, an officer's wife said to him, "You're so good-looking you should be pickled." It was a very superficial relationship which ended when his training at Willy was completed. But it added to my confusion about my relationship with Joe: how could I make a commitment to Joe when I had just developed a huge crush on someone else?

Then something happened that pulled Joe and me closer. One day in late January 1953, after classes had ended, I was sitting at my desk grading papers. There was a knock on the classroom door. I opened it, and there stood a tall, handsome officer in a Naval uniform, with a pretty young woman at his side.

"Hi. I'm Jack Guth, Joe's brother. Are you Gil?" Jack and his bride, Joanie, were on their honeymoon and had stopped by to meet me.

The three of us spent the evening together, and Jack talked a lot about his big brother. He told me how Joe had broken all kinds of sports records in high school and college, how he had always been Jack's hero, and what great admiration and respect Jack had for him. Jack was very much like his brother Joe, with a wonderful sense of humor and a very outgoing, winning personality. I suggested they try the after-dinner liqueur to which Joe had introduced me. It was drambouie, and to this day, Jack still calls it "dramboonie." Jack and Joanie stayed at the officers' guest quarters on base that night, and left the next morning to resume their trip. It had been a very enjoyable, and in some ways poignant, evening. Their unexpected visit intensified my wistful thoughts of Joe. And now he was going to be gone two more years. I didn't know what to do.

Sometimes I felt so uncertain and scattered it affected my ability to maintain a calm demeanor with my second graders. I heard myself reprimanding them for minor misdeeds. Sometimes I lost control and yelled at them simply out of frustration. Another day I told them I was going to leave the room and go get the principal to come and talk to them, which I did.

```
                                         27 Jan 53

Dearest Gil:
After five consecutive hours of class I'm
dulled to the point of stupor. A huge hole
was drilled in my head and libraries of
information were stuffed in.

Tonight the movie house is the Chaplains', so
no movie. To the rescue of the weary
schoolboy came a whole volume of short
stories by Gilberta Cosulich, the famed
author. As I groaned with complete
```

satisfaction at the prospect of lying in the sack and reading the stories, motor mouth Archuleta said that I had the evening as fat as a 40 pound robin.

Speaking of being fat, I've put on most of the weight that I lost in Korea. Went over there at 165# and came here at a mere 140. I'm now back up to my fighting weight, not, however, approaching the blimposity of a 40-pound robin.

Gilberta, you're going to have to do something about yourself or US or something because you can't keep hollering at those children, or you'll give them a neurosis or psychosis or a schizoid or something.

While we're on the subject I feel it mandatory to tell you that the trick you pulled on the sweet little innocents was cowardly. It doesn't sound like you. Running to the principal, a beastly thing to do. Fight the battle of the classroom with honor, and if they win, or you lose because of a poor tactic (in which I think you were in tactical error) lose graciously.

Another trend I've noticed in your letters is the beer guzzling. As I remember you would hardly touch a bottle, and I'll tell you, from experience, that you'll not find the solutions to your problems in the bottom of a beer bottle. Alcohol can have serious effects on a person's physique and mental attitude. Beware of the evils of drink. I'm teasing.

As I sit here thinking about us I don't seem to be me anymore because part of me is you. Please tell me what you want to do Gil.

Your Joe

It was obvious that he was going to continue pressing for a decision on my part. As much as I cared for him, I was beginning to feel we were moving into a corner, with no solution in sight.

His letters were still filled with vignettes about his life at Komaki Air Base, Japan, his classes, his friends, and flying. I still looked forward to them with anticipation, and eagerly checked my post office box every day.

Sun Jan 31, 53

Dear Gil:

I've been trying to write you every other day even if it is just a short note, but yesterday was a lost day. We were in the classroom at 0800 for the last hour of lecture and then began three hours of tests. An hour for lunch and then four hours to finish the test. That was at 1700 and then I took off for a night cross-country. By the time I got back to the barracks it was ten and after a beer I promptly flaked out. This is the reason I didn't write but as a good soldier would say, "No excuse sir."

An event that happened to Archuleta while on the cross-country made him the object of the most continuous razzing I've ever heard. It will follow him the rest of his life. Col. Bower and Arch took off as Able 1 and 2. Lincoln and Scofield as Baker 1 and 2. Myself and Huffman as Charlie 1 and 2. On down the line was Dog, Easy, Fox, George, and How, making 16 of us in the air. We took off at five minute intervals and after reaching altitude all monitored the same radio channel, a thing Arch evidently forgot because about 20 minutes out we heard this: "Able lead, this is Able 2. Do you see anything behind me?"

"What, what, no this is Able lead, no I don't see anything behind you. What is it?"

"I don't know but something is chasing me."
Then complete radio silence and at the same
time we all realized that the thing Arch
thought was following him was the moon. It
was real bright, a full moon, and Arch
thought it was something chasing him. All the
way back there were catcalls of "What's that
behind me?" and "Something's chasing me!" and
"A flying saucer's after me!" Needless to say
Arch has not heard the end of it and the Moon
Boy is very embarrassed about it.

Joe also wrote some critiques of my writing selections that I sent him, which he seemed to like:

Have read all your stories and think that
some of them are fine. I agree with most of
Miss Turner's comments, and I've enclosed
some of mine. Ask your instructor, Miss
Turner about my comments. Gil, this is what I
meant when I said we could do some good work
together. You see some good things and add
things that I don't see and I can do the same
with you. We could turn out some good work.

I was glad to learn that he liked my stories, and I found his critique and comments very helpful. His letters continued to reveal his efforts to keep his morale up, especially when the demands of flying, classes, and adjusting to life in Japan were overwhelming. And also when there were long intervals between our letters, or when he didn't find the words he wanted to hear in mine:

5 Feb 53

My Gil,

My spirits are so low I probably wouldn't
write except that I have nothing to do except
wait for the mail tomorrow.

A crisis has developed here, among the
various personalities, and I'm standing alone
and losing. You remember my telling you I was
second in command in our flight. Then I was
number one boy, but by the time you receive
this I'll probably be #99 again. Strictly a
matter of personalities.

Added to this was a flying experience
yesterday which took my blond hair and turned
it grey. All weather flying, and not to go
into details, but a water glass of whiskey had
no effect on my jangled nerves after landing.

While this was going on Bud Gustine came here
to visit me, and from what he says all the
other troops will be home next June. Gus has
53 missions as do most of the others and the
whole situation just makes me sick.

All this would be tolerable, unimportant
even, if I could be sure of Us. Gil, honey,
I've never needed anyone or anything in my
whole life as I need you now. And day after
day I tromp to the P. O. and have no mail
from you. It's been over a week now, no mail
today, so I'll just wait until tomorrow.

To top it all off, my ears have been giving
me trouble. We fly so damn high that the
eardrums are strained to the breaking point,
and every night I wake up to this throbbing
and my heart throbbing for you.

I have the feeling that you've taken unkindly
to a letter I wrote you recently, but remember
this, Gil, I love you, truly love you.

Until I feel better again. Your Joe

Feb 11 53

Dear Gil:

This is the third time I've started this letter in addition to two attempts at short notes telling you I would answer with a long letter later. The long letters never got completed because I kept changing my mind as to what I wanted to say, the short ones because I always had to go fly as soon as I got started.

It will be evident from this letter that my morale has improved 100% over the stupid thing I wrote a few days ago. Also that I'm moody and temperamental, which will be borne out by this new attitude.

Before that short note of yours honey I had waited and waited for a letter from you. I was so miserable it was almost unbearable. I was angry, very angry. I hounded the orderly room to see what time the mail was coming in, then cursed the post and all associated with it. I hated flying and everyone here, hated to do anything except sit in my room and pout. Then I did get your short note, but I was still angry because it didn't help much and I still hadn't heard what I wanted to hear. I wasn't angry with you because as you said you were ill, but I was angry with the situation in general. Angry isn't correct, Gil, anger was part of it but I think frustration describes it better. It was the weekend then and no mail would be delivered until Monday. A long weekend indeed.

My morale was at its nadir and in the past when I didn't hear from you my spirits would drop but they couldn't get any lower. Something had to alter. Gil, honey, I've waited for five long months for you, waited for you to say the things that would make US what I wanted, what I hoped We wanted, but

Gil I've just about given up on US. Dear sweet Gil, I'm not angry with you and I still love you just as much as I always did, but I refuse to wait as I was, so completely unhappy and despondent.

Actually nothing has really changed and this letter could have gone unwritten but we agreed to write what we were thinking. During these months I was waiting for you to say the things I wanted to hear, I'd spend the whole of my waking hours dreaming about the things we would do and the life we would have. All these dreams based on the supposition that you also would soon tell me of these things. But I can't wait any longer at the expense of unhappiness and being a social and human detriment.

Darling, the only thing that is different is that I'm not waiting for you to say these things any more and I'm not dreaming these unfulfilled dreams and unfounded plans. If things with you ever change that will be the time for us to make plans and if not???

I am in a melancholy but peaceful frame of mind. The cold winter has passed here and the sun is shining and it's warm. My civilian clothes got here and those make me feel like a human being instead of a military automaton. I feel almost at peace with the world except that my pride is hurt slightly. I feel defeated at not being able to make US work out.

Until I hear from you I remain as ever

Your Joe

A SIXTEEN-SHIP FLIGHT OF F-84G'S FLIES LOW OVER NAGOYA, JAPAN.

When that letter arrived I read and reread it over and over, trying to understand what he was saying. I felt hurt and confused. I finally concluded that he wanted to ease off on our courtship by mail, so that he could start thinking of other things and stop expecting me to commit to marrying him. Of course the delays between our responses to each other's letters did nothing to help us understand each other's feelings. While he was waiting for my response to this February 11 letter, he wrote the following:

12 Feb 53

Dear Gil:

I waited until the last minute yesterday
before I mailed you the letter I wrote. I
wanted to be sure I was ready to face the
possible consequences of complete severance,
something which I have been unable to face in
the past. I mailed it. I now don't know what
to expect.

Today, I got another letter from you telling
of Jack and Joanie's visit. I'm real pleased
that they stopped to see you.

On our small calendar February 14 is in red
and (a pox on schoolteachers for not teaching
me history), I thought it was because it was
Washington's birthday. My own little
valentine to you:

For this I should have
Planned ahead
But if you were here now
I'd take you to
My arms and give you a
Huge kiss

Thank you for the valentine. I liked it very
much.

My golf clubs should be here in a week or so
and as soon as we are finished with this
first phase of this training I'm off to the
golf links.

Love, Joe

18 Feb 53

Dear Gil:

Got a letter from you yesterday and another
today. Thank you and thanks for the second
valentine. As you said in your letter
troubles build up to the breaking point and
then everything starts being all right again.
They did and now things seem better although
they weren't solved the way I used to hope
them to be. I don't seem to have much to say
about these things, sort of apathetic. If you
were a millionaire and you could go anywhere
you wanted to go, where would you go?

Since I came out of the depths of despair and
stopped feeling sorry for myself flying has
become a great deal more interesting. Have
read an article in Mechanics Illustrated
Magazine, titled The Most Dangerous Jobs in
the World. The figures were compiled by the
national ratings of the jobs they wouldn't
insure. Number One was military jet pilot and
test pilot. The article seems to finally
recognize and most everyone here seems
pleased cause we're walking around saying,
"Who has the most dangerous job in the
world?" "I do, the fearless jet pilot." It
adds quite a bit of prestige to be number one
in the world in something.

This and an idea I had prompted an article.
Yesterday I wrote "Riding the Red Mach," an
article about today's jet pilots. It is only
four pages long and I found a public
stenographer to do the typing and
corrections. I would have sent it to you but
I've sent you so much stuff lately that I
didn't want to overburden you, especially
with your own work and school and everything.
I'm going to send it to an aviation magazine
in a few days. Hope something comes of it.

Guess I'm getting cold blooded or numb to the

news of my friends getting killed. It doesn't bother me as much as it used to. Last Saturday I took a flight to Itazuki, the rear echelon base of the 58th in Korea, and I saw Gary Dickerson, Henry Karnes, Bud Liebelt, and Pat Keig. We only stayed for a short time but I got all the poop and Korean news. The news is that two more of my best friends have bought pieces of real estate in Korea. Billy Graham and Billy Fain. You met both of these boys, I'm sure. Of the seven who left Greenville to go to Willy there are only three of us left, Jack Denton, Grady Hinson, and myself. Walker, Corbett, Rase and now Graham have gone.

I am now taking lessons in Japanese. Japanese is really going to be easy just a matter of learning the vocabulary. Unlike German, Spanish and English, there are no irregular verbs. They are all conjugated the same way, and the conjugation is simple since they have only the present and past tense. The instructor said we could learn the whole language in four to six weeks if we applied ourselves.

Gil, try as hard as I might and do as many things as I can and think about as many things as possible, load my brain to its capacity, I still can't help thinking about you. It's nice to get letters from you.

Love, Joe

20 Feb 53

Dear Gil

Got another welcome letter from you today telling all about Valentine's Day. Also got a letter from Mother and she said she heard from Joanie, telling of their visit with you. Mother quoted some things from Joanie's letter and it seems that both she and Jack were very impressed with you. Haven't received a letter from Jack or Joanie as yet so I can't get the poop first hand. You must be a very nice person from what they say. Tell me all about you sometime.

Archie has a ukulele and we have been writing songs. With a lot of patience and little talent we have turned out some things that we think will wow the troops at the next beer bust. At present we are working on a verse to make us heroes and also keep us First Lieutenants the rest of our lives.

Will try and write soon.

Love, Joe

23 Feb 53

Dear Gil:

Last Saturday we went to Korea. We usually go over there, at least fly over the peninsula, in order to get our combat area income tax deduction. We didn't go to my old base K-2 but went to K-13 instead. Visited my old friend Jim Palmer. He knew some of the details about my assignment and after I filled in the rest we cried on each other's shoulders.

We started back to Komaki but the weather socked in and had to land at Itazuki.

Did you know a Lt. by the name of Guyer?
While we were at K-13 we saw him take off,
catch fire, explode and crash. He was in
Baker Class. Had just fifteen missions to go.

I hate you. I hate Joan. I hate my Mother. I
hate all women!

You remember my visit with my friend Howie
Pierson at Yokota AB? While I was there he
got a telegram from his intended saying that
she had gotten the passage money, booked
passage and was sailing the next day. She was
to be there in about two weeks at which time
Howie was to call me so that I could arrange
to get off two days in order to be a
groomsman at their wedding. I waited two weeks
with no concern and then three, thinking that
they needed time to get settled and make all
the arrangements. That was two weeks ago, and
I've been concerned, but did not call knowing
that Howie would call if anything had gone
wrong or if he needed me in any way.

Get this! He got a cablegram from her from
the ship saying not to meet the ship and that
she would give back the passage money, but
not to meet the ship. He did, of course. She
had fallen in love and married the first
mate! Need anything more be said?

Haven't studied my Japanese lesson for class
tonight but am going to go at Japanese with a
new vengeance so that I can be fluent and
suave and get a good Japanese girl for Howie.

1ST LT JOE GUTH (ON THE RIGHT) RETURNS WITH FELLOW PILOT AFTER AN F-84G MISSION.

1ST LT GUTH HAS A REFLECTIVE MOMENT.

```
                                                27 Feb 53
Gil:

I'm so tired I think I'm going to cry. I have
a great deal to write about, all the flying,
moving from our room, the rebuilding of the
building, my new car prospects, etc., but I'm
going to bed. Please excuse this typing. I'm
punchy.

Have been hoping for a letter from you (in
spite of my determinations) although that is
not why I've not written, honestly, no time.

With or without a letter from you tomorrow I
will try to write, although I probably can't
because I'll be in the Philippines, Manila,
and I'll be too tired again.

Don't even know what I'm saying so I'll
close.

Gil darling—I'll save it.

Your Joe
```

Joan and I decided early in 1953 that we would not sign teaching contracts at Willy for the following school year. We would be completing two school years there, and felt that it was time to make a change. She applied to be a part of the Hormel Girls, a very competitive program which involved travel, making sales presentations, and performing with the Hormel dance troupe all over the U.S. With things looking so uncertain between Joe and me, I decided to apply for a teaching job in San Francisco—a city I had always admired. The process took several weeks and involved a lot of applications, paperwork, and letters of recommendation. It even required a photo of myself and a telephone interview.

About this time I wrote to Joe in response to his letter of February 11, in which he told me that he couldn't wait any longer "at the expense of unhappiness and being a social and human detriment." I told him that I understood, and that I was sorry that it hadn't worked out as he had hoped. I told him I had applied for a teaching job in San Francisco, and that I was waiting to hear if I had been accepted.

I didn't hear from him for about two weeks. His next letter shows his angry reaction to what I had written to him. It appeared to him that I was attempting to break off our relationship, when in reality what I was attempting to do was to let him know that he was free to stop making definite plans about us for the time being:

10 March 53

Dear Gil:

I received your letter as you have probably guessed by my not answering for such a long time. You have also probably guessed my reactions, and correctly, too. When I read your letter, once, I threw it, all your old letters, everything associated with you, dreams and plans of you coming here into the trash can.

Because of my childishness I don't have your letter here to refer to, but my bitterness and jealousy have turned to wondering and confusion.

We were supposed to be trying to find out how we felt about Us, and I said I wasn't going to wait THE SAME WAY I had been any longer. I said nothing about not writing or still trying to find out about Us.

You dropped Us like a hot potato as something you were glad to be rid of and seizing the opportunity divorced all interest in me. Is that what you intended? This is the only thing I can believe because if you had any interest or concern I would have heard from you again. I was still writing.

If this is the way it is, so be it. Is it? If so, let me know of the things of yours I have and I'll send them.

Many things of tremendous importance have happened, but rather than be a bore I'll close.

Joe

When I received that letter, I was very hurt and upset. I wrote him, trying to explain what I had meant to convey to him. That I had not "dropped Us like a hot potato" or "divorced all interest" in him. I feared that whatever I wrote might only make things worse:

2 April 53

Dear Gil:

Your letter did not make things worse. I was pleased to find out that I had not been so mistaken in my judgment of you. After your other letter I thought I had erred completely in judging you. That is why I was so angry. However, I don't know that it improved things more than before we started all this. I do think we can straighten out the misunderstanding we have just had, but I don't know about solving the problem of Us. I doubt it Gil.

I doubt it, Gil, and that is why I decided not to wait the same way any longer. I was waiting for you with the solution in the plans for the future. The plan, the solution, was for you to come here to me in Japan. We wouldn't have to wait, only until June when you would have finished your semester, if you wanted to. It could have been done. All pertaining problems could be solved except your uncertainty. I've tried to stop considering it, stop thinking about it, stop thinking about you in my future. This isn't easy to do, but I stopped making plans and refused to think of the future as far as we were concerned. Every time a thought of you came into my mind concerning the future I forced it out, made myself think about something else, and when there was no diversion I bit my lip until it hurt so much I finally wondered what the hell I was doing. I read books, technical aircraft manuals, magazines, Japanese, anything to keep from thinking about it. To make things worse I had

three weeks of free time, no flying because
of problems with my tooth, which I'll explain
later. I played golf and since there was no
one to play with during the week I practiced
every day all day, snow, freezing rain or
shine. Gil I beat that golf ball until my
hands were sore and blistered, but I stopped
thinking about you. Not you, exactly, but the
plans I had and all thoughts of the future.

There are several improbable solutions. You
could finally realize what you wanted. I
could manage to get back to the States some
way so that we could have a few days
together, when I'm certain we could solve it.
We could manage some way for you to come here
for a while and solve it the same way as my
coming there. Just let it die a natural
death. Leave it suspended until something
happens.

I almost managed to get back to the States on
a testing team to Las Vegas, but it fell
through. You could have met me in Las Vegas
and I'm sure after a few days we would have
known what we wanted. A bad break that I
didn't get it.

I've been at this letter for days and I still
do not have it exactly the way I want it, but
the more I think about it the more I get
confused so I'll send it.

I'll write later and tell you of all the
news. Some news about flying, our new dog, my
tooth, golf, stateside prospects, etc.

Love,
Sincerely, Joe

That letter helped somewhat toward clearing up our misunderstanding. But it seemed to me that going to Japan to "work things out" required more of a commitment than I was able to make. We continued to write, but not as frequently as we had previously.

In early April I received a letter saying that "over a long list of candidates," I had been chosen for the teaching job in South San Francisco. I wrote a letter of acceptance, thinking that there was no solution to Joe's and my problems in sight.

---

3 April 53

Dear Gil,

Want to write you of some of our news before it all gets too stale and loses its zest. First I think and most fitting is Beauregard.
Beauregard is our new dog. A while ago I got my record player, audio and radio clock. Instead of just waking up and going to bed we now fade away from the day and slowly become aware of the next day to the quiet music of "Top of the Morning." My morale has improved 100% and this place doesn't seem so lonely and apart from the rest of the world.

Am buying a new Chevrolet to be delivered here. Am getting it real cheap compared to the prices in the States because we don't have to pay all the taxes imposed there.

I hadn't planned on getting one for a while because I had uses for the $2000 but the other plans didn't work out too well and I really have use for a car.

Gil, this isn't much of a letter and I know it lacks a lot of what you want to hear, but I'm out of practice writing to you. I don't even know if you will want to keep writing if you get dullards like this one. I don't exactly know what I want to say nor what I want to do. Be patient. I was with you. (Sounds like you should be writing this instead of me.)

Tomorrow is Saturday and I'm not on the flying
schedule and if I can get away early enough I
can spend all day on the golf course.

I'd better close this thing. You said you were
going to write the news but I haven't gotten
anything from you. Will write again after the
weekend and tell you if I finally got into the
seventies or still hacked around in the
eighties.

Be a good girl. Joe

The delays between our letters and lack of continuity kept both of us filled with doubt and uncertainty. It was beginning to look like an unsolvable dilemma. And then it happened—an event which would change the course of both of our lives forever.

* * * *

Chapter Six

HEAVEN SENT CHANCE

Joan and I had just risen to get ready for school. It was Thursday morning, April 16, 1953. The telephone in our apartment rang. "Miss Cosulich? This is the Western Union operator. I have a cablegram for you. I'll read it to you, and we'll also send you out a copy." He read me the following:

```
PFA032 25/28 PD INTL O.SF TOKYO VIA RCA 16 1139

TF HIGLEY EXTENSION 623 GILBERTA COSULICH


CIVILIAN BOX 1154 W.A.F.B. CHANDLER ARIZ




DEAREST GIL HEAVEN SENT CHANCE FOR US MEET ME LASVEGAS

IMMEDIATELY CABLEGRAM OR TELEPHONE FOLLOWS LOVE


JOE. 928PM
```

Those words, from that moment on, were immediately, indelibly engraved in my memory, and they have remained there ever since.

Stunned, I rushed to Joan's room and read the cablegram to her. I didn't know what to think, what to do, or what to expect.

"You've got to tell Mrs. Lowers about it right away so you can leave as soon as he calls!" Joan exclaimed. I knew she was right. Joe might only have a couple of days, and I wanted to be ready for his arrival.

When we got to school I explained to the principal what had happened.

"I don't know how long he'll have, Mrs. Lowers, but I want to be ready to see him, even for a short visit," I said anxiously.

Smiling, she responded, "You can leave as soon as he calls. I'll cover your classroom until a substitute can arrive."

I kept one ear tuned to the classroom intercom all day. I was unable to concentrate on my work. I was excited and at the same time apprehensive about what all this would mean. The kids of course picked up on my distraction, and they began to talk to each other, wander around the room, and not pay attention to their lessons. As the day progressed they were beginning to get out of control.

"Boys and girls!" I heard myself shouting. "Get back in your seats at once. If you don't go to your seats and get on with your work, there will be no story hour today!" I had completely lost the quiet calm that I was usually able to maintain with my second grade class, and I was resorting to threats.

"Why doesn't his call come?" I thought desperately. "When he calls, what will I say? What will I do? What will I wear?" Just a few hours before, he was, to my knowledge, in Japan, and our recent correspondence had all been pointing to the strong probability that we might never see each other again, much less continue the romance which had barely gotten off the ground.

The day ended at last, and Joan and I went home. There on the floor outside the door of our apartment lay the cablegram. I tore it open and the words were exactly as they had been read to me that morning. I read it over and over, trying to make sense of everything, and trying to imagine what was going to happen.

I waited anxiously all evening for his call, but it didn't come. I tossed and turned that night, unable to sleep. Finally at 1:00 a.m. Friday the phone rang, and I knew it was Joe.

My heart was racing as I picked up the phone and heard him say, "Hi, Gil! I'm calling from Honolulu. We're about to leave for San Francisco. Wait for me to call you from there, and I'll tell you where to meet me."

We didn't have much time to talk, because he was about to board his plane. "I'll be waiting!" I assured him. I didn't know what would happen, but I was filled with the excitement and the anticipation of seeing him again.

That day was as difficult to get through as the previous one had been. But somehow I managed to keep my second graders from running completely amuck. I watched the classroom clock tick off the hours interminably. Finally, school ended for the day. I started closing the classroom windows before the children filed out of the room, and, as they were leaving with their usual "Bye, Miss Cosulich!" I kept giving each one an impatient little push, trying not to show my eagerness for them to be gone. With all of them gone at last, I picked up my belongings and, closing the door behind me, left my classroom and went home.

It was 5:00 p.m. when Joe called from San Francisco. "My CO, Lieutenant Colonel Deward Bower, and I will be arriving at the Phoenix airport at midnight tonight. His wife will be there to meet him, too. Meet me there in the Menace."

"Okay!" I said, and then he had to hang up.

I had no idea how long he would be in the U.S., how long his visit with me would be, or if he would be returning to Japan. These thoughts and myriad other questions kept churning around in my head while the evening hours passed. I killed time by fixing my hair, talking to Joan, and looking in my closet.

I couldn't decide what to wear. I only knew that I wanted to look spectacular to meet Joe. After many deliberations with Joan I finally decided on my best navy and white suit, and my high-heeled white and navy spectator pumps, remembering how much he liked to see me in high heels. It no longer bothered me that, wearing them, I would be almost as tall as he was. My hair had grown to below my shoulders, and I let it fall into a soft pageboy from the barrette holding it away from my face.

"Are my stocking seams straight?" I asked Joan. She gave me a quick once-over, nodded, and I was out the door and into the Menace.

Driving toward Phoenix, I tried to review the past several months, the misunderstandings, the frustrations, the apologies. As the Sky Harbor Airport came into view, I could feel my heart starting to pound. Somehow it didn't matter that our relationship had come close to being severed. All I could think about was that I would, very soon, be seeing him again.

I waited for his plane under the starlit Arizona sky outside the boarding lounge. As the plane was landing, I noticed another person standing there, a young blond woman.

"By any chance are you meeting Colonel Bower on this incoming flight?" I asked her.

With a broad smile, she said, "Yes, I'm Bonnie Bower."

She was Joe's commanding officer's wife. We barely had time to introduce ourselves before the plane was taxiing toward us. It stopped, and the passengers disembarked.

I saw Joe walking toward me, smiling broadly, holding out his arms to me. His body looked fit and muscular in his crisp khaki uniform. I could feel his strength as he pulled me to him and wrapped his arms around me. We stood kissing and holding each other until he stepped back, and, holding both my hands, said softly, "Oh, Toots, you look so good to me."

I stood smiling at him as he touched my hair, my cheek, my arms. In the dim light from inside the terminal I could see how intensely blue his eyes were, how dazzling his smile was.

My joy at seeing him again wiped away all the uncertainty and confusion of the recent months. The only thing that mattered was that he was here, and I was with him. The other couple, after their hellos, came over to us and said, "Won't you join us for a drink?" We longed to be alone, but out of courtesy we accepted their invitation. We followed them to their hotel, and spent a short time with them. The two men told us that they had flown from Japan with two other pilots, plus the squadron's weapons officer and the intelligence officer. The two pilots had flown on to other locations to meet or pick up their wives. They were all to rendezvous in Las Vegas on Monday afternoon so that the six of them could report for duty at Camp Desert Rock, sixty-five miles northwest of Las Vegas, on Tuesday morning. What I didn't know until later was that the colonel told his wife that night, "When we see Joe again he's either going to be the happiest or the most disappointed man on the face of the earth."

Driving back to Willy, Joe explained that theirs was a top secret assignment, one that he couldn't even talk to me about, other than that they were assigned to observe a nuclear test blast in the Nevada desert outside Las Vegas. The reason for his being there wasn't as important to me as the fact that, suddenly, happily, he was here with me.

When we arrived at the apartment at Willy Joan got up to say hello to Joe, and it was agreed that he could sleep on the couch in the living room rather than go to the Transient Officers' Quarters for what was left of the night. We talked until almost dawn, hugging and kissing, gazing into each others' eyes. It didn't matter any more that our correspondence over the past several weeks had been filled with misunderstandings and disappointments.

There was an urgency in his voice and demeanor as he explained to me that he would be in the States for only two weeks, the first week on duty near Las Vegas, and the second week on leave. Then he would return to Japan, along with the five others.

"Gil," he said, taking my hand. "Will you marry me? Now... while I'm here?"

I looked into his face, those clear blue eyes gazing earnestly back at me. I knew that I loved him. I didn't know how, or when, we could manage a wedding with his reporting date in Las Vegas just two days away. But I did know that I wanted to spend my life with him.

My heart pounding, I whispered, "Yes, I will!"

We decided that the thing to do was to drive to Tucson the next day, Saturday, and talk to my parish priest, to see if we could get permission to be married in Las Vegas. We met Bonnie and Colonel Bower for brunch Saturday morning. We didn't tell them anything about our plans. We honestly didn't know what was going to happen.

"See you on Monday, Joe!" Colonel Bower called as they drove away. And then we left in the Menace for Tucson.

The drive to Tucson was filled with non-stop talking, planning, laughing, and not just a little anxiety about the many hurdles that might be ahead of us. We pulled up to my family's home. My mother, who was living in Tucson at the time, came out to meet us. My grandfather, my aunt Catherine and my uncle Manny stood on the front porch as we walked up the steps, welcoming us with hugs for me and hearty handshakes for Joe. They had heard a lot about him during the year and a half I had known him.

After visiting with the family for a couple of hours, I could tell that Joe was an instant hit with all of them. We didn't tell them where we were going when we left for our 6:00 p.m. meeting with the parish priest. We knew that there was a possibility that our request to be married in Las Vegas might be turned down.

Father John Kelly was a tall, slender young Irish priest. He listened intently as Joe explained to him that this assignment had occurred very suddenly. He told the priest that he must report to Las Vegas two days later, and that he would be in the U.S. for one additional week after his assignment was completed. Since it was customary at that time for a marriage to take place in the home parish of the bride, we were asking for a special dispensation allowing us to be married in Las Vegas.

"I must call the Bishop," Father Kelly said, leaving the room. We waited nervously for almost ten minutes. When he returned, I tried to read his face, but he was expressionless. I just knew that our request was refused.

He said, "The Bishop said I can marry you tomorrow. Here. In the rectory."

We both exclaimed, "Tomorrow!"

"Can you get the necessary documents?" he asked. "Gilberta's Baptismal Certificate from the Cathedral, the marriage license?" Without hesitation, we told him that yes, we could get the necessary documents. We could do it all.

The first thing we did was to go to Paulo's Restaurant for dinner. From there I made several phone calls... the first, to my family, to tell each of them the news. I could tell from their reactions that they were very happy for us, and not too surprised. I asked my grandfather if he would give me away.

"Yes, I will, Honey," he responded. "Joe is a good man. He'll take good care of you."

Looking back, this all seems hard to believe, unreal, in some ways surreal. But, amazingly, everything seemed to be falling into place in our favor. While in college I had worked during the summers at the Pima County courthouse, in the Registrar's office. I called my former boss, Johnny Johnson, at his home. His daughter had been a classmate of mine.

I heard him turn to his wife and say, "It's Gilberta Cosulich... she wants to get married." I asked him if he could help us get our marriage license before 3:00 p.m. the next day, a Sunday. He told me to call back in ten minutes. By the time I called him back he had arranged an appointment with the county clerk for us to get a marriage license on Sunday morning.

After dinner we returned to the house, where we were welcomed by the family with open arms. It meant a lot to me that they all seemed to like Joe so much.

My mother showed her happiness by offering ideas about where we could go on Sunday to find a dress, shoes, flowers, and other details needing attention. We called a former classmate of mine to ask if he and his wife would be our witnesses. Once again Joe slept on the couch in the living room, this time in my family's home in Tucson.

The next day, Sunday, April 19, 1953, was our wedding day. We went to 7:00 a.m. Mass at St. Augustine's Cathedral, where I had been baptized and attended church as a child, and where my grandparents had been married. At Father Kelly's request, the Cathedral's business office was open, and the attendant there provided a copy of my Baptismal Certificate. Since this was wartime, all kinds of allowances were being made which were not usually given. My mother and I drove to the one department store which was open on Sundays, hoping to find a suitable white dress and shoes. My mother, who had been in and out of my life while I was growing up, was caught up in the happiness and excitement of the event. She and I shared that day with joy.

"He seems like such a wonderful man, Honey," she said.

I had always heard that true love could move mountains, and I felt like a mountain had been moved when we found the perfect white linen, street-length dress with a white unlined coat to match, and a pair of beautiful, white linen, high-heeled pumps.

GILBERTA POSES IN HER WEDDING DRESS, APRIL 19, 1953.

But I was getting a sore throat. I knew from past experience that once a sore throat got hold of me I would be miserably sick and in a horrible, sneezy, coughing state which would make it impossible for anyone to want to be near me, including my soon-to-be husband.

I made a call to my doctor, who had known me since my childhood, and explained the situation. He said, "I'll meet you at my office in twenty minutes."

After a throat swabbing, and with medications in hand, I met Joe at 11 a.m. in front of the courthouse. We were relieved to see that, as Mr. Johnson had promised, the clerk was there to issue our marriage license to us. Another mountain moved.

We had a little time back at the house so I could change into my wedding dress and have a short visit with the family. Someone asked, "Joe, do you have a ring?"

"Ring?" Joe said. "No, I don't have a ring!"

My uncle Manny exclaimed, "I have a ring!" Manny went to his room and quickly returned with a narrow gold band. He had returned from World War II hoping to marry the love of his life, but had met with disappointment. He had kept the ring, and as he handed it to Joe, he told us, "Here. You can have this. And you can keep it."

Then it was 2:00 p.m. and we were ringing the doorbell of the church rectory. We signed the necessary documents, and since weddings were not held inside the church on Sundays, and since a Mass was not required for marriage to a non-Catholic, we met the family in the living room of the rectory. In addition to those that Joe had met the night before, my other aunt, Carmel, and her husband were there. Our witnesses and one neighbor were the only others besides my family who were present. It was three o'clock. Time for our wedding.

I hadn't even had time to call Joan back at Willy. Things had happened so fast that, although I thought of her, there just didn't seem to be a spare moment to call her and ask her to drive to Tucson for our wedding. Besides, we had the Menace with us. It took her some time to forgive me for not letting her know what was happening. I've always regretted that she, my best friend, was not there that day. As fate would have it, I would be halfway around the world the day of her wedding, a year later.

Joe placed the tiny gold band contributed by Manny on my finger, and the quiet little ceremony was over. I remember feeling like I was outside myself, observing what was happening. We don't even have any pictures of the event. Catherine, who appointed herself photographer for the day, had forgotten in her excitement to put any film in the camera.

After champagne and cake back at the house we said our goodbyes and left for Phoenix. On the way we stopped at Willy to tell Joan what had happened.

I opened the door of our apartment and tossed my orchid corsage into the living room.

"Why didn't you call me!" Joan said, her eyes glistening with tears of surprise and happiness. "I would have come!"

I explained how everything had happened so fast, how sorry I was that she wasn't there. I told her how much I hoped that she would understand, and I asked her to forgive me.

As I hurriedly packed some clothes I wondered if what I put into the suitcase would be okay for two weeks of what would probably be some very festive events.

We went to the principal's home and told her the news. Mrs. Lowers' eyes filled with joyful tears for us as she assured us that she would get a substitute teacher for me for as long as I needed to be gone.

Everything, so far, had fallen into place for us.

On the way into Phoenix, all kinds of thoughts and imaginings were racing through my mind. I had heard many wedding night stories, and now, here I was, having had virtually no time to ponder, prepare myself, or reflect. It was my wedding night.

We stayed at the Desert Hills Motel. The first thing Joe did was order room service... we were both starving. He ordered a hamburger for me, and a ham and Swiss cheese on rye sandwich for himself.

I remember thinking, "I've never known a man who ordered a ham and Swiss cheese on rye before." To me it was another indication of Joe's sophistication and knowledge of the world.

My aunt Carmel had given me her wedding nightgown and negligee that afternoon. Her mother, my grandmother, had made it for her when she married her sweetheart, Matt Schmitz, after he returned from

World War II. As I put it on in the bathroom, I wondered how I would look to my new husband.

My apprehensions about that night were soon dispelled. I had never been intimate with a man before, and Joe knew it. He treated me with gentle respect and love, and told me how unbelievably happy and grateful he was that, at last, we were together.

* * * *

Chapter Seven

LAS VEGAS HONEYMOON

It was Monday morning. We left Phoenix and drove back to Willy to meet Bonnie and Colonel Bower at the main gate, as we had agreed. When Joe told them we'd been married the day before, Colonel Bower exclaimed, "Outstanding!" He pumped Joe's hand, grinning broadly.

"Bonnie!" he shouted. "Meet the newlyweds!"

She jumped from their car and rushed over to give both of us a joyous hug.

"We had our fingers crossed!" she said, beaming. "Congratulations!"

They followed us to the apartment, where we dropped off the Menace and said goodbye to Joan and Judy. As we got into the Bowers' car, Joan stood on the balcony with the dog sitting beside her.

"Bye!" she and I called to each other. And then we drove away, headed for Las Vegas.

Joe and I spent a lot of the travel time dozing in the backseat, with my head on his shoulder or resting in his lap.

We stopped for lunch, and when we had a moment to ourselves back in the car, Joe told me quietly, "I'm so proud of you. I know that the weekend was hectic for you, and last night wasn't easy, but you are still so sociable and pleasant. I love you so much, Gil."

His words warmed my heart. Though so much had happened in just three days, I felt secure in the knowledge that this was the beginning of a new, exciting, and joyful time in my life.

We arrived in Las Vegas and pulled up at the Last Frontier Hotel and Resort. As we were getting our bags out of the car, the other two pilots on the assignment from Japan came out of the hotel with their wives to greet us: Bob and Mary Willerford and Lowell and Ellwyn Rogers.

"We have a couple of newlyweds with us," Colonel Bower told them. "Joe and Gil were married yesterday in Tucson!"

"We're going to have a party!" exclaimed Bob Willerford, pounding Joe on the back and shaking his hand vigorously. "Congratulations!"

"Hey, Joe, you really pulled it off!" said Lowell Rogers with delight, grabbing Joe's hand.

Jim Davis and A.B. Aldridge, introduced as the squadron's special weapons officer and the intelligence officer, arrived a short time later. I didn't know what their non-flying duties were at that time, but I got the distinct impression that they were an important part of this team.

All ten of us stayed at the Last Frontier Hotel, and the fabulous week began. The glitzy nightlife of Las Vegas captivated all of us every evening as we celebrated by taking in the casinos, the restaurants, and the shows. I could sense the special camaraderie between the six men. They seemed to share a bond which went beyond friendship. It was unique to anything I had ever seen before.

That first evening, before we went out, Joe called his parents in St. Louis to tell them the news. They were thunderstruck. They hadn't known until the moment he called that he was in the States, and not in Japan. He tried to explain to them how all this had unfolded so quickly, and told them that we would fly to St. Louis to see them after his assignment was completed at the end of the week. After he explained it all to them, they seemed to regain their composure. Since his mother and I had corresponded a few times, we had a brief but friendly chat before hanging up.

She was cordial as she said, "Gil, we're so excited and happy for you both! We can't wait to see you!"

I thought to myself, "This must be a real shock for them. I hope they'll like me!"

That first evening we saw the performances of Dorothy Dandridge and Eddie Bracken at the Last Frontier. It was a lush and glamorous evening. The ten of us were a happy, high-spirited group. There were frequent and funny toasts to Joe and me and to our marriage. We were the center of attention wherever we went.

"There are more people with us on our honeymoon than there were at our wedding!" Joe remarked at dinner, drawing laughter around the table.

I felt like I was radiating with love and happiness. It was like being in the middle of a dream. A few days before I had been teaching second grade at Willy, with no thought of seeing Joe anytime soon, if ever again. And now here I was, married to him, celebrating our marriage with his friends in the glitziest city in the nation. I knew and cared very little about his assignment there. I only knew that we both were very, very happy.

In our hotel room, the Bowers' and our room were joined by a closet. That evening Colonel Bower and Joe surprised each other by meeting in the closet when they went in to hang up their coats. Both of them stood in surprised silence for a moment, until they both burst into laughter at the ridiculousness of it all.

The next morning the six men had to get up very early to drive the sixty-five miles to Camp Desert Rock. Joe still couldn't tell me why they were going to observe the nuclear test shot, or what it had to do with their assignment in Japan. But I didn't care. All that mattered was that I was now married to him, and we were together.

They began their four-day training to observe the test shot. It was to take place out in the Yucca Flat desert at the end of the week. It wasn't until much later that I learned the reason for this assignment.

During the day I went sightseeing and shopping with the three other women in the gaudy city of Las Vegas. In the evening, when the men returned, it was time to celebrate again. The second night it was Nelson Eddy at the Sahara, the Desert Inn Latin Quarter Review, and then a drive around Las Vegas with the Bowers. Thursday evening it was Italian dinner and Van Johnson at the Sands. In between times we were caught up in the excitement of our honeymoon and the camaraderie of our group.

The six men didn't return at the end of the day that Friday. They stayed overnight for more training at Camp Desert Rock. Then came a pre-dawn, twenty-five-mile drive out to Yucca Flat for them, into the heart of the U.S. Atomic Energy Commission's Nevada Proving Ground.

The three other women and I rode in Bonnie Bower's car to the desert to watch the 5:00 a.m. atomic blast that morning. It was called "Shot Simon." It was Saturday, April 25, 1953.

Seated in Bonnie's car a few miles outside Las Vegas, we saw a blinding flash of light, illuminating the sky over Las Vegas and the barren desert surrounding the small city. Seconds later, we heard the boom, like a thunderclap, from the blast. And then in the distance we could see the huge orange and black fireball rising into the brightly lit, pre-dawn sky. As it rose, it took on a mushroom shape, and the colors seemed to change: black to purple to lavender, orange to dusty rose. Then everything turned to a dirty brownish color. We were awestruck, and we knew that we had just witnessed something far-reaching and significant.

Joe told me later that they had been in trenches less than two miles from the blast. They were told that they were the closest that any group had previously been to a nuclear detonation at the Nevada Test Site. They were dressed in flight suits, and were not wearing any protective clothing, gloves, or eyewear. They had been instructed to firmly place their hands over their eyes while down in the trench, but when the blast occurred they would still see a bright white light. He described how the trench had quivered, shaken, and then heaved, how the thunderous shock wave had jarred them, and how they had been covered with dust. After the blast they were loaded onto a bus and driven around within "ground zero" of a previous shot, with dust sifting into the bus from the road.

A couple of hours after the blast the six men met us back at the hotel. They had all showered and changed back into their blue Air Force uniforms. They were all anxious to depart to begin their week's leave before the return to Japan. Saying goodbye to the Rogers', the Willerfords, Davis, and Aldridge, we all told each other, "See you in Japan!"

It was hard to believe I would soon be there. I thought of it as a far-off place full of mystery and the unknown, a place I would never have dreamed of seeing.

We had Chinese dinner with the Bowers that evening before they left for Phoenix. As we watched them leave, I wondered how long it would be before we saw them in Japan. Each wife would have to wait until her husband found suitable housing before she could join him. I had no idea how long that might take.

The next day, Sunday, we were having breakfast and Joe said thoughtfully, "You know, I could fly us to St. Louis. Let's go out to the airfield and see what kind of plane we could rent."

There was a small Piper single-engine plane available to rent. I looked at it dubiously as Joe walked around it, climbed into the cockpit to check out the controls, and, jumping down, he said, "We wouldn't have any problem flying to St. Louis in this."

"That little thing? But it's so small!" I cried. I guess my face showed him how very apprehensive I was, because he said, "You'd rather not, wouldn't you."

I was so relieved when he made reservations for us to fly commercially that I must have visually heaved a sigh of relief. I didn't care that flying was what he did for a living. I only knew I didn't want to fly all the way to St. Louis in that little crate.

So we arrived in St. Louis on a commercial flight that evening, and I met Joe's parents for the first time at the airport. They were a very youthful-looking couple, and it was obvious how close they were to their son.

His mother's eyes filled with tears as she said, "Gil, I knew I would like you from your letters."

Joe's dad shook Joe's hand and embraced him. "Congratulations!" he said. "We sure are glad you came!"

We visited his Granny, aunts, and uncles. I felt warmly welcomed, and thought to myself what really solid, good people they all seemed to be. Joe was obviously delighted to be with his family, and was especially attentive to his Granny. She was sitting in her rocking chair next to me when she gave me two prized possessions: a Peruvian blanket that Joe had sent her from South America when he was serving there during World War II, and her recipe for creamed spinach, which Joe loved. He watched baseball on TV with his dad while I got acquainted with his mother, grandmother, aunts, and uncles. In the midst of this whirlwind his family gave us a wedding shower and a big party. I met many of his friends from high school, college, and the service.

THE NEWLYWEDS VISIT JOE'S PARENTS IN ST. LOUIS, APRIL 26, 1953.

Everyone seemed so fond of Joe, his sense of humor, and his way of being so full of fun. It was another week of celebrating and sightseeing. He took me to the Jewel Box, the Art Museum, Forest Park, and all the main sights of his hometown of St. Louis. I went with him to the beautiful Famous-Barr Department Store, to the men's department. There he bought a classy, grey pinstriped silk tie. I was very impressed with his sense of style, and his big-city demeanor.

Then the week ended, and it was time to fly back to Phoenix. We said our goodbyes to his family and friends, promising to write, to send pictures. His parents took us to the airport where we said goodbye, with no idea of how long it would be before we would see them again.

IN THE YARD OF JOE'S PARENTS' ST. LOUIS HOUSE.

We spent that last night together in Phoenix. The next morning we took the hotel shuttle to Sky Harbor airport for Joe's flight to San Francisco, from where he would return to Japan. At the airport, saying goodbye, he promised to find a house for us immediately so that we could be together again as soon as possible. We clung to each other, not knowing when that might come about, not wanting the time together to end. He turned to go and looked back, waving and smiling as he boarded the plane for San Francisco. I waved and threw him a kiss, trying to smile. We had been married two weeks.

* * * *

Diary of a Fighter Pilot's Wife
During Korea, Cold War, Vietnam:

Little white gloves and frilly hats and
calling cards

Receiving lines and rigid protocols

Fine dining and wines

Escargot in silver chafing dishes

Manhattans and martinis in vats

Dancing all night in glamorous gowns

Thrill of adventure

New stations, new countries

Culture shock, cantankerous heating systems

Unpredictable plumbing

Sudden TDY's

Subsequent crop of new babies

Unfamiliar doctor's face between the soles

Of your feet in delivery room

Loneliness, waiting, coping

Sheer stark terror

Grief.

—Louise I. Duquette

AIRBORNE:

A GLOBAL FLIGHT

1953-1969

* * * *

Chapter Eight

THE REUNION

Watching Joe's plane taking off, lifting and disappearing from sight, I felt as though I had just awakened from a dream... an amazing, unbelievable dream. I looked down at the narrow gold band on my left hand, and rubbed my fingers over and around it.

"This all really happened. In just two weeks," I thought. "You're married... to Joe Guth. You are now Gilberta Guth, Mrs. Joseph R. Guth."

Now I understood what the term "swept off my feet" really meant. I, indeed, had been swept off my feet. I now understood how wartime urgencies could bring about sudden marriages. And I knew that I had made the right decision.

Joan picked me up at the airport in the Menace.

"You look so happy!" she beamed as I got into the car. "I have some exciting news, too," she continued. "I was interviewed for the job with the Hormel Girls caravan. I got the job, and I'll be leaving this summer!"

As we drove back to Willy, there was much to share. Once at our apartment, we continued to talk well into the night, both of us relating all the events of the past two weeks. I told her of the week in Las Vegas; meeting Joe's comrades and their wives; flying to St. Louis; being with his parents, relatives, and friends. And then his departure from Phoenix to return to Japan, and how I would be leaving to join him as soon as he found us a house.

171

Joan and Lt. Lynn Lane, the young student officer she had been dating for over a year, had become quite serious. But like all of the graduating flight students at Willy, he had been transferred to prepare for combat in Korea. He was sent to Nellis Air Force Base, near Las Vegas, where he was training to fly the F-86 SabreJet, the swept-back wing fighter which Joe had described as the "air-to-air combat jet." It was the plane Joe had hoped to fly in Korea. From Nellis, Lynn would be in that pipeline to Korea for a one-year tour.

Joan was happy about being accepted by the Hormel Girls. It would be an exciting career change for her as she waited for Lynn's return. The qualifications were extremely high, and the selection process very competitive. It was a job that would take her on a totally different path from teaching, but would allow her to follow her lifelong dream of being a dancer. It involved considerable traveling throughout the U.S., and performing in stage presentations and sales meetings to promote the products of the Hormel Meat Company.

Joan and I realized that both our lives were changing drastically. Events were happening that we never could have imagined in our wildest dreams. We'd been like sisters since childhood. We knew that our paths were now going to take us to opposite corners of the world, with no idea when we might see each other again. But we both were filled with happy anticipation about the changes that lay ahead.

The next day, Monday, was a school holiday. I drove to Phoenix to visit my uncle George, to tell him about my marriage to Joe and my plans to go to Japan. My happiness seemed to enliven George, usually a quiet man, and he expressed genuine delight and gladness for me. George had always encouraged my interest in writing, and he said, "Gilberta, you're going to have a wonderful life. Just think of all the interesting things you'll be able to write about!"

One of the first things I had to do was to notify the school district in San Francisco that I would not be signing a contract for the coming year, due to my marriage to Lt. Joe Guth.

There were two weeks remaining in the school year at Willy. When I walked into my classroom the next day, my second graders were filled with excitement. My new name, "Mrs. Guth," had been printed on the blackboard, but to them I was still Miss Cosulich.

"Oh, Miss Cosulich," one of my students said. "We thought you'd be wearing your wedding dress!"

They all had signed a beautiful congratulatory card for me, which I still treasure. I was happy to see them, and I was touched by their show of affection toward me.

Over the next few days I eagerly waited for a letter from Joe. He wrote these right after his arrival back in Japan:

8 May 53

My Dearest Gil,

This is going to be a very short letter. I'm so tired. There isn't much to tell about the flight. It was very, very long, and very, very boring, and I'm very, very tired from it and I love you very, very much.

"Anna" is playing over and over and I have a hundred memories of you, although we were together only a short time. So many things, Gil that I wanted to say and do. The minute you were out of sight at the airport I wanted to tell you to have that drink I suggested and that you wouldn't be drinking it alone, but I would be with you. So many memories, I can almost see you and feel you. I do so hope it won't be long before we are together again.

With all my love, Mrs. Guth

Love, Joe

Monday 10th or 11th 53

My Little Darling,

A fast recap. We arrived here Friday about
1600. There was a birthday party for Major
Hornsby, but I was too tired and I just moped
around drinking beer and thinking of you.

Flew today for the first time in a month and
I liked it. Went to Itazuke to deliver some
papers on an engine, took the mail to our
troops stationed there and checked an island
for possible use as a gunnery range.

On the way back I rolled and looped and
played like a bird. I was happy, and it felt
good.

In between times I found some (inadequate)
information on your coming here. Have all the
necessary papers. Heading the list of
requirements is authorized and approved
housing. All the rest of the forms are easy,
being purely documentary. Housing is the big
nut to crack.

Col. Bower didn't tell me of all the
incongruous labyrinths, but I'm not going to
sit on my duff and hope it will all work out.
I think it will, but it makes it too long to
just sit and hope.

I have a few leads, some with Americans, some
with Japanese. Will follow up on all of them.
As to government housing, we'd be eligible
around December or January. All I have to do
is find something until then.

Gil honey, it may seem like it may be a long
time before I find something, but this is the
type of thing I can do and I'm sure I'll find
something soon or work it out some way.
Loving and wanting you so much I know I'll
get something. Of course it may be a real

shack and all you may have to keep you warm
in the winter is me. OK.?

Went to the PX and they didn't seem to have
any rings of the kind we wanted. They
referred me to a Japanese jeweler, but none
of the people there spoke English. We may
have to wait until you get here to find
something you would like. I'm going to keep
trying though, and I think I will have much
better success in the Tokyo area.

Reading this over it seems like I've done a
heck of a lot in three days. I'm anxious to
get some free time so I can really devote my
energies to house hunting. I'll get one if I
have to canvas house to house for one.

Rogers had sent a vague postcard from Las
Vegas to the troops here and hinted at
catastrophe for me. All the troops thought I
had either gotten married or lost all my
money in Las Vegas. They all seem to think I
did the right thing. Some have accused me of
getting married just to shorten my stay here.
Will explain that later.

Gil I'm punchy and am going to close. Have a
hundred nice things and thoughts to tell you
but will have to write of them later.

I love you, my wife, love you, love you, love
you.

Love, Joe

His letters over the next weeks were filled with details about his search for a house. He described following up on numerous leads that fell through. He was trying every possible tactic to hurry the process along. He also wrote beautiful expressions of his love and longing for us to be together:

It was pointed out to me today that I'm too impatient in that it took some of the guys months to find something and that I've stirred up more action in three days than most of them did in a month. I can understand that partly in that they couldn't have near the incentive to work for that I have, but I'm a man of action, action, you hear, and I want action! Will report again tomorrow.

Was elected the captain of the 9th golf team. We have a match Saturday and I'm seeded #1 on the team. As one of the smart alecks said today, that's the only way Guth can make Captain, elected golf captain. I ought to have punched him.

All of this letter seems so practical with no sentimental thoughts but rest assured Mrs. G. that the tender thoughts of you are not numbered but are continuous. Always behind me is the thought that we have finally come to be one and I'm like a new man. Then I catch myself staring into the mirror and reflecting that someone loves me and wants me and that I belong to someone. It's a very fine feeling, young lady.

My heart was touched by his tender words, and I waited for his letters eagerly each day. And I was most anxious for news about his finding us a house.

After a few days, a handful of my students were starting to call me "Mrs. Guth." The last two weeks of school passed, and then it was the final day of classes. As they filed out of the classroom for the last time, I hugged them goodbye and most of them said, "Bye, Miss Cosulich!"

I felt a little nostalgia as I watched them leave, knowing that I would never see them again, nor would I see this classroom, this base, nor, in all probability, many of the friends I had made over the past two years.

During our last days at Willy, Joan and some of our fellow teachers planned a bridal shower for me, and several of our friends came from Tucson. It was a joyful time as I opened the beautiful gifts for Joe's and my home-to-be. There were linens, kitchen equipment, and decorative household items. As I opened them, I tried to imagine what my new home in Japan would look like.

We finished up our year-end reports and closed up our classrooms. Joan and I packed up our belongings and prepared to leave what had been our bachelor working girls' home for two years. We loaded everything into the Menace that we could and left most of the furniture we had borrowed from our families for the next teachers who would occupy the place. We said our goodbyes, locked the apartment, and got into the Menace. As we left Willy through the main gate, I read the sign for the last time: *You Are Departing Williams Air Force Base Drive Carefully.*

Back home in Tucson, I waited for two and a half months to join my husband overseas. My mother had left for Paris right after our wedding, to visit my uncle Philip there and begin a new job. My grandfather, aunts, and uncles expressed their happiness for me as I began preparing to leave for Japan.

Joe's letters continued to be filled with details about my trip to Japan and about his search for a house. He sent pictures and panoramic scenes of possible houses and their surroundings, accomplished by taping three or four photographs together.

We both were writing almost every day, telling of our longing to be together, and of the details about my trip to join him. The delays in mail delivery caused its usual problems, but no longer dimmed our happiness:

```
                                         15 may 53

Dear Citizen Guth,

Tonight readers my editorial takes the
prosaic form of a crusade. Prone as I am to
laud the great organizations of our great
nation it cuts me deeply to have to openly
denounce this organization but it's high
time, high time I say readers that this
diabolical institution gets its due. Woe be
unto me for the words of criticism heaped as
flaming coals on the heads of innocent
children of these sadists but it is their
```

fathers that have brought them the disaster, for as soon as you my readers learn of the intended heinousness you will rise as one against the decadent Bastille we know as the US Post office. For years we have hypocritically turned the other cheek in hopes of at least a slight elevation in the financially draining quagmire but the employees and the directors, yes the directors too, more so to blame because of their supposed leadership abilities, have sunk deeper in the quicksand of inefficiency. Now readers, now the road has ended. Now is the time, it's ripe, to tear the walls of the Bastille down, burn the inquisitors, drown the witches of the Air Mail system, stab the effigies of the parcel post system, burn in oil the insurers of the never arriving mails, but most of all send a letter to Lt. Guth from his darling and sorely missed wife.

Who could resist such a plea. If I only owned a newspaper I would write such an expose. If I don't get a letter from you tomorrow I'm going to make an effigy of Postmaster General Hershey and stick pins in it and then slowly pummel it with golf balls. It isn't not getting the letters so much as knowing they're held up somewhere by some goof sitting on his duff and most of all that I can't do anything to rectify the situation.

Good news of a promise. We have a house. Promised. Jerry Bingham arranged it with Lt. Abbot. He has a house that he has lived in for almost a year with three children. Two bedrooms, living room, ante room, bath, kitchen, etc. He works in the housing section and has the ungarbled word that the government housing is going to open up at Gifu and he is one of the first in line since he has been here so long. We're not eligible since I've only been here 6 months. If he does get the house in Gifu it will be next

week and he will then sublease his former
house to me at which time I'll put in our
application. The week after that the board
will meet and approve the application and the
paper work will begin. Soon after that we
will be together again.

Playing golf in a tournament tomorrow. Flew a
long mission to Korea today, another day
saving income tax, but all I want is you,
that's all I think about. Honey, I want you
here with me, now, and I don't want to wait
for two or three months. Now that I'm
thinking about you again I can't think of any
more little things. I love you more each day
and am gladder each day that I married you.
Have been sitting here thinking about you.

Love, Joe

His search for a house kept turning up leads which looked promising. Some of these appeared to be certain enough for him to turn in the necessary application papers for me to join him. However, government transportation involved a four-month wait. Since I still had a valid passport from my summer in Guatemala, he started looking into the possibility of commercial travel by sea, at our own expense:

19 May 53

Hi Honey,

I had planned to spend this evening writing
an easy casual letter to you and get a good
night's sleep. Wanted to write you 'cause I
got four letters from you today. However, the
9th won its second golf tournament today.
That's 2 out of 2. Col. Bower didn't make our
team. He is #7 and we usually just field 5 or
6. However, he is real nice about it and lets
us off to represent the 9th. He does get a
lot of publicity from our winnings however.
Heard a Colonel say to him tonight, "Heard

your boys won another golf match today. What
the hell are they supposed to be, pilots or
golfers?!"

That's the reason this is going to be a short
letter. Am real tired and after a full shrimp
dinner and three coffees and Drambouies I'm
drowsy, too.

Sorry I didn't get to meet Uncle George. Glad
his intended cookbook to us has a wine fare.
As to the books, bring them all and let's
begin our library. It will be a little
cumbersome at times, but I think it will be
necessary eventually. OK?

Before I forget. Got a letter from Mother,
and I'm so pleased with you about your
writing her I can't even think of a
comparison.

She said, "This has been one of the best
Mother's Days I have ever had. Joe, you sure
married a wonderful and thoughtful girl." She
then tells of your cards and gifts to her,
Dad, and Granny. Also said she had to cry
over some parts. To quote again, "Oh, Joe,
sometimes I think I'm dreaming to think I got
two such grand girls for daughters. I know
I'm lucky. Not every Mother has that luck.
Dad sure likes Gil. Our friends the Brueners
were over last night. You should have heard
Dad telling them what a swell girl Gil is."

Honey you know how that pleases me. Besides
loving and wanting you very much I want to
thank you, just as one person to another. I
think it's wonderful how you have treated
Mother and Dad. Thank you very, very much
darling. I want your folks to like me too,
but I'm not nearly as responsible a person as
you and I'll need some goading to live up to
your standard, but I promise to be dutiful as
soon as I settle your coming here.

```
When I make the final settlements on our
house, transportation over here for you,
financial adjustments, the myriad of paper
work, a ring, the golf tournament, flying and
making up the work I missed I'll write Jo,
your Mother, think of a present for Manny and
all the others, announcements, people,
places—I'm rambling. I love you, my darling.

Your Joe
```

Amid all the happiness and excitement of planning for me to join him in Japan, his successes as a pilot, as a golfer, and the joy of our marriage, tragic events continued to happen. The Korean War was still being waged:

```
Some bad news. A short paragraph. My best
friend was killed yesterday. Grady Hinson was
shot down, a direct hit while on his dive
bomb run. Not much more to say other than it
leaves something missing in me.
```

This meant that of the seven student officers who went from basic training at Greenville, Mississippi to Willy for advanced pilot training, only Joe Guth and Jack Denton had survived. Once again the dangers of Joe's profession were driven home to me, as I realized how easily he could be one of those who had been lost. At the time, however, I refused to let those terrible thoughts linger too long. It frightened me too much to think about it.

As the years passed Joe would continue to mention those names occasionally. Many years later I was looking through his Class of 52-Charlie yearbook from Willy, and I discovered that he had marked the dates on which his close friends had been killed under each of their young-faced, eager-looking pictures. I knew then that these losses of his friends, so long ago, had affected him much more deeply than he ever discussed. They were all so young.

As I was preparing for my new life overseas, every day was filled with details requiring attention. And every day I eagerly waited for a letter from Joe. They were always filled with news and loving words. But the slow mail delivery continued to complicate things for us as we dealt with the details of my trip to Japan:

Monday May 25 '53

My Dearest Wife,

Today I got four letters from you and everything is O. K. again. You know, Honey, I've gotten only one letter from Mother and I'm sure she's written more. Mail delivery, Bah!

I'm just waiting for your GO sign about your passport, ideas and wants about coming here commercially. If you agree, I'll go to the steamship lines, buy you a ticket and send you a wire as to where, when, and how. If your passport is still good, let me know when you could be in San Francisco ready to go.

Rumors have it that Komaki Air Base will get a section of houses, 60 of the 95, at Camp Gifu. If that is so we will probably get one and will be able to live in government quarters.

Howie Pierson just called me. He is down from Yokota Air Base on their track team. He's coming out for lunch tomorrow. He will be surprised to hear that I'm married, and slightly bitter I suppose after his unfortunate experience about bringing his girl over here to get married and her falling in love with the first mate.

Sometimes I'm selfish and think, "Now I've got her and nobody can take her away and nothing can separate us." I'm glad I have you, so very, very happy with you.

Got all the pictures you sent and I like them very much. Soon as I got back I got your picture out again. Have now put one of the

colored pictures your Uncle George took at
Christmas on each side of your big one.
Everyone who sees them remarks on the
question of how I got such a good-looking
girl. My quick retort to that is, "yeah—she's
plenty smart, too."

Have one page in the album entitled Miss
Cosulich and have the three pictures of you
and Jo in your flight suits on it plus the
one of you and Jo in your Spanish hats and
the two of you and me together. Will title
another page later on MRS. GUTH.

Will sure be glad to own a car here. Even if
we don't get government quarters for quite a
while it will be O. K. with a car. Car or no
car, new or old, I want you. Oh, honey, I
miss you so much, impatient mostly I think.
Knowing how wonderful it was to be with you
and how peachy it will be I can hardly wait.
The two weeks we had was just sort of a tease
preview of what there is to come. Love me,
Honey, because I need you very badly. You're
all or more than I hoped for, in every way I
can think of. Every time I think of life and
all its concerns I think of my Gil.

Until the next letter, lover. I love you.
Your Joe

Joe's efforts to find a house for us were meeting with setbacks and frustrations. But he was determined to get me to Japan as soon as possible. It appeared that ship travel at our own expense was the only way that it would work:

Some new developments, not good. The house I thought we had has fallen through.

If you think like I do four months is too long to wait for government transportation.

If you come here commercially you'll get here a month or two earlier, with a clearance to stay six weeks on a visitor's visa. But if you do come at our expense I do not have to have a house and it's the house I'm having trouble with. If you come at our expense I will have from now until then to find a house plus the six weeks on your visitor's visa. That will be ample I'm sure, sure as I'm sitting here.

I'm in a rush to get to town and start stirring up the little people I had working for me to try to find another house.

Honey, I've not done too good so far, but things are a little different here. I'm really trying. Be patient.

I love you
Joe

The next several letters were full of details about my trip over by ship, his efforts at finding a house and all the bureaucratic problems associated with the endeavor. As always, the mail delays complicated things but we were both determined and undeterred by all the red tape:

For the last three days the mail has been delivered, but I can't say promptly. Yesterday I got your May 23 letter and today I got your May 15 letter, but as long as I keep getting them I'm happy. Got a letter from Mother too, and honey you have really made a hit with her. All her letter of four pages was about was you. All the nice letters and cards and gifts you sent. We both love you very much, me especially.

```
Howie Pierson is here in Nagoya as an entrant
in the Far Eastern Track and Field meet. He
should win the discus throw and a trip back
to the States. Think he has recovered from
the injury of his girl marrying the first
mate, but that was a hard blow.


More soon.
Your Husband
```

I bought a copy of the book *The Air Force Wife*, and started pouring through it, eager to learn about how to be a good wife to an Air Force jet pilot. I became a little concerned that there might be some resentment if I, a new bride, got to Japan sooner than some of the wives who had been waiting a long time. Also, it occurred to me that I might get to Japan sooner and we might get government housing sooner if I got a teaching job in the American school there. Joe responded to all of my questions and also expressed his opinion about the book I was reading:

```
                                        May 31, 53

Dearest Gilberta:

Got home a little late and a little tipsy too
so I didn't see your letters until this
morning and they almost cured my headache.
You are making me very happy and are really
keeping my morale up with your frequent
letters. Wish I could write as often.

I was really happy to hear that your passport
is still good. Now I can swing into action.
Tomorrow I'm going to the travel agency and
find out about a ticket. I will try to get
you a ticket on a freighter sailing about the
first of July. Glad you heard about the
freighters and I'm pleased to find out
someone you know made the trip and that it's
nice. I will buy the ticket here and let you
know of the sailing date. Before I pay for it
or make final arrangements I'll try to call
you and confirm it from your end. I assume
```

you can be ready by about the first of July.

Yes, please try and get all your shots as soon as possible so that you can be ready to leave as soon as we get the ticket information.

No, Gil, I don't want you to teach, especially if you don't want to. There is no reason for you to have to teach here as long as we're satisfied to live in a Japanese house rather than government housing. I am, and I'm sure you will be too as soon as you see them. I'm not sure it would do us any good to try to get government housing even if you would teach.

Darlin' there will be absolutely no hard feelings about you getting here as soon as the other wives. There is no reason for them to have any feelings one way or the other 'cause I'm bringing you at my own cost and they could have done the same thing but they elected to wait for government travel. No reason to think of it again.

Don't get too involved in that Air Force Wives' book. From what I've understood a lot of it is bosh.

Your letters have been coming along and are being delivered promptly now. Hope it keeps up.

Didn't feel like playing golf today. It was cloudy and rainy, plus the fact that I shot so badly yesterday that I think I'm getting stale. Spent the whole day sketching and drawing up plans for a record cabinet. I think I'll be able to use the woodworking shop on the base. Think it will be about two months before our new car gets here. Sure wish it would get here soon. We're liable to have a lot of inconveniences for a month or two after you first get here. The house we will probably get will not be available to us

until maybe August or September. Until then
we will have to stay in a hotel or a house if
I can find one.

About all the stuff we'll have: When I talked
to the ship agent he said you would be able
to bring 175# of personal baggage. Now that I
think about it you will probably need that
weight for your personal things. Here's a
suggestion. After we find out what ship and
when you will be sailing pack up everything
and mail it to me here. In fact, you can
start sending things right away if you want
to.

Beauregard our dog is dead, been dead for two
months. While I was back there in the US the
troops found him on his back with his feet
straight up in the air, rigid. I didn't want
to tell you about it. We all miss him.

I love you, and I can't wait until we're
together again.

Love, Joe

A highlight during those days of waiting was the night he called me from Japan. It was wonderful to hear his voice during that brief call. He sounded like he was very close by as we verified some of the travel plans and exchanged loving words. That call made me all the more eager to begin the journey to Japan, so I could be with him again:

                                    Monday 1 June 53

My Darling,

It was so good to talk to you today. When I
first got back here before I got any of your
letters I sometimes thought We were a dream.
After getting your letters you seemed real,
but after talking to you today you seemed
really vivid. I can still hear you talking
and could almost see you. Oh honey, I want
you here so much I can hardly wait to see you

and hold you again.

I went to the ticket office to see about
getting you a ticket to come here
commercially. Mr. Wataknabe, the agent,
thinks that the American President Lines are
the best and his sailing schedule showed that
there is a ship, the President Arthur,
sailing the 4th of July. I thought that you
would be able to get ready in a month. It's a
cargo ship and it is in the same class as a
freighter as far as accommodations. He showed
me a brochure and it looked real nice. He is
making a reservation for you on that ship.

In some ways the 18th of July seems close (it
will take you that long to get here), and
then again when I think of another six weeks
without you it seems so long. I can hardly
wait to have you with me again.

Oh! I've been meaning to tell you to go ahead
and sell or destroy the Menace. I had been
considering bringing it over here and using
it until our new car came over but the new
one should be here soon after you get here
and after thinking about the expense and its
condition I think it would be a bad bet.
Think it's about time the old doll had a turn
in the pasture anyway don't you?

Your loving husband, Joe

He encouraged me to bring Judy to Japan with me. He suggested this not only because of my fondness for my dog, but also for her to be with me during the day "in case we're living in an isolated place." His search for housing continued, and he assured me that by the time I arrived he would have something, even if we had to stay in a hotel for a few days.

I had to have a metal crate made for Judy, since she would be taking the voyage outside on the stern of the ship. She needed to have shots, a veterinarian's certificate, sufficient food for the trip. The crate was built for her at Davis Monthan Air Force Base, near Tucson. Judy and I both had our shots at Davis Monthan as well. These were only a part of the myriad details that needed attending to and, squeezed between all these tasks were wedding showers given by relatives and friends, followed by the required writing of thank you notes.

My uncle Manny took my grandmother's trunk to the garage and relined it with linoleum and repaired it for me to pack our wedding gifts and my clothes in. It had been hers since her marriage to my grandfather in 1902.

"She would want you to have it," Manny said. "It's of no use to anyone around here."

I was touched by the fact that he had thought of it, and by the effort he put into refurbishing it. Manny had always treated me like I was his own daughter, and I loved him dearly.

Because of the time lapse between Joe's and my letters, our correspondence was filled with many repeated questions, answers and reports of details accomplished and acknowledged.

His mother and I corresponded, and her happiness for us permeated her letters. It was good to learn how devoted Joe's family was, and how close he was to them.

Then came a sudden change in the July 4 scheduling of my departure. He wrote this letter on June 10, and I received it a week later:

Called the ticket agent today and here is some vital news. He suggested you come by the cargo ship President Polk rather than the Liberty Ship President Arthur. Honey that ship leaves the first of July. I know that gives you less time to get ready but you will be here sooner. That is what I want even if you have to leave some things undone and have to do it by correspondence or have some things shipped over. I saw the brochure and it looked real nice.

If you can make the sailing date and if you can make arrangements to get Judy to San Francisco and then on the ship we will be together by the middle of July and we can

> then start living as we should, as man and
> wife. That honey is all I'm living for and
> dreaming about. After our second honeymoon in
> Tokyo of course.

This news meant that my preparations to leave had to be speeded up considerably. The *President Polk* was part of the American President Lines' fleet of cargo carriers that provided accommodations for up to twelve passengers. We were assured that these accommodations were very comfortable, and in fact, luxurious.

With barely two weeks to prepare, I rushed through all my carefully planned lists of "things to do," including getting Judy's requirements completed, packing, getting train reservations, hotel reservations in San Francisco, finding and reserving space for Judy at a San Francisco kennel near the pier, the goodbye calls and visits, and last minute shopping. My aunt Catherine was going with me on the train to spend a couple of days with me in San Francisco while I waited to board my ship.

Catherine and I were very close. She had been a teenager when I was born, and was like a big sister to me. She had helped my grandmother look after me while I was growing up. We knew we would have fun together in San Francisco.

The last letter I received from Joe before leaving Tucson was dated June 12, 1953:

> Hi Honey,
>
> Went to the PX and in answer to your questions
> about the availability of things over here, I
> verify what I said about the naiveté of the
> book you're reading on "The Air Force Wife."
> The PX has irons, toasters, ladies' dresses,
> knives, pots, pans, radios, silverware and
> loads of other things you'll be able to spend
> our money on.
>
> I think of you all the time and I'm plagued
> with trying to imagine meeting you at the
> pier at Yokohama. Never been there so I can't
> do too well, but I can almost imagine you.

The day of departure arrived at last. We had Judy put in the baggage car in her crate, Catherine and I boarded the train, and we waved good-bye to family and friends as we pulled out of the Tucson station.

We stayed at a small San Francisco hotel near Union Square called The Franciscan, and planned for two days of sightseeing. One evening when we returned from dinner, there was a message for me to call the American President Lines' Passenger Services office immediately. The *President Polk* was in drydock for repairs, and I would be leaving, instead, on the *President Taft* on July 10. An extra nine days in San Francisco! I wired Joe, drew additional money from the bank, and Catherine and I started our unexpected extra days and nights of savoring the sights of San Francisco. We packed an incredible amount of fun into those next nine days in the city, going to the theater, taking daytime and nighttime tours, shopping, sailing on the Bay, and dining at some of the famous restaurants.

As the day for my departure approached, I decided to get my hair done. I knew my long hair would turn frizzy in the ocean air, so I wanted it put up into a chignon, out of the way and manageable. We found a hairdresser near the hotel, and Catherine waited for me while I had it done. Catherine was a hairdresser, and as she sat and watched, I wasn't sure she totally approved of what the operator was doing, but my hair got put up and out of my way in a style that I could keep and probably duplicate during the long sea voyage.

Finally, on July 10, Judy and I boarded the *President Taft*. Judy, in her metal crate, was loaded onto the stern of the ship by a crane. I could hear her barking and whimpering, confused by what was happening to her. I walked up the gangplank and went to the rail. Catherine and I were waving and throwing kisses to each other as the ship rumbled away from the pier. We were both fighting back tears as we kept waving good-bye, until the ship turned into San Francisco Bay, and the pier she was standing on was out of sight.

The ship sailed under the Golden Gate Bridge, headed for Yokohama Harbor, Japan. I was shown to my cabin then, and was pleasantly surprised at how comfortable and private it was. There were eight other young wives aboard, and we were treated to a first class voyage. We were told that we would be dining with the ship's officers in the Captain's mess, and were given the meal schedule. Meals were signaled by a steward, walking up and down the passageway to our quarters, playing a small handheld xylophone.

I unpacked my belongings and left the cabin to go check on Judy, who was overjoyed when I took her out of her crate for a walk around the deck. It was also an opportunity to meet my fellow passengers. Some of them were standing at the rail, walking the deck, or sitting in deck chairs watching the coast of northern California fade from sight.

Soon it was time for our first meal in the Captain's mess. There were four officers in addition to the Captain. They were all in their dress uniforms, standing respectfully as we entered, waiting for the Captain to signal us all to be seated. Conversation flowed easily during the meal, which was delicious. The men all seemed interested in getting acquainted with us and making us feel at home.

As the days passed, I became aware that the *President Taft* was fertile ground for a shipboard romance. One or two of the young women seemed to be quite taken with all the attention. I thought of Joe's friend, Howard Pierson, whose fiancée, on her way to marry Howard in Japan, had fallen in love on just such a voyage, on just such a ship, and had married the first mate.

However, most of the young women were like me, so eager to be with our husbands that we didn't succumb to all the flattery and attention. I spent most of my time reading, visiting with my fellow passengers, and looking after Judy, who needed to be walked several times a day, fed, and cleaned up after. She would welcome me with her overjoyed panting and tail-wagging whenever I went back to the ship's stern to tend to her.

I was intently engrossed in reading Nancy Shea's book, *The Air Force Wife*, despite Joe's comment that it was probably "bosh." I was determined to be a good Air Force wife, so I took everything Nancy wrote as gospel:

Flying is a highly specialized career. It takes more than just the ability to fly. The pilot's actions at the controls must be instinctive, quick, sub-conscious; his judgment in an emergency must be perfect. His mind cannot be disturbed by worry over unpaid bills, the ten-

sion of making it home for a party or 'bust,' or news phoned to him by an unthinking wife that Johnny fell out of the tree-house and broke his arm. The arm will heal, but a mistake in judgment on the part of the pilot may claim the lives of many.

All of these points, which may seem minor to you in your youth, may assume serious proportions and clutter up the mind of your pilot husband, thereby making him less efficient. To do his best, your husband must have a congenial, happy home life. His mind must be free for the work in hand. In other words, when he takes off he wants someone to come back to, someone who cares and understands. No husband enjoys coming home to listen to complaints or being heckled because he did not make it in time for the Smiths' dinner—particularly if his delay was caused by weather, orders or something else over which he had no control.

As I read the book, I made up my mind that I would do everything in my power to create a stable, happy home environment for Joe and me. I felt the importance of "keeping his mind free" of worry, tension, and "clutter."

As instructed in the book, I had ordered printed calling cards for myself in Tucson. I carefully absorbed the correct protocol for "calling" on commanding officers' wives, the proper dress for different occasions, including white gloves, hats, and other fine points of military life as it existed in the 1950s. I was going to be the perfect Air Force wife... the quintessential fighter pilot's wife.

After what seemed an interminable fourteen days we arrived at last in Yokohama Harbor. It was July 23, 1953. We had to remain on the *President Taft* for several hours, waiting for the ship to be docked. The extra hours gave us more time to fret, to primp, and to debate whether what we were wearing was the perfect outfit for reuniting with our husbands.

We kept knocking on each others' cabin doors to ask, "Do you think this dress is all right, or should I wear the blue one? Should I wear a hat? Do you think this dress will be too warm? May I borrow your nail polish? Does my slip show? Are my stocking seams straight?"

Everyone's anticipation and impatience were growing by the minute. We paced the deck, searching for some sign that the ship was moving into its docking space. I imagined what it would be like to see Joe, to run into his arms, to kiss him, to be with him at long last. We waited three long hours, and finally, the docking space was ready. Our ship lumbered in and tied up at the wharf. We could finally go ashore.

I walked across the gangplank and into the waiting area. There stood Joe in his crisp summer uniform, holding out his arms to me. We ran to each other's arms, laughing, kissing, hugging happily, so happy. We stood holding each other for a few minutes, and gazing into each other's eyes. Then we went to pick up Judy in the baggage room. Joe opened her crate, grabbed her collar, and snapped her leash onto it. But in her joy at seeing us she broke loose from his grip and jumped up, muddying that spotless uniform of his, panting happily and frantically wagging her stub of a tail. As we pulled her out of the terminal and onto the sidewalk outside, she was jumping up and down with happiness, and wrapping her leash around both of us.

Joe had arranged to leave her at a kennel across the street for a few days, so we started across the very wide, very busy Yokohama street. Halfway across, Judy decided she had to "go," and squatted down to take care of that need. Joe tugged at her leash.

"Come on, Judy! We can't stop here!"

With cars honking and racing by us, Joe pulled her the rest of the way across on her rear end. We were laughing as we finally got her to the kennel, and, glad to finally have her out of our way, we got into a taxi.

We took one look at each other and threw our arms around each other, holding on tight between kisses and saying, "I love you." Then Joe took a small blue velvet box from his pocket and gave it to me. I opened it to find the beautiful gold and diamond ring he had designed himself and had made for me in Tokyo. He put it on my finger next to Manny's narrow gold band, and we clung together for the remainder of the ride to our hotel, not talking... just kissing, hugging and holding on to each other as though we'd never let go again.

* * * *

Chapter Nine

THE HEART TAKES A HIT

We stayed at the luxurious New Grand Hotel in Yokohama for a few days, promising to love each other forever. On our second evening there, we were having a candlelit dinner in the hotel's beautifully decorated dining room. I was wearing a low-cut, sleeveless black blouse with a full, black and gold skirt. Joe was looking at me across the table.

"Miss Sweet Breasts of 1953," he said. I looked up, surprised. He took my hand and said, "I admire you and respect you, and I love you."

My heart at that moment was touched in a way that I have never forgotten. Remembering the candlelight, his touch, and his face as he said those words to me years ago still evokes the sense of loving and being loved that I felt that evening. In the years to come I would not see his face look that way often. I learned that he usually kept his feelings to himself, and found it hard to express his emotions. But that night he looked vulnerable, open, his eyes soft, his expression tender.

Our romantic reunion continued for a few more days. Then one evening Joe said, "I want you to meet a good friend of mine."

We met Joe's friend, Howard Pierson, and his date at the Latin Quarter in Tokyo. Joe and Howard had become friends in Greenville, Mississippi, while they were in basic Air Force pilot school together in the Class of 52-Charlie.

Howard was a big man, six feet four, who had played football at the University of Alabama before entering Air Force pilot training. Joe had written me about his friend, "Howie," who seemed to have recovered from the trauma of losing his fiancée to the first mate on her voyage to Japan.

His date was a very beautiful, petite young American woman who stood four feet eleven. She was a court reporter for the Judge Advocate General's office at Far East Air Command Headquarters in Tokyo. She didn't appear to be surprised or embarrassed by Howard's unconventional behavior, nor his habit of calling her "Pygmy," the endearing nickname he'd given her. When we entered the Latin Quarter that evening, Howard was told that he must wear a tie, so he asked Pygmy for her scarf and tied it in a big bow around his neck.

After dinner he said, "Come on, Pygmy, let's dance!" Grabbing his tiny partner, he swung her off her feet and whirled her around the dance floor. It was a fun and memorable evening, and I was happy about meeting one of Joe's closest friends. Joe's friendship with Howard was to last a lifetime, although the romance between Howard and Pygmy did not.

The next day we left for Nagoya, a large city about 250 miles southwest of Tokyo, where Joe was stationed at nearby Komaki Air Base, flying F-84G Thunderjets in the Special Weapons assignment. I didn't

DINNER WITH HOWARD PIERSON AND DATE SHORTLY AFTER GILBERTA ARRIVES IN JAPAN.

know until long after we returned to the States what their mission had been: their planes were armed with nuclear weapons to be used against any future enemy. At that time the possibility of their being used was real, since the Cold War was posing a constant threat to the U.S. Each pilot was assigned a certain target, and each one had his own "escape and evasion plan," in case of being shot down over enemy territory. Joe's plan, he told me much later, was to disguise himself as best he could, hide out during the day, and at night, get a boat and make his way toward the sea. Since he had been an airplane navigator in World War II, and had served on a special assignment to a Merchant Marine ship as ship's navigator, he was an expert at celestial navigation. His escape plan was to sail at night using the stars as his navigational guide to safety. I wondered, when he told me about his plan, how far he would have gotten in an Asian country with his blue eyes and blond hair.

However, during the year and a half I spent in Japan, I lived in blissful ignorance as to what the men were training to do and what they might be called upon to do.

On July 27, 1953, just days after I arrived in Japan, the Korean "Police Action" ended with an armistice, an uneasy truce. During the three-year war, 36,900 Americans had died, 7,000 had been taken as prisoners of war, and more than 8,000 remained missing. The armistice did not affect what the U.S. government saw as our continued need for readiness. The continuance of the Cold War required troops, pilots, and planes to remain in a state of combat readiness. So Joe and the thousands of other pilots and ground troops were to stay, almost as if the armistice had not taken place.

Japan was a fascinating, unusual, and strange place for me, a new bride. Our first home was the upstairs of Jane and Pat Farrell's apartment. Pat was one of the pilots in the 9th Fighter Bomber Squadron, and like Joe and me, Pat and Jane had only been married a short time. I cooked our meals on a tiny, three-burner stove which was hung over the stairwell. Joe shaved at the same small sink in which I washed dishes.

Early every morning the noodle man rode by on his bicycle, blowing on his flute and waking me from the sleep which I had usually just sunk into after a restless, stifling night. Japan in August was very humid, hot and uncomfortable. I was used to the dry climate of my native Arizona, and I found myself exhausted, with no energy, as my body struggled to acclimate.

Jane Farrell and I visited during the day. A southern girl, she baked fresh rolls every day for her husband's dinner that night. Thinking that this was what a good wife was supposed to do, I watched her, got her recipe, and began baking fresh rolls every day. I would roll the dough out and set it in a bowl, place the bowl in warm water, let the dough rise for several hours, and bake the rolls in our electric oven in time for dinner. I was very proud of my bread baking, and Joe told me how good he thought my rolls were. It never occurred to me that the electric oven was generating additional heat during those humid summer days, and he was too tactful to mention it.

Jane and I occasionally explored Nagoya. We went to lunch at the beautiful Kanko hotel, which had been taken over by the U.S. forces at the end of World War II. It served as the Nagoya Officers Club, and was a very luxurious place, with its lavish lobbies, restaurants, and ballrooms. We explored the little stalls at the Nagoya market, where the native clothing, souvenirs, and fascinating items for the home were on display.

I bought Joe a kimono like the ones worn by the Japanese men. It was made from a blue and white, printed cotton material, with the traditional wide kimono sleeves and sash that tied around the waist to keep it closed.

One evening, Joe changed from his uniform into his kimono and said, "Let's go to a movie."

"Aren't you going to change?" I asked.

"No, I'm going just the way I am," he said. "All the Japanese men wear these, so I can too."

The kimono hit him at just about mid-calf, revealing his muscular, hairy, slightly bowed legs. With his blond hair and blue eyes, he was a strange sight to the Japanese. I watched their reactions as we walked the two blocks to the bus. Many stopped and stared. Once on the bus, he was the object of more curious gazes. I learned that this self-assurance of his spilled over to all aspects of his life. He didn't let other people's reactions embarrass or perturb him.

Our stay in the little Japanese rental was brief. After three weeks we were given housing at Camp Gifu, a U.S. Army base about twenty miles northwest of Nagoya and fifteen miles from Komaki Air Base.

It was beautiful, clean government housing, a duplex with everything furnished: living room, dining room, kitchen, two bedrooms, and a bath. The kitchen was completely equipped with dishes, glassware, and silverware for twelve, right down to the demitasse spoons. All of us were treated to the luxury of hiring household help, which made up for some of the inconveniences of living in the totally unfamiliar surroundings of Japan. It was especially helpful for those families with children, who needed frequent access to childcare due to the extremely active social life we were leading.

The Willerfords, the Rogers', and the Bowers, all of whom had been with us on our honeymoon in Las Vegas, lived close by. Across the courtyard from us lived another pilot in the 9th Squadron, Pete Petersen, with his wife Pat and their eighteen-month-old baby girl, who looked so much like her father that she was called "Miss Pete." The pilots were all close comrades because of their work, and within a very short time the wives also became close friends. We offered each other support and friendship, especially when the men were on flying assignments that took them away from home for days, or longer, at a time. And we were always ready for a party at one or another's house.

I was learning that military life would provide an instant social life, as well as immediate friendships, no matter where the future would take us. It seemed like the beginning of an idyllic, fairy tale existence. I had married the man I loved, and I was making some wonderful friends; we were living an exciting life in a country full of interesting sights; we were young and happy; and the Korean War was over.

Then something happened which cast a shadow over our seemingly carefree lives. Joe came home early one afternoon. When I saw his face I knew that something terrible had happened. His jaw was clenched, and he looked pale. It was a look that I hadn't seen before. I wasn't prepared for the news he brought.

"Petersen was killed this afternoon," he said hoarsely.

I stared at him in disbelief. How could this be? I'd had coffee with Pat at her house just that morning. She had shown such delight in her baby girl, and we had shared so much as we talked about our lives in Japan, our husbands, and the coming social events.

"Oh no!" I cried. "What happened!?"

"He was turning on final approach and crashed off the end of the runway."

I felt weak with shock. Joe took me in his arms and we stood clinging to each other. He was trying to be strong, trying not to show his grief and distress.

His voice cracked as he said, "Colonel Bower and the chaplain are with her now."

I looked across the courtyard to Pat's home, and the thought of what she must be feeling at that moment sickened me.

"What can we do?" I sobbed.

"In a few minutes we'll go over," Joe said. "You're close to Pat, and it will probably help for you to be with her."

Looking outside, I saw Bob Willerford walking into his home, and I knew that he would be telling Mary this awful news which I had just heard from Joe.

I attempted to regain some composure before going over to Pat's house. We went to her door and were let in by Colonel Bower. Joe went to Pat and put his arms around her wordlessly, holding her as she shook with grief. I took her in my arms and just held her. Both of us were crying. There were no words that could be spoken. Her look of anguish spoke eloquently of her devastating loss.

Over the next few days, the wives mobilized. Bonnie, the squadron commander's wife, provided us with her good example of strength, support, and willingness to be of any possible help. We took turns being with Pat, taking care of her baby, answering her phone, taking food to her, being sure that she ate something, that she tried to rest. We saw to it that she was never alone.

Pete had graduated from the U.S. Naval Academy at Annapolis. It was arranged that his body would be flown back to the States for burial at Arlington National Cemetery in Washington, D.C. Pat and her child would leave Camp Gifu as soon as arrangements could be made for her household belongings to be packed up and shipped. Families were not allowed to remain in base housing without their "sponsor."

A memorial service was arranged at the base chapel at Komaki. As we all crowded into the chapel I remember thinking, "This can't be true... it can't." I felt as though my idyllic life had suddenly been interrupted by this unthinkable event, and I realized, for the first time, that it could be any one of us walking into the chapel on an officer's arm, pale and drawn, dressed all in black.

Following the memorial service there was a reception at the Officers Club. People went up to Pat, unable to speak, wordlessly expressing their grief by taking her in their arms, crying and allowing her to cry with them.

Joe and I were sitting down when Pat came over and sat down beside us.

"Joe," she said. "I want you to do something for me."

"Sure, Pat... anything," he answered.

"I want you to drive me out to where Pete's plane crashed."

Joe looked stricken. "Oh, no, Pat. You don't want to do that."

She replied, "Look, Joe, I'm a nurse. I know what death is like. I want to see the place where Pete died."

She would not relent in her request, in spite of Joe's strong efforts to dissuade her. Joe went over to where Colonel Bower was standing, and the two men spoke quietly for a moment. Returning to where Pat and I were sitting, Joe took her by the arm to lead her out to our car, and I followed. The three of us got in, with Joe and Pat in the front seat and myself in back.

We drove the short distance to the end of the runway. The sun had just gone down, and in the twilight we saw a small blackened crater where Pete's aircraft had impacted. The wreckage had been cleared away. Pat got out of the car and Joe jumped out after her. I followed them to the edge of the crater, and the three of us stood there in the twilight, looking at the wound in the earth. "My heart is broken right... down... the middle," Pat faltered.

Joe put his arm around her shoulders, and told her, "The heart doesn't break, Pat. It takes a heavy hit, but it doesn't break."

Pat started to weep, and we stood there with her, both of us holding her, trying to find the words that might offer her some degree of solace. But there were no words. Just the twilight, and the sound of Pat softly sobbing.

As the darkness began to deepen, Joe said, "Come on, Pat. Let's go back." We returned to the club, where Pete's flying comrades, their wives, and other friends continued to go to Pat, murmuring softly to her through their tears, holding her.

Over the next few days Pat's house was filled with packers, movers, and those of us who wanted to be with her to help in any way possible. Her belongings were moved out, we said our tearful goodbyes, and then she and "Miss Pete" were gone.

```
                    HIGH FLIGHT

    Oh, I have slipped the surly bonds of Earth
    And danced the skies on laughter-silver wings,
  Sunward I've climbed and joined the tumbling mirth
    Of sun-split clouds-and done a hundred things
      You have not dreamed of -- wheeled and

                    Soared and swung
      High in the sunlit silence. Hov'ring there
    I've chased the shouting wind along, and flung
    My eager craft through footless halls of air.
      Up, up the long, delirious, burning blue
  I've topped the wind swept heights with easy grace
        Where never lark, or even eagle flew.
    And, while with silent, lifting mind I've trod
      The high untrespassed sanctity of space,
    put out my hand, and touched the face of God.

              --John Gillespie Magee Jr.,
    RAF fighter pilot, killed in action World War II
```

* * * *

Chapter Ten

WHO WILL BE NEXT?

This was my first of many such wrenching experiences that were, I learned, a part of life for a military pilot's wife. Ahead was the challenge of learning to live with the terrifying knowledge that there would always be another such experience in the future. And how to deal with that awful question: who will be next?

But life gradually returned to a fairly stable routine following Pete Petersen's death. The pilots got back to their strenuous flying schedules immediately, and the social whirl again got underway. They continued to train, practice, and hone their skills, still exuding the same attitudes of invincibility as before. No one spoke of what had happened to the Petersens. I wanted to talk about it, to share my grief. But I knew I shouldn't bring it up to Joe, who was dealing with his own feelings about it, and gearing up each day to go out and fly again. There seemed to be an "unwritten protocol" which precluded such talk, not only among the pilots, but also among their wives.

Whether getting together during the day at each others' homes for coffee, attending Wives' Club functions or evening social events, the loss of Pete Petersen and the departure of his family was not discussed. We just didn't talk about it. It seemed that everyone was on their own to deal with it according to their own inner resources. I began to understand the need for the pilots, as well as their wives, to maintain a positive, optimistic attitude, in spite of the ever-present dangers. To do this I started to rely heavily on my religious faith to help me garner the necessary strength. I was to learn that I would meet this challenge many times in the future. The friendships continued to flourish, and I realized how much we all depended upon each other for optimism and support.

Soon it was Thanksgiving, and we invited several of the bachelor officers over for dinner... my very first Thanksgiving dinner, prepared and served all by myself. One of the invited guests was Joe's good friend, Howard Pierson. He had been transferred to Nagoya to become aide-de-camp to the Commanding General of the Japan Air Defense Force. He was going to bring the turkey, so I prepared all the side dishes. I arranged the table in what I thought was a beautiful setting, with linens, candles, flowers, crystal, and china. Joe made the cocktails, and we awaited the arrival of our guests, Dave, Jack, Howard, and Doc Gorman.

Joe welcomed them warmly as I came out of the kitchen to greet them. Howard stood holding the turkey—a frozen solid one. I was flabbergasted. I stared at it, totally at a loss as to how to salvage my first Thanksgiving dinner.

Rising to the occasion, Joe said, "No sweat, Toots. The Officers Club is putting on a big Thanksgiving dinner. We'll call them and tell 'em we're coming to buy a whole cooked turkey."

So Joe and Howard left for the Officers Club. The other three guests stood in the kitchen, having a drink, laughing, and generally enjoying themselves. I put the finishing touches on the other dishes and served some hors d'oeuvres, waiting anxiously for Joe and Howard to return with the turkey.

Arriving with the cooked turkey, Joe and Howard joined the others in the kitchen. While I finished the last minute preparations, Joe carved the bird. I went to the dining room to get the serving dishes. Suddenly the exuberant voices in the kitchen fell silent. There was a long pause, and then I heard Joe say something to the others in low tones, followed by loud guffaws and an exchange of comments that I couldn't hear.

The fresh rolls were baked the last minute, and the carved turkey and all the trimmings were carried to the table. Joe lit the candles, poured the wine, and we sat down to what I saw as my perfect first Thanksgiving dinner.

There were many compliments throughout the meal.

"Gil, everything is so good!" proclaimed Joe.

"I especially like the rolls," said Howard.

"They are delicious!" declared Dave.

"Exceptional!" exclaimed Doc.

"Light as a feather," said Jack.

Joe told me later that, while he was carving the turkey in the kitchen, he saw one of the guests washing his hands over a large bowl in the sink. It was the bowl holding my rising dough for the dinner rolls.

"Listen, you SOB's," Joe had ordered, "you're going to eat every damn one of those rolls. Not only that. You're going to tell her how delicious they are!"

In those next months after Thanksgiving, our house became a gathering place for many planned and impromptu get-togethers.

Al Schneider, the new squadron operations officer, and his wife Gayle had arrived and were our new neighbors. Al and Joe became golfing buddies, and Al's wife, Gayle, and I often met them in Nagoya at the Kanko for dinner or a party after their golf game.

Joe and Al each bought the components to build themselves some high-fidelity stereo systems. One Saturday Al came over to help Joe put together our stereo system, and a party to try out the new equipment ensued. The living room soon became filled with friends stretched out on the floor, and on every chair and sofa, listening to the musical sounds emanating from the new system. We played long-playing records by Frank Sinatra, Eartha Kitt, Doris Day, Perry Como, and instrumentals by the big bands—Benny Goodman, Tommy Dorsey, Tex Benecke, and Harry James.

Al was a jazz enthusiast, and while sitting on the floor with his back against the sofa, he would close his eyes, relishing the beautiful jazz sounds floating through the room.

"Hey, look at Al!" one of our guests exclaimed. "He's fallen asleep!"

"Hell no, I'm not!" declared Al. "Can't you see my foot? It's keeping time with the music!"

Joe made sure that every guest's glass was always full, and I saw that there were plenty of snacks to nibble on. As everyone began to get hungry, Gayle and I made a big pot of spaghetti and a huge salad.

The next day Joe helped Al assemble his stereo system, and another party was in the making. It was obvious that the men were always ready to escape their high-energy, tension-filled days. And the wives welcomed the socializing and friendship that the get-togethers afforded.

Sometimes Joe and I played recordings of the great operas, sitting quietly together, holding hands, absorbing the story and the magnificent music. One evening we were listening to one of our favorites, Pucini's *Madam Butterfly*. The emotional, stirring aria by Butterfly, "*Un bel di*," "One Fine Day," with its sad undertones of impending betrayal and tragedy, always moved me to tears. Joe put his arm around me and, as though to address the betrayer, growled, "Pinkerton, you rat!"

Because I didn't care for bridge, I decided to find a productive way to fill the daytime hours. I took a job teaching at the Education Office on base. My students were enlisted men who needed to prepare for an academic test that would qualify them for their next promotion in rank. The first day I walked into the classroom I could sense that they were dubious about me. They were all quite a bit older than my twenty-three years. Many of them sat with their arms folded, and appeared resentful that this young officer's wife would be trying to teach them anything, and what could she know anyway? I was determined to meet the challenge, and worked hard preparing the required material, relying on my professional teacher training. I tried to maintain the calm demeanor that had worked well during my two years of teaching second grade, ignoring their doubtful expressions. I taught them high school English, composition, and mathematics. There was no doubt that they were highly motivated to prepare for that test. My sense of confidence increased as they were gradually won over to the fact that this Mrs. Guth was a real teacher, and was there to help them.

When the time came, I administered the test to them, and all of them waited at their desks for me to finish scoring their papers. One by one, I called them up to my desk to tell them their scores. Much to my joy, everyone in the class achieved the score required for promotion. As each man left the classroom after learning that he had passed the requirement, his grin, handshake, and expression of thanks told me how much the class had meant to him.

F-84G'S TAKE FLIGHT OVER JAPAN NEAR MT. FUJIYAMA.

"Great! Thanks a lot!"

"Boy! That's a relief!"

"Thanks, Mrs. Guth!"

It was while teaching that class that I realized how much I liked working with adults, and I decided then that I probably would not return to an elementary classroom.

The pilots continued their intense flying duties. Sometimes Joe was gone overnight, or for days at a time. When he returned, he would walk in the door in his flight suit, exhausted. His face would bear the markings from his oxygen mask—deep lines under his eyes and around his mouth where the tight mask had been in place for sometimes as many as nine or twelve hours at a time. He explained to me that on these long flying missions they would do in-flight refuelings, hooking up to tankers in midair and taking on additional fuel for continuing the mission.

One evening we were filing some personal documents at the dining room table. He started talking about in-flight refuelings, and, picking up our marriage license, he sketched a picture on the back of it showing how in-flight refuelings worked. I was awed that he, in his jet aircraft, flying at such speed and such altitude, could connect with a tanker midair, take on fuel, disengage, and continue his flight. It was a glimpse into the incredible skill required to perform in this amazing profession.

As the holidays approached there were many festive get-togethers. In addition to gatherings at our homes, the Kanko Hotel was the site of holiday parties, dances, and sumptuous dinners and buffets.

"Pygmy" had been transferred from Tokyo to Nagoya shortly after Howard was, and we saw a lot of them, along with the many other friends living at Camp Gifu. Once again it was an active, happy, and busy life.

And then after the first of the year, thrilled and excited, we learned that a baby was on the way.

* * * *

Chapter Eleven

ICHIBON

Joe named the little one-to-be "Ichibon," which means "Number One" in Japanese. My pregnancy didn't limit our active social life at all. Many of the young wives became pregnant during those months, so maternity clothes were very fashionable. We were able to have some stylish maternity outfits made-to-order by availing ourselves of the highly talented Japanese seamstresses. They could recreate clothes by simply looking at the magazine pictures we showed them. They made beautiful maternity evening dresses, dresses for afternoon Wives' Club events, and outfits for every day.

Fortunately I stayed in excellent health while pregnant, so we were able to travel to some of Japan's beautiful historical sites and other spots of interest. It was in Kyoto that Joe's interest in cultivating bonsai trees was kindled. It was to become a hobby he enjoyed for many years. He said the art of bonsai helped improve his patience, a characteristic that he admitted was not one of his strongest.

We loved taking the sightseeing tours around Kyoto, marveling at the ages-old monuments and the little shops. We were struck by the diligence and incredible patience of the craftsmen as we watched them working. The sights, sounds, and smells of the narrow streets teeming with pedestrians and bicycles made me feel almost like I was watching a movie, and not actually walking around in this ancient foreign land. Since the Japanese alphabet had no similarity whatsoever to ours, it was impossible to acquire any points of reference from reading street signs, advertisements, or signs identifying the products of the various shops.

Joe had taken some lessons in Japanese, and I was beginning to pick up a few words and phrases. Our attempts to communicate always brought smiles, nods, and polite bows from the residents, as though they were pleased that we were at least trying to speak their language.

It was still hard for me to believe that I was going to be a mother. On April 1, 1954, little Ichibon made his presence more obvious with his first kick. What would he (or she) look like? Would he (or she) be dark-haired and green-eyed like me, or blond and blue-eyed like Joe? We were awed by the whole idea of him (or her), who was due to appear around September 13. On April 19, our first anniversary, Joe got his captain's bars. It was a happy, exciting time for us.

In May we took a vacation trip to Tokyo. We flew via Japanese Airlines, and stayed a week at the San Bancho Hotel, a tiny, cozy, western-type hotel that we loved.

Among the many places we visited were the Latin Quarter, where I had first met Howard and "Pygmy" the year before. We went to Maxim's Italian Restaurant, the huge Tokyo Base Exchange, the Imperial Hotel, Ketel's German restaurant, the Linen Shop, Bohemian Club, Silver Shop, Kofu-en Bonsai Nursery, and countless tiny, fascinating handcrafts shops. We took tours, shopped, and in the evening we went dining and dancing. We were very much in love, and were overjoyed about the baby we were expecting.

By this time I was very obviously pregnant. One night we were at the Imperial Hotel for dinner and dancing. Joe was holding me as close as he could, given the growing Ichibon between us. The orchestra leader had been watching us, somewhat amused. He looked down from the bandstand and asked, "When is the baby due?"

"In September," Joe replied without missing a beat. He continued holding me, dancing in perfect response to the romantic music. He was a smooth, skillful dancer, even with a heavily pregnant woman.

We hired Mitsuko as a housemaid. She was about twenty-one, tiny, beautiful, and bright. We knew we would be able to depend on her to help take care of Ichibon, as well as keep our little duplex spotlessly clean.

Along with our friends, Al and Gayle Schneider, we decided to buy some rattan furniture. It was made in the Philippines, and we ordered enough pieces to completely furnish our living room. The pieces were all sectional, and we were to learn that the versatility of all the sections would serve us well in our many years of military moves. In fact, it presently furnishes the family room of our home, having had numerous slipcover replacements over the years. One piece that Joe ordered especially for me, in my pregnant state, was the two-piece chaise lounge. The comfortable way it supported my pregnant body earned it the nickname "Pregnant Lady's Chair" from Joe. Whenever our friends came to our house, he would always escort whoever needed it to the Pregnant Lady's Chair, and there was always someone in the group who qualified.

One evening a group of friends was gathered in our living room. Howard and Doc Gorman decided they were going to have a contest to pick the name for our expected baby. After much bickering and discussion, the names that they felt deserved the award were Gunther for a boy, and Ruth for a girl—Gunther Guth or Ruth Guth. They were proud of their selections, but Joe and I were not as enthusiastic.

One August day Bonnie Bower and Mary Willerford (who was also expecting a baby in September) gave me a surprise baby shower, under the pretense of a tea for the wife of the wing commander. I walked into Bonnie's living room and there sat my friends, smiling and exclaiming, "Surprise!" Seeing all the beautiful little baby things, many handmade in Japan, I was struck with the amazing reality of the fact that I was, indeed, going to be a mother! That evening, when I showed all the little things to Joe, he too appeared to be awed by the reality of it. Joe had painted the baby's room a pale yellow, the bassinet was ready, and the bath and changing table and crib were in place. We had diapers, baby oil, cotton balls, and all the many supplies listed in my baby book. Even my suitcase was packed and waiting. We were ready, with three weeks still to go until the mid-September due date.

With Joe's August 31 birthday approaching, I decided to give him a surprise party. I took advantage of his being away on an evening flight on August 25 to call twelve couples to invite them to the party. As I was calling the last guests I suddenly became aware that something very unusual was happening with my body. By the time Joe got home at 8:30 we were sure something was going to happen, so we called the doctor on duty at the Air Force Hospital in Nagoya. I was glad to find that the doctor on duty was Captain Walters, who had been caring for me throughout my pregnancy.

"Just relax," he said. "Nothing's going to happen for another week or so. Just take it easy, and by tomorrow you'll feel fine."

So we spent the evening on the couch, me attempting to read a magazine, and Joe "concentrating" on a book. By 10:30 we were sure that the baby was on the way, so we called the hospital again.

The doctor asked me a few questions, and then calmly told us, "Maybe you'd better come on in, but take your time. Nothing will happen for at least eighteen hours."

We put my waiting suitcase into the car, and dropped by the Willerfords' and the Bowers' to tell them. Finding a moment alone with Mary, I asked her to call our friends and cancel Joe's surprise party for me.

We began the slow and arduous drive on the muddy and bumpy road to Nagoya. But we were in no hurry. Joe drove carefully, and I was comfortable. We talked a lot about names. We were in agreement about a boy's name, but still hadn't decided on a name for a possible girl.

Arriving an hour later at the hospital, Joe checked me in. It was midnight. The hospital was a huge complex, staffed by highly skilled American doctors and nurses, as well as some native Japanese personnel who served as nurses, aides, and other supportive functions. We had complete confidence in the quality of care.

Joe had brought along a thermos of ice, a bottle of Scotch, and a good book, but he didn't have much of a chance to enjoy them.

He was allowed to stay with me in the room, and he occupied himself by "timing pains" and making a written record of the intervals, until they were coming too fast. He said, "I don't know when one ends and the next one begins!"

Joe was soon told he must stay in the hall, and good, kind Dr. Walters came in. With a reassuring smile lighting up his handsome African American face, he said gently, "Sugar, I think you're ready."

In the delivery room Dr. Walters was kind, but quite firm when he thought I was getting cold feet about my decision to follow the principles of "natural childbirth." I had studied a book on it, had told him I was determined to follow its instructions and had asked his support in my decision. Our friend Shig, the Chinese American Air Force nurse was there, and also a sweet, kind-eyed Japanese nurse whom I'll always remember with gratitude.

It was 4:47 a.m. (0447 military time), August 26, 1954, when our son arrived. At first I couldn't believe he was really here, until the doctor said, "It's a little boy."

I saw him immediately... first, his little blue feet clasped in the doctor's hands. His body looked so odd—sort of like a big bluish sausage. I tried to reach for him but was told there were things that had to be done to take care of him.

While I waited for them to bring him to me I told the doctor worriedly, "Dr. Walters, I don't know how to make formula." I had been planning to study that procedure during the last week or two before the birth.

"You'll do fine," the doctor smiled.

"Does he have ten fingers?" I asked.

"Nurse, count that baby's fingers," said Dr. Walters.

"There are ten of them Doctor," was her reply.

"Does he have ten toes?" was my next question.

"Nurse, count that baby's toes," said the doctor, chuckling.

"There are ten," she said.

"Let her see him," the doctor told her.

We named him Joseph Harry Guth. The name Harry was chosen as his middle name in honor of my grandfather, Harry Lesley, who had been like a father to me all my life. There was never any question that his first name would be Joe.

His little worried-looking face peeked out from the blanket, and I whispered, "He looks just like Joe! You're going to be such a wonderful person, just like your Daddy Joe."

They gave me a shot that made me sleepy, and I heard the nurse say, "She's asleep." To this, I promptly announced, "Oh no I'm not! I want to see my husband."

When I was back in the room I felt very drowsy, but was happy when Joe tiptoed in and asked, "Are you mad at me for what I did to you?"

"I love you more," I replied sleepily. I told him it had been hard work. We talked for a minute or two more before he went to the nursery to take another look at our son. I heard him tiptoe back in to get his cap.

He kissed me goodbye, saying, "I love you, Gil," and tiptoed out.

I tried to sleep, but I kept thinking about all that had happened. I had a Rosary clasped in my hand, and wanted to say the Rosary to tell God how happy I felt, but I was too tired, so I just held it and felt the happiness. Never before had I felt so close to our Creator, or so completely happy.

We had "rooming in," which meant that the baby was kept in a crib by my bed during the day, and taken to the nursery each night. I nursed him, held him in my hands, and just looked at him. I felt such joy that it still brings tears to my eyes to recall it. He was beautiful... our little blond son, such a pretty face, a perfect little body. His skin was sort of a light bronze color, his hair like the light fuzz of a peach on his little round head. I was so happy I thought my heart would break.

* * * *

Chapter Twelve

SAYONARA

Throughout the next five days in the hospital, Dr. Walters dropped by to see how Little Joe and I were doing. One day when we were chatting we discovered that we had a common interest—creative writing. He asked me if I would read some of the things he had written, and I was delighted. He brought in a few of his articles and fictitious short stories which I read during the free times when I was not looking after the baby. I was complimented by his willingness to hear my feedback. This common interest was a bonus to the fact that he was a very kind, talented physician, a person whom we would never forget.

Joe was visiting one day when the doctor dropped by.

"I've always wanted to take a ride in a jet," said Dr. Walters.

"Sure, Doctor, I'll take you for a ride," Joe answered, and they agreed to set a date in the near future.

A few days later it was time for Little Joe and me to go home. During the ride back Joe and I talked about our new baby, excited and happy to be taking him home. We didn't realize then how much a baby would change our lives. Joe kept glancing over to look at him as he drove us over the bumpy, winding road back to Gifu.

"He sure is cute, isn't he," Joe commented.

"I think he's beautiful," I said.

Mitsuko was waiting for us, and ran out to meet us when we pulled up.

"Hi, Baby Joe!" she exclaimed softly, holding out her arms. I put the baby in her arms, and she gently took him, looking down at his beautiful little face. "Baby Joe" became his nickname from then on. We all went into the house, I on Joe's arm, the new baby held tenderly in Mitsuko's arms. We went up the stairs to the waiting nursery. Mitsuko and Joe watched as I changed him, then laid him in his bassinet. The three of us stood there for a few moments, looking at him and feeling the wonder of it all. I felt tired, so Joe took me by the arm to our bedroom. While I was pregnant we had ordered solid mahogany bedroom furniture, copied from a picture I liked, to be built by Japanese furniture makers. During my hospital stay it had been delivered, and Joe and Mitsuko had replaced the austere government bedroom set with the beautiful new furniture. They had installed the new curtains and bedspread I had ordered, and placed a huge bouquet of flowers on the new dressing table.

I stood in the doorway, overwhelmed by the surprise and the new beauty of our bedroom. Joe and Mitsuko stood grinning, admiring their handiwork and their success in surprising me.

"Oh! It's so beautiful!" I exclaimed. "Thank you, thank you! What a great surprise!" I gave them both a big hug, gratefully lay down on the bed, and promptly fell asleep.

While I was sleeping Joe left to spend an hour or two checking on things at the squadron. I was awakened from my afternoon siesta by the faint cries of Baby Joe, letting me know that it was time for his mid-afternoon feeding. I was beginning to realize that everything from now on would be different, that the new responsibility of caring for our child was going to occupy much of my energy and my thinking. I remember wondering for a moment just how much it would affect the idyllic life Joe and I had been leading together.

The first few days were a little difficult as we waited for my milk supply to become adequate to fill Baby Joe's requirements. The sleep deprivation, breast pain, and fatigue were all-consuming.

"Don't do anything else," Joe said. "Just nurse him and take care of him and of yourself. Let Mitsuko take care of everything else."

I didn't even go downstairs for several days. Friends started to call, asking when they could come to see the new baby. Mary Willerford was the first to drop in, and when she saw Baby Joe, she exclaimed, "He's beautiful! Look at that beautiful skin! It looks like he has a suntan!"

The arrival of Mary's own baby was imminent and, since she already had two children, I felt that she could answer many of my questions and concerns very ably.

"Mary," I said worriedly, "sometimes the baby's feet look a little blue. Why is that?"

She smiled and said, "It just means that his body's thermostat isn't quite working yet. It's a good idea to keep at least a light cover over him so that his body heat is maintained."

Mary, a beautiful girl with dark hair, alabaster skin, and huge brown eyes, had met Bob while he was a cadet at West Point. She was from New England, and they had married immediately upon Bob's graduation, when Mary was only eighteen. Now at twenty-two, she already had two children, with a third on the way.

Several of the wives came by with homemade soups, casseroles, and desserts. Everyone said they thought the baby was adorable, and that he looked just like Joe.

"He's the most beautiful baby in the world," I thought.

My dog Judy was awed by our baby. We let her sniff his little feet, and after a few days she got used to having a new presence in the house. In fact, whenever he cried, she would run to the nursery, and then to me, tail wagging, looking up at me expectantly, as though she was telling me that he needed attention.

Joe and I spent a lot of time reading Dr. Spock's book on childcare. We came to rely heavily on his ideas about infant care, feeding, handling the unexpected, and the importance of relaxing around the new baby.

Since his birthday party had been bypassed due to Baby Joe's arrival, we invited the twelve couples I had originally called to come over for a belated birthday celebration. Everyone brought something to the potluck and there was an abundance of food for all, including a birthday cake.

Judy jumped up on her perch on the leather hassock to watch the proceedings. She loved it when guests came over because, being such a well-behaved dog, she got a lot of attention. Joe said she was a real lady because she would sit quietly and never bothered anyone nor begged for food.

Sitting in the living room, surrounded by friends with the stereo playing all our favorite tunes, I felt a surge of gratitude that we were such a close-knit group, and that this indeed, was our family. This would prove to be true many times in the years to come. The true meaning of friendship would be revealed countless times. In each place we lived we would meet a handful of people who would be added to our family of friends, a family which stayed in touch even though years might pass before seeing each other again.

The guests took turns holding Baby Joe, admiring him, gazing at him, and gently touching his soft cheek. Even the men, some of whom were not yet fathers themselves, got a kick out of holding him, rocking him, talking to him, and chuckling when he made baby faces in response to the funny noises they made over him. The birthday party was a huge success, and of course the new baby and his father were the centers of attention. Joe took a lot of ribbing about the fact that the baby looked so much like him.

"Hey, Joe, you really marked this poor kid," said one buddy.

"Boy, I sure hope he doesn't grow up to have your nose," said another.

One night a good friend of Joe's was passing through and Joe invited him to come home with him, stay for dinner, and spend the night. We moved the bassinet into our bedroom, and our guest stayed in the nursery, sleeping on the foldout couch we'd placed there for just such emergencies.

Before we all retired for the night, Joe took the baby to the changing table in the nursery, and invited our guest to go with him. I heard them talking in low tones and laughing softly. Joe told me later that they were both marveling at our boy's perfect little body. Joe was very, very proud of his newborn son.

Japan's September rains began, bringing with them a big challenge for Mitsuko—how to get the diapers washed, hung out to dry, and brought in before the afternoon downpour, since we had no dryer. Mitsuko sometimes had to make a mad dash for the clothesline as the dark clouds signaled that the shower was imminent. Occasionally the rain arrived so suddenly that she would drop whatever she was doing, say, "Oh no! It's raining again!" and then race outside to rescue the diapers before they became soaked. Often our living room, dining room, and kitchen were decorated with diapers placed everywhere in an attempt to dry them out.

In early fall we went to a football game in Nagoya between our own Nagoya Comets and the team from Johnson Air Force Base. Several of our friends were on the team, including Doc Gorman, who had been one of the guests at our memorable first Thanksgiving dinner. Many of our friends were sitting in the stands near us. Suddenly we saw a handsome, well-built black man bounding up the steps of the stadium toward us.

It was Dr. Walters, shouting, "I want my baby back! Joe, you never took me for my jet ride. Give me back my baby!" When we recovered from our surprise we all started laughing, and everyone sitting around us picked up the call.

"Hey, Joe! You'd better take him on that ride... he's really mad!"

Joe promised the doctor he would make good, which he did a few days later in a T-33. Joe told me they were "all hooked up, intercom, oxygen, seatbelts, shoulder harnesses, helmets, and parachutes."

"Hey, Doc," Joe told him over the intercom as he prepared to land the jet, "you should forget that doctor stuff and be a pilot."

"Maybe I'll do both!" Dr. Walters said delightedly.

"He really liked that ride," Joe told me later. "I wrung it out—cloverleafs, Chandelles, Cuban eights, loops, Immelmans—all the tactical combat maneuvers—and he loved every minute of it! And he didn't barf!"

In mid-October a big dinner party and dance was held at the Officers Club, with a fashion show put on by the wives. I modeled a red and gold brocade Chinese dress, tight-fitting, copied by one of the Japanese seamstresses. I was happy that my figure had returned to normal so quickly. I had my hair cut in a short bob, with straight bangs across the forehead. Mary Willerford, whose baby had arrived just three weeks after ours, was the fashion announcer. She, too, had quickly gotten her figure back, and with her cultured Bostonian accent and wearing a frosty net formal dress, she was perfect for the job, confidently announcing each of us as we walked down the ramp. Our husbands watched proudly in the audience as we modeled the beautiful fashions of the 1950s—the full-skirted, feminine dresses and evening gowns, with me in my Chinese dress coming on last. The band played the popular music of the day, providing a romantic background with tunes made famous by Frank Sinatra, Perry Como, Eartha Kitt, Tommy Dorsey, and Benny Goodman.

Following dinner, Joe held me tightly as he swung me around the dance floor, humming in his enthusiastic but slightly off-key way.

"We have the world by the tail, Gilberta," he said. I smiled at him and nodded, feeling like, indeed, everything was just perfect. It felt like this was what our lives would be like forever.

Soon we were waiting for orders to return to the U.S. According to government regulations, newborns were not allowed to be moved PCS (Permanent Change of Station) before they were six weeks old. So we were kept wondering where Joe would be assigned. He took the uncertainty in stride, because he had done it so many, many times. I, however, felt like I was on pins and needles—anxious, not knowing if I would be on the East Coast of the U.S., the West Coast, or anywhere in between. Even though this uncertainty about pending new assignments would be a part of our lives for years to come, I never became accustomed to preparing for a PCS without any idea where we would be going.

THE WIVES PRESENT A FASHION SHOW AT THE KANKO OFFICERS CLUB, NAGOYA, JAPAN, 1954.

GILBERTA MODELS A CHINESE-STYLE DRESS AT THE KANKO. MARY WILLERFORD ANNOUNCES.

GILBERTA AND JOE DINE WITH MARY AND BOB WILLERFORD, AL AND GAYLE SCHNEIDER (SEATED).

At last, orders arrived. It was to be Turner Air Force Base, near Albany, Georgia. Next, we were waiting for travel orders, which finally arrived with instructions to sail on the USS *Buckner*, a huge troop transport ship with accommodations for families. We would be leaving on November 12, when Baby Joe would be two and a half months old. Joe talked to me about how glad he was that I was nursing our baby, since we would have a lot of traveling ahead of us. We agreed it would be the safest, healthiest, and most convenient way for all of us.

The next weeks were spent planning, sorting, and packing. It was my first experience with a major move of our entire household. PCS moves required certain special preparations. We had our "hold baggage" set aside. This contained a minimum of household and personal necessities which would travel with us on the USS *Buckner* and be delivered to us immediately upon our arrival at Turner.

Joe's beautiful dwarf bonsai trees, which he had been tending so carefully, had to be crated up and sent to the port to be quarantined for six months before being shipped to our stateside address. Our furniture and other household belongings were to be put into storage when they arrived in the U.S. and held there until we found permanent housing at our new place of assignment. Our travel baggage was set aside also, since I'd been warned by my more experienced friends to hide anything I didn't want the movers to take. Government movers, I was told, were paid by the package, and were known to wrap up everything in sight, including full ashtrays and deep fryers full of cooking oil. It was good advice, as I found out later when our washing machine arrived at our destination with the last load of diapers still inside it.

Travel arrangements were made for Judy, too. She was to be sent on to Yokohama, in her metal crate, and kept at the port kennel until we boarded the ship. She again would make the journey on the stern of the ship, and we'd be responsible for walking her, feeding her, and cleaning up after her, just as I had done on the voyage over.

We were to be driven by Air Force vehicle to Nagoya and then travel by train to Yokohama, where we would board the USS *Buckner* for the two-week voyage across the Pacific.

Since many of our friends were also leaving or about to leave for the States, there were many get-togethers and parties those last few weeks. It was as though, with the goodbyes getting closer and closer, we all wanted to spend as much time together as we could. I tried not to think about saying goodbye to our friends and to Mitsuko, who had become a good, loyal friend and companion to us and to our baby.

Saying goodbye to Gayle and Al Schneider, Mary and Bob Willerford, and Colonel and Bonnie Bower was especially hard, since we had become such close friends and had shared so much with all of them. I had learned a lot from Bonnie, a seasoned officer's wife, so outgoing, without a pretentious bone in her body. We had shared many social activities with Gayle and Al, and he was one of Joe's closest golfing friends. We had often gotten together with Mary and Bob, and Mary's confident answers to my concerns about baby care had been a great comfort to me.

As the time grew short, I began to realize how much I would miss all these spontaneous, warm friendships. The last get-togethers were filled with emotional goodbyes and tears. None of us had any idea when, or if, we would see each other again.

Finally, moving day came, followed by the day of our departure. I stood holding the baby, looking at our empty duplex, our first home. I imagined all the friends sprawled across our living room listening to music, of dinner parties, of our first Thanksgiving and Christmas there, of bringing our new baby home, of the beautiful furniture Joe had surprised me with. Now the rooms were all empty. Our belongings were on their way to our destination halfway around the world. Albany, Georgia seemed so far away. Judy was gone, shipped on ahead to Yokohama Port. I watched Mitsuko as she busied herself finishing up the cleaning, which had to be done according to specifications. Before Joe could clear the base the building inspector would come to verify that we had fulfilled all the requirements for leaving the place absolutely spotless.

And then it was time to leave. Mitsuko took little Joe in her arms, kissed him, touched his cheek and said, "Goodbye, Baby Joe. You will grow up to be a good boy." Then she and I hugged, holding on tightly, both trying to smile. But neither of us could hold back the tears. Joe hugged her then, thanking her for all she'd done for us. She walked out to the waiting Air Force vehicle with us, watched as we got in, and stood there as we drove away. Looking back I could see her waving and heard her calling, *"Sayonara!"* until the car turned the corner and she was out of sight.

* * * *

Chapter Thirteen

THE VOYAGE HOME

The USS *Buckner* was an enormous troopship used for transporting armed forces to and from the Far East. During peacetime, accommodations were made for families going to and returning from the overseas bases scattered throughout the world.

As we boarded the huge vessel, I was awed by its size and the vast number of troops it was carrying. Our private quarters in the family area were small, austere, and spotlessly clean. A small crib had been placed there, and there was a desk, a dresser, and two narrow bunk beds. The top bunk never got any use. We clung to each other on the narrow lower bunk at night, sometimes listening in the dark to the constant rhythmic sound of the huge engines churning away below us, each day taking us closer to the United States. On the ship there was a base exchange, a hospital and dispensary, and officers' and enlisted men's dining halls.

Between caring for Baby Joe, seeing to Judy's needs at the stern of the ship, mealtimes, and walking the decks for exercise, our days seemed busy and were passing quickly.

Late one night after we'd fallen asleep Baby Joe suddenly began to cry. I jumped up to tend to him, but nothing seemed to comfort him. His cries turned to a scream, and he felt hot. I took his temperature—104 degrees. By then Joe was up, and, beginning to panic, we threw on some clothes and wrapped the baby in a light blanket. He was burning up with fever, screaming at the top of his little lungs. With Joe carrying him, we ran out of our cabin and down the seemingly endless gray passageways of the ship to the emergency room of the ship's hospital. The doctor on duty checked him over, and couldn't find anything wrong.

"Something is wrong with this baby," said the doctor, "and I'm going to find out what it is, even if it takes me all night." The doctor went over the baby with stethoscope, light, and tongue depressor, gently probing the tiny body with his fingers. Joe and I stood there watching, filled with anxiety and fear. We were in the middle of the Pacific Ocean. What if something was very seriously wrong? What if this small ship's hospital couldn't handle the problem? What were we going to do?

Peering with his examining light for the third or fourth time into the baby's tiny ears, the doctor said, "Ah, there we are. An ear infection. It's just starting, and it's so small I didn't see it at first. We'll have to give him a penicillin shot."

In the future Joe would relate this scenario to friends. "That doctor took this enormous hypodermic needle full of penicillin, and he jabbed that tiny little butt with that huge needle so hard—it still hurts when I think about it!"

We were instructed to sponge Baby Joe off with cool water, and to bring him back every day for the rest of the voyage, to be sure the penicillin was working.

That was our first experience with a sick child waking during the night screaming with pain. Being on the high seas made it even more memorable, and we never forgot that experience or the cold panic we felt as we raced down those long gray passageways, carrying our baby to the ship's small hospital. As our family grew, we would know dozens more of such childhood emergencies.

Periodically during the trip there was a fire drill. Everyone had to put on a life jacket and go out to the nearest deck, including tiny infants. Joe took pictures of Baby Joe, totally engulfed in the life jacket belted firmly around him, with only his tiny face peering out.

The remainder of the voyage progressed uneventfully, and the nearer we got to San Francisco the more excited I became about returning to the U.S. Finally, we were approaching the Golden Gate Bridge. We stood at the rail, Joe holding the baby, and watched the glistening San

BABY JOE ABOARD THE USS BUCKNER ON HIS WAY TO SAN FRANCISCO.

Francisco skyline come into view. The enormous ship, towed by tug-boats and with the fireboats blowing their welcoming whistles, was guided under the brilliant orange bridge into the Bay, and nudged into its berthing dock. Since that day I have never crossed the Golden Gate Bridge without remembering the thrill of passing under it, bringing our new baby to the United States.

We spent a couple of days seeing the sights of San Francisco. The baby's recovery from his ear infection seemed to be progressing nicely. His temperature was normal and he was nursing without any problems. Seeking a little respite, we got a bonded babysitter through the hotel, and the two of us took in some of the nightspots. We spent some time at the Top of the Mark, where Joe had partied with his fellow pilots on their way to Korea a little over two years before.

While we were at the Top of the Mark Joe showed me the "Weepers' Corner," the alcove surrounded by windows from where one could see the gorgeous San Francisco Bay. I thought of the wives and sweethearts who had watched the troopships leaving under the Golden Gate Bridge on their way to combat during World War II and the Korean War. I was struck with the poignancy of that spot.

We savored the beautiful views of the city at night, dined and danced. We were glad to be back in the United States, and together. Life seemed good.

A couple of days later we boarded a train for Los Angeles. We were to stop for a visit with my friend Joan and her husband Lynn, whom she had married the year after our wedding. The Korean War ended before Lynn was assigned to Korea as a jet pilot, and they had been sent to Vandenberg Air Force Base, California.

We got off the train and walked down the hall to the station waiting room. Joe was carrying little Joe, and I had the diaper bag, filled with baby necessities.

When Joan saw us she exclaimed, "I didn't expect to see Joe carrying the baby! Joe, I'm so surprised! And impressed! You're a real Daddy!"

There was so much to talk about, so much catching up to do, and of course the baby received a lot of attention. It was good to be with my lifelong friend Joan again, and to see her happily married to Lynn.

The next day we boarded a train for the day's trip to Tucson. As our taxi pulled up in front of the house, Pop came out to meet us.

"Let me see that baby!" he exclaimed, taking little Joe in his arms and laughing with pleasure at seeing his first great-grandchild. My two aunts and three of my uncles were also there to welcome us. I felt like I'd been gone much longer than a year and a half.

"That's some baby!" said my grandfather. We spent time visiting with relatives and friends, taking pictures of the baby with each and every aunt, uncle, cousin, and especially with the baby's great-grandfather, my Pop.

We also took pictures of my great-aunt holding Baby Joe. She was my grandmother's sister, and had been a nun for most of her life. She looked so much like her sister, that when I looked into her face, I could almost see my beloved grandmother.

One day Pop was watching me feed little Joe a bottle of milk.

"It seems like only yesterday that you were a little girl playing with dolls," he said, chuckling. "And now you have a baby of your own."

After a ten-day visit it was time to be on our way. Pop and the rest of the family stood on the porch waving as we drove away in the taxi taking us to the train station. The train ride to St. Louis took several days. We quickly settled into a routine—caring for the baby in our compartment, reading, having meals in the dining car, and watching out the window as we sped across the country.

Joe's mother and father met us at the St. Louis train station. When I placed her first grandchild in her arms, his mother's eyes welled with tears and she murmured, "Oh, thank you!"

Joe's dad seemed thrilled with his first grandson and namesake. We were with them for our first Christmas in the U.S., and saw many of Joe's friends and relatives, including his grandmother, who like my Pop, posed for many pictures with her first great-grandchild. Baby Joe was now four months old, and everyone, including Joe and I, thought he was the most beautiful baby in the universe.

When it came time to leave we picked up the new car we'd ordered, a 1955 Chevy, and started on the trip to Albany, Georgia.

I was not prepared for the culture shock that awaited me in that small southern town.

* * * *

Chapter Fourteen

A LONG, LONELY TIME

Joe had been assigned to Turner Air Force Base near the town of Albany, Georgia to fly the F-84F Thunderstreak. In Albany, we initially sub-leased a duplex apartment, unpacking only our "hold baggage," the minimal personal items and few household necessities which had come with us from Japan on the USS *Buckner*. Our furniture and other belongings were put into storage, awaiting our assignment to more permanent housing.

My days were filled taking care of our baby, fixing simple evening meals, and occasionally visiting with my next door neighbor, Janet. She was also a pilot's wife, and a mother of three. Nostalgic for the glamorous life we had led in Japan, I asked her one day if she and her husband would like to go out to dinner and dancing with us some evening. "Oh, no," she said. "We can't afford to do that." I was baffled by her response. Joe handled our money and as far as I knew, we had always had enough to do whatever we wanted.

We soon began to socialize with the pilots from Joe's new squadron and their wives. There were dinners, parties, and wives' gatherings to go to, but I felt like I was starting all over, meeting new people and trying to find a few whom I could really call friends.

We had only been in Albany a few months when Joe was selected for Squadron Officer School in Montgomery, Alabama. It was consid-

JOE PRIOR TO TAKE OFF IN HIS F-84F.

ered an essential step to a successful Air Force career, and was an assignment sought by all aspiring young officers.

So we packed up, cleaned the apartment, and left for Montgomery. We were to be there for the three and a half months required to complete the Squadron Officer School program.

Montgomery was filled with apartment buildings, many of them short-term rentals to accommodate the constant turnover of young officers arriving with their families, completing the program of classes and field training, and then leaving, making room for the next influx of arrivals.

Our Montgomery apartment was a tiny, two-story, two-bedroom place, simply furnished, but with all the basic necessities. A huge ceiling fan in the hallway of the upper floor of the apartment helped us combat the oppressive heat and humidity of Montgomery, but the fan was so noisy that it often kept us awake throughout the stifling night. Unable to sleep, we spent many memorable nights as lovers.

All of our neighbors were there for the same reason we were—to complete Squadron Officer School, "to fill the squares," as the pilots called it. "The squares" referred to certain requirements to be fulfilled for a young officer to be in line for promotions and/or choice assignments. These essential steps to a successful Air Force career included, in addition to Squadron Officer School, completion of Command and Staff College and Air War College. All flying "minimums," or periodic training requirements, had to be maintained as well as tactical flying experience in order to stay "current."

Additionally, college degrees were a must, and graduate study was encouraged, along with civic involvement. Joe would be well on his way to filling the "squares," having completed a college degree, maintained his "minimums," and having flown in tactical combat squadrons. Although he did not care for the "political" aspects of the military rank system, he understood that these were "hoops through which they had to jump" to further the chances for a successful military career.

After the exciting, privileged life we had led in Japan, the pace here seemed slow, routine, and humdrum. Joe became heavily involved in the classes and trainings of the Squadron Officer School program. My days were occupied with caring for Baby Joe, now nine months old, and I missed the freedom of being able to leave him with Mitsuko any time I wanted. It was hard to cement friendships with the other young women I met there, because all of us knew we would be scattering to the four winds after completion of the brief Squadron Officer School program.

I began to feel that my life had taken a dramatic turn. I looked forward with anticipation to Joe's return at the end of the day. I eagerly listened to him tell how he had spent the day, about his classes, his instructors, his assignments. It was as if I could vicariously share the excitement of his program just by listening to him talk about it. Occasionally he would ask me to type or edit an assignment for him, and I welcomed the intellectual challenge that it offered.

Joe's mother and father once visited us for a couple of days while we were in Montgomery. I was grateful to have their company, and they loved spending time with their new grandson. It seemed that we all were getting to know and enjoy each other more each day they were there.

One day after Joe left for work, his mother sat at the table and watched as I put away the breakfast things and started a load of laundry.

"Gil," she said, "you're such a nice little housekeeper!" I knew she meant the remark as a compliment, but I was taken aback. I had never thought of myself in those terms, probably because in Japan Mitsuko had handled all the details of housekeeping. It sharpened my awareness that I would no longer be living the carefree existence I'd enjoyed in Japan.

"I became really spoiled in Japan," I thought to myself. Although I might have occasional household help and babysitters here in the States, the keeping of the home, hearth, and family would be totally my responsibility. Joe's mother, Gussie, was a legendary homemaker and cook, and spoke often of how much she had loved keeping a home for her husband and her two boys, Joe and Jack. I wished I could feel as fulfilled as she described. Instead, I felt bored just caring for a baby and a small apartment, and depending on Joe's company in the evenings for my happiness. I wondered if there was something missing in me that prevented me from feeling that sense of fulfillment which she so obviously had enjoyed.

Joe's parents left a couple of days later, on their way to Florida to look into moving there, since Joe's dad had recently retired. I stood at the door, the baby in my arms, and watched them leave, waving and smiling. I knew the long, lonely days would be starting again, and I felt depressed.

One day Joe came home and told me he was one of a few men in his class who had been selected to go on TDY (Temporary Duty) to Tyndall Air Force Base in Panama City, Florida for ten days. They were to conduct classes and do flying demonstrations for a group of West Point cadets considering an Air Force career.

"Ten days!" I exclaimed. Bursting into tears, I cried, "What am I going to do without you for ten days!"

Putting his arms around me and trying not to smile, Joe said, "Toots, ten days isn't long at all. I'll be back before you know it." In the days preceding his trip, I wept every time I thought about his being gone. To me, ten days might as well have been a year.

Finally, the day came for Joe's departure. I gloomily watched him leave when the taxi taking him and a couple of other men from the building drove away. While he was gone, every time I heard a romantic song on the radio, I'd burst into tears, especially Roy Hamilton's "Unchained Melody":

> *Oh, my love, my darling,*
> *I've hungered for your touch*
> *a long, lonely time.*
> *And time goes by so slowly*
> *and time can do so much,*
> *are you still mine?*
> *I need your love,*
> *I need your love.*
> *God speed your love to me!*

Even the fact that I had a car didn't help, since an infant's schedule made long excursions out of the question. I became friendly with the wife of one of the other men who was sent to Florida, and we gravitated toward each other, seeking friendship and support during the days alone.

Finally the ten days were over, and Joe returned. I was ecstatic when he arrived. He plunked his bags down in the living room, and took me in his arms.

"Oh, I'm so glad you're here!" I exclaimed between kisses.

He tiptoed into the baby's room to peek at his son, grinning and touching the smooth, rosy cheek of our sleeping infant.

"He's really grown, hasn't he!" Joe said.

He went back to completing his Squadron Officers' training. I welcomed editing and typing his final papers and reports. It pleased me that he would ask me for my opinion about the wording of his ideas, and he seemed to respect my comments and suggestions. During the last few weeks of the program, the men competed in physical competitions and games, including minor events like three-legged races and egg-throwing contests. Joe and his training partner, Bob Jordan, won all of the top awards, a story Joe loved to repeat over the years.

Soon it was time to pack up, clean the apartment, and head back to Albany, Georgia, where Joe's assignment as a pilot in the Thunderstreak would continue. We said goodbye to our neighbors, and as we drove away, I realized that we would never see any of them again.

At Turner Air Force Base, we stayed for a couple of weeks in temporary quarters, consisting of trailers parked near the flightline. Every time a jet landed or took off, our little trailer would shake violently. The noise would wake the baby, interrupt our conversations, and make it hard to sleep at night. Finally, our name came up on the list of those waiting for "Capehart-Wherry Housing," small, comfortable, government-contracted houses just outside the base, available for rent to military families. It was named after Senator Kenneth Wherry of Nebraska who, in 1949, introduced the bill in Congress which resulted in its funding. Its purpose was to meet the critical housing shortages that existed after World War II as the nation sought to maintain a large, peacetime fighting force.

I was excited the day we moved into our Capehart house and saw the moving van, filled with all of our own furniture and belongings, pull up in front of the house. We hadn't seen our things since leaving Japan, and it felt like Christmas as the movers carried in our rattan furniture, the beautiful mahogany bedroom set, our pots and pans, dishes, appliances, and the rest of our clothes. I found the load of diapers in the washing machine that Mitsuko hadn't had time to hang outside. They were stiff as a board, just as they looked at the end of the spin cycle. I smiled as I thought of Mitsuko. I missed her.

The next several days were spent unpacking, setting up and becoming what I learned to call "operational." Joe took a few days off to help, but soon he was back at his job at the squadron. I made some drapes for the living room, dining room, and bedroom, proudly settling into our first real stateside home.

After a few weeks Joe's beloved bonsai trees arrived. He was concerned about their condition, fearful that the time in quarantine had been damaging to them. So, determined to revive them, he started on a carefully executed treatment program for them. Working in the garden and with his little trees seemed to help him unwind at the end of the day.

Joe never appeared to have any trouble fitting into the close comradeship shared by the pilots. The wives, too, seemed eager to include the newcomer, so after a short time we began to feel more like a part of Joe's squadron. I still missed our friends in Japan and all of the fun we'd had living there, but I was gradually beginning to sense that we belonged at our new station. I came to understand that this "instant friendship" was vital to our sense of well-being because of the transient lives we were leading. I welcomed the new friendships that I was beginning to form, especially since the pilots, engaged in their intense flying schedules, were sometimes away for days or weeks at a time.

One of the long flights they took was to Alaska. The pilots' wives put on a floor show for them prior to their departure. I was in a routine wearing Joe's fur-lined flying parka, black fishnet stockings, and black high heels. Another young wife and I danced and sang the song,

It's a hot night in Alaska,
You can even feel the heat down in Nebraska!

Our show was a hit with our audience, and their enthusiasm made us feel like we had given them a good sendoff.

At an invitation issued to all the officers stationed at Turner, Joe and several of his golfing buddies joined the Albany Country Club to take advantage of its verdant golf course when their schedules permitted. Joe came home from his golf game one day and, chuckling, told me about his day with his caddy, a boy of about twelve.

"After the first nine, this kid turns to me and says, 'Mister, I'm tired. Will you carry me?' I couldn't believe what he was asking me. I didn't carry him, but I let him leave my clubs and go on back to the clubhouse."

One night at a dance at the Country Club, I left our table to go to the ladies' room. Several of the local club members were chatting together inside, and as I repaired my lipstick in front of the mirror, one of them turned to me and said, "Hi. Are y'all new members?"

"My husband is an officer at Turner... a pilot. He loves your beautiful golf course," I replied.

"Oh," she said. "My Daddy would NEVER let ME go out with soldiers!"

I stared at her, incredulous at her rudeness. As she turned and left, an older woman standing nearby said to me, "Don't pay any attention to her, Sugah. She's always like that!"

I was hurt and angry. In spite of the periods of loneliness and the turmoil and disruption of the frequent moves, I was developing a sense of great pride in Joe and in his service career. I was also becoming proud

GILBERTA APPEARS IN A WIVES' FLOOR SHOW AT TURNER A.F.B., GEORGIA.

of myself for the support I was learning to give him as he faced the physical and mental demands of flying. That rude comment was like a slap in the face, which I never forgot.

A few months later I realized that I might be pregnant again. Joe was watching me clear the table one evening when he said, "You're pregnant, aren't you?"

His comment surprised me, since I hadn't felt sure enough yet to tell him that I might be.

"I think I am, Honey," I said. He got up from the table, came over to me and put his arms around me. "That's just great, Toots. Now Joey will have someone to play with."

I felt relieved that he was happy about having another baby. He put in a little lawn in our back yard, and built a small white picket fence around it so that Joey, as we were beginning to call him, could play safely and I could keep my eye on him from the kitchen window.

One day I heard a commotion on the street outside our front door. Going to the door, I saw men in jail uniforms doing street repairs right in front of our house. There were two men dressed in guards' uniforms, each one holding a rifle. It was the first time I had ever seen a prisoner chain gang doing street work in a residential area, and I was shocked and frightened. I ran to the back and out into the little yard where our son was playing, picked him up and took him into the house, locking the doors and closing the blinds.

I thought, "What if one of those rifles goes off, maybe even accidentally, or what if there is trouble with one of the prisoners?" I was relieved when I heard Joe's car pull into the driveway that evening, and his familiar "Hello, Gilberta!" as he came through the door.

I told him what had happened that day, and he listened quietly.

"If you are ever scared when I'm not here, call me at work. If I'm flying or not there, tell one of the other guys what's going on. You don't have to be scared and not let anyone know." What he said made an impression on me, and I learned in the years ahead that what he said was true. There was a comradeship among these men that went beyond friendship—they also cared for each other's families.

I had some difficulties early on in my pregnancy. I was starting to bleed, and the doctor said there might be danger of a miscarriage. I remember the doctor asking me, "Do you want this baby?"

"Oh, yes!" I exclaimed.

"Then stay off your feet for the next month, until we're sure everything is okay again," he said. Joe and I were both scared by his words, and did our best to follow his orders. This was difficult with a toddler in the house, but my new friends rallied and made it possible for me to stay off my feet most of the time every day, until Joe got home from work and could take over. After a month we were able to return to a more normal routine. I breathed a prayer of gratitude for our friends, Bunky Harper, Bensie Krone, and Biddy Pitts. What if they hadn't been around, I thought? What would we have done?

Joe's parents came to visit for our first stateside Christmas in our own home. Joey, of course, was again the center of attention. Our second baby was due the end of April, so Joe's mother and dad assured us that they would be on hand to help with Joey when the new baby arrived.

Early in the year Joe led a flight of four on a cross-country speed run in the F-84F Thunderstreak from coast to coast. They broke the existing speed record, crossing the United States in three hours and fourteen minutes. I was very proud of his accomplishment, and he was elated about the success of the flight.

I was becoming aware of the extremely high standard Joe placed on himself... always striving to win, to be the best. It was soon after the speed run that I first observed how this demand for excellence would spill over into how Joe related to our children.

We had taken little Joe to a nearby park. He was about nineteen months old. Our dog Judy explored nearby as Joe started to play catch with our little son, tossing a colored rubber ball to him from a few feet away. Joey held out his hands to catch the ball, and it slipped through his little fingers. He toddled over to pick it up.

I called to him, "Good, Joey. Now throw the ball back to Daddy!"

"Let me handle him," Joe told me. "Here, Joey. Now I want you to catch this." I watched as again the ball slipped through Joey's small hands. He ran to pick it up, and threw it back to his father, who said,

JACK HARPER, JOE GUTH, WAYNE DOZIER, BOB KRONE SET SPEED RUN RECORD IN THE F-84F.

"Joey, you have to catch the ball when I throw it. Don't let it fall through your fingers."

I could feel the hair on the back of my neck starting to bristle, and I said, "Joe, he's only a baby."

Joe turned to me impatiently and said, "Would you just let me handle him, please?"

Joe's show of impatience with me hurt and surprised me. I also felt hurt for our little son. It was obvious that he was trying hard to please his Daddy.

What I didn't know then was that Joe's self-expectations of excellence would sometimes manifest in his expectations of excellence in his children as they were growing up. Each of them would handle it in a different way, according to each one's personality. But for me it was always a source of hurt and concern that our children's self-confidence might be affected by such high demands. This issue would come up often between us in future years.

About six weeks before the new baby was due, Joe was assigned to gunnery training at Ramey Air Force Base in Puerto Rico. It was March 15, 1956. I sat watching quietly as he packed his bag. I was learning to put up a brave front at times like this.

"I'll call often," he said. "If anything happens, just call the squadron, and they'll get hold of me right away."

"Okay," I said, attempting a smile. "I'll write and tell you everything that's going on."

Joey was playing in his room. His father went in, picked him up, kissed him and said, "You be a good little man, Joey, and Daddy will see you soon."

One last hug and a kiss, and then it was time to drive him to the flightline. The wives and children all watched as the twenty planes of the squadron took off. The pilots were all wearing their helmets, so they all looked alike. But Joe had told me how to identify which plane was his by the number on the fuselage and the wing. I was holding Joey, and showed him which plane was his daddy's as it taxied from the flightline onto the runway.

"Wave at Daddy, Joey. That's his plane, right there," I told him. It was thrilling to watch as Joe and the nineteen other pilots took off and flew out of sight. We were all left standing there, watching them fade from sight and listening as the sound of their engines grew fainter, until we no longer could hear them.

Joe's first letter from Puerto Rico arrived a few days later:

Hi, Toots:

The sight of you all waving goodbye was pleasing and I'm glad you were there to send us off.

The flight itself was a sweat-sweat what with low oil pressure, low fuel, etc. but as we sang that night, over and over again, "20 got off and 20 got here, 20 got off and 20 got here!"

The party that night was really a fighter pilots' party. You know how it goes, same

```
tune, only with more fervor.

Love to you, very much, and the little man.
Hello to Judy. Please water the bonsai trees.
Will write more in a couple of days.

Love, Joe
```

In his next letters Joe wrote of their routine at Ramey, of flying, of practicing at the gunnery range, and of his attempts to make the time pass by reading and going to movies in his spare time. He also wrote of his plans to take me on a trip to Atlanta after our second baby was born, on a sort of second (or third) honeymoon. He told me to be looking into finding reliable childcare so that we could be gone for a few days.

On the afternoon of March 23, the phone rang. It was Joe, calling from Puerto Rico. "Hi, Gil. I wanted to call you and talk to you before anyone else does. I had a small accident, but I'm fine. I don't want you to worry. Really. Everything is fine." His voice was calm, reassuring.

I sank into the couch. I was stunned by his words and imagined a crash, a fire, an explosion. I imagined that Joe was burned or injured. He said in an even voice, "Everyone is going to be calling you. That's why I wanted to talk with you first." I was eight months pregnant, and I knew he was trying to keep me calm. He went on to describe in detail what had happened, assuring me over and over that he was okay, except for a small bruise on his heel.

He was right. The phone started ringing. The first call was from Captain Pitts, the squadron operations officer, assuring me that Joe was fine. Then Major Santry, the squadron CO. Then all the wives started calling. Two of them came over, saying they didn't want me to be alone. They invited me to have supper with them, one of them even offering to spend the night at my house if I wished.

Joe's accident was another lesson for me about the strength of military friendships. I was grateful for all the support extended to me during what could have been a very frightening time.

Several days later I received this letter from him, describing the accident. He understood how I had become fascinated by the details of his profession. He knew that somehow it would be reassuring to me to read his words explaining exactly what had happened:

24 March 56

Hi Toots:

Got your letters of the 18th and 20th and one from Mother, too. I'll bet Joey did look cute in his new Easter suit. I miss that little guy.

About the accident. Had hydraulic failure, declared an emergency and did everything by the book. The landing was good with speed just right. Since I didn't have flaps and I was still fairly heavy on fuel the landing was faster than normal. I used the drag chute but it fell off the aircraft. Without boosted brakes because of the hydraulic failure, and an inoperative drag chute, and faster than normal landing speed, I ran off the end of the runway. It's 9,000 feet long but has no overrun and no barrier. I was going fairly slow, but the nose gear sheared off and when the aircraft fell on the pylon tanks they ruptured and caught fire. Up to this time I was calm, cool, and collected. When I saw the flames I did get a bit excited but blew the canopy off, unstrapped the seat belt and jumped out. The fire trucks were there almost immediately and put it out before it could explode but not before it ruined the aircraft. I don't think it will fly again.

They think they have found the trouble with the hydraulic system and also accounted for the drag chute failure. We'll know more soon.

It was good to talk to you even though the connection was poor. Last night we really had a celebration. Everyone was very happy that I got out of the thing and we were really in a celebrating mood.

```
Harry Archuleta and Leo Thorsness were the
funniest things Samba-ing together that I
have ever seen. We sang songs, drank and told
lies. I had to tell the story so many times
that by the end of the evening it was just a
little less spectacular than the Lindberg
crossing.

Have to hurry to the show with Mad Dog Santry
and Elephant Dozier.


Will write more soon.
Love, Joe
```

I imagined the celebration he described, the camaraderie, the bravado, the singing and the drinking, all intended to blow off steam and relieve the tension of their dangerous job.

Joe returned from Puerto Rico shortly before our baby was due. We invited a pilot friend and his wife to dinner one evening, and during dinner I became aware that the baby could be on the way. I was beginning to feel light contractions. Our guests left, and as we were finishing up the dishes I said, "Joe, I think it's time to go to the hospital."

We had arranged with our friends, Bunky and Jack Harper, that they would take care of Joey, so we called them and told them we were on our way.

At the base hospital, Joe sat in the chair in the labor room, timing the contractions, until I told him, "Joe, get the nurse!" After being checked I was wheeled into the delivery room. I had not met the doctor on duty before. I was disappointed that my own doctor, Dr. Ravinski, the chief of the OB-GYN clinic, was off that night.

At 3:36 a.m. on April 30, 1956, our son, John Edward Guth, was born. When I first saw him, I said, "A little boy! Hi, Sweetheart. Now I'm outnumbered!" The nurse chuckled and took the baby to attend to him. The doctor, I noticed, was very quiet, and seemed to be intensely occupied with looking after me.

"Get Ravinski," he told the nurse urgently. By then he appeared to be quite worried.

"What's happening?" I asked.

"Don't worry. You'll be all right," he said. Everyone in the room seemed very intense and busy all of a sudden. I began to feel drowsy and weak. A short time later the door to the delivery room swung open and Dr. Ravinski burst in. He quickly began to issue orders, and started kneading my stomach. I was feeling weaker. Someone gave me a shot. I don't know how long I was there. When I opened my eyes I was in the hospital room and Dr. Ravinski was standing there with Joe.

"Is this the way you do natural childbirth, Gilberta?" Dr. Ravinski asked, smiling.

"What happened?" I asked.

Joe took my hand as Dr. Ravinski explained that I'd had "uterine atony," a failure of the uterus to "clamp" after giving birth, making it impossible for bleeding to stop.

An injection of a medication combined with Ravinski's kneading of my abdomen got the condition under control. "You had us all pretty excited!" the doctor said.

He told me I might feel crampy for a while from the medication, and he wanted me to stay in the hospital for a week. He patted my shoulder, shook Joe's hand and left.

"It's okay, Toots," Joe said. "I've called Mom... she's taking the next train. The Harpers said they'll keep Joey as long as we need them to." He looked worried, and sat there for a long time, holding my hand as I drifted in and out of sleep.

The next day Joe brought his mother to see me. Gussie was smiling as she entered the room, but was holding back tears as she kissed me. Our new baby son John was brought in, and the three of us took turns admiring him and talking about how different he looked from Joey, but how beautiful he was—another perfect little boy.

By the time the week was up I was eager to get home. They hadn't allowed Joey to visit, and I was anxious to see him.

"Mom is really taking good care of Joey," Joe said. "You should see how she combs his hair."

We cooked up a scheme for introducing Joey to his baby brother in a way that would not be traumatizing to him. Joe's mother took him into the backyard to play just before Joe, the new baby, and I arrived from the hospital. We put little John in his bassinet in the back bedroom, I sat down in the living room, and Gussie brought Joey in, saying, "Your Mommy's home, Joey!"

Joey happily toddled over to me, calling, "Mommy! Mommy!" I lifted him into my lap, kissing him and cuddling him.

"I'm so glad to see you Joey!" Joe and his mother stood watching, smiling at the joy of reunion between mother and son.

"Would you like to see your new baby brother, Joey?" I asked him. He nodded excitedly, and we took him into the room where his infant brother lay sleeping.

"His name is John," Joe said. "Isn't he nice, Joey?"

The little boy reached out to touch his brother, and Joe said, "We have to be very gentle, Joey. Just pat his little back, very, very gently, like this. Don't touch his face. He's very delicate."

Joey's eyes grew large with awe as his little hand gently patted his brother. "Ooooh," he said.

Gussie's help and support over the next week was a godsend. She cooked wonderful meals, looked after Joey, and kept the house spotlessly clean.

One day she said to me, "Gil, I'll never forget the night Joe called us to tell us you were in the hospital and that you'd had some trouble. He kind of sobbed when he told us, 'All I want is for Gil to be all right.'"

I was touched. Joe had a way of always being in control of things, as though nothing could worry him or hurt him. I knew that he loved me, but he seldom showed his emotions in the way she described. I kept her words in my heart, and often thought of them in the years ahead, especially when I felt that he was keeping his emotions to himself.

At the end of the week Joe's dad arrived, and he, too, helped entertain Joey, taking him for walks and playing with him. I was again getting used to the routine of caring for a newborn infant. Soon it was time for them to leave, and I tried to find the words to thank them for all they had done. I watched as they drove away, standing there with Joey in my arms and baby John asleep in his bassinet.

Joe returned to work, and I faced the challenge of caring for a toddler and a newborn infant. I tried to grab sleep whenever I could, since baby John was waking up during the night for feedings. Bunky came over and took Joey to her house one afternoon so I could sleep while

John was between feedings. I was getting concerned that he wasn't getting enough milk, so I talked with Dr. Ravinski about it.

"Don't make a federal case out of it. Just put him on formula and he'll do fine," Dr. Ravinski said in his calm, reassuring way.

Don't make a federal case out of it. I knew he was right, but I couldn't help feeling great disappointment at not being able to supply all of the breast milk nourishment John needed.

"You've got two babies to look after," Dr. Ravinski said. "It will be easier on you if you put John on formula, and he'll do just fine, and you won't be so tired." So I reluctantly took his advice, and indeed, John did just fine.

Joe was temporarily assigned to be Safety Officer of the wing. One of his duties was to investigate crashes and review the evidence, attempting to determine the causes of an accident. It was an assignment he hated and was glad when it was completed. I realized that for Joe, investigating crashes meant taking a firsthand look at the risk of being a pilot, something he and his fellow pilots didn't like to think about.

One day while both babies were napping I heard the distant sound of sirens. Going outside to the front porch, I looked toward the base and saw that familiar sight, a column of black smoke rising from the direction of the runway. Suddenly I heard a child's voice calling, "Mrs. Guth, Mrs. Guth!" It was the six-year-old girl from next door, running across my yard to where I was standing.

"Will you drive me over to the base? I want to see if that's my daddy that crashed!" She was crying, almost hysterically. Her teenage babysitter came out of the house, calling to her.

Kneeling to comfort her, I said, "Susie, I'm sure that's not your daddy. Your Mommy will be home in a few minutes. You'll see. Everything is all right."

Just as her mother drove up, the phone rang. It was Joe, saying that yes, there had been a crash, that it wasn't anyone we knew, and that he would be home at the usual time. I told my neighbor what had happened, and she picked up her sobbing little girl and, thanking me, carried her into the house.

I was stunned that such a small child would understand the significance of that column of black smoke. For the first time, I thought of how Joe's career could affect my own children. I resolved to insulate them from worry about the dangers of their father's profession. Watching them closely for signs of anxiety whenever Joe had to leave on dangerous assignments, or when there was an accident on the base where we lived, I became practiced at maintaining the calm, confident demeanor I was learning from Joe.

* * * *

Chapter Fifteen

SEMPER FI

We decided to have a house built in Albany. We selected a plan, engaged a contractor, and were waiting to sign the final papers. The day of the signing arrived that fall of 1956. I was feeding Baby John when Joe came home midday, smiling broadly, his face flushed with excitement. Not at all like he had looked when he was the bearer of tragic news.

"Toots! I've been selected to go on an eighteen-month exchange duty with the Marines!"

Holding the baby spoon in midair, I stared at him. "What does that mean?" I asked.

"It's a great opportunity, Gil. Only two pilots from each service are selected each year. I'll be able to qualify to fly off of carriers!"

He could barely contain himself as he continued, eyes shining, "It's something only a few Air Force pilots ever get the chance to do. We'll be going to Cherry Point, North Carolina. It's a big Marine air station near Morehead City."

I was overwhelmed. I spooned another mouthful of applesauce into John's tiny open mouth.

"What about the new house?" I asked softly.

"No problem. Any contract can be broken when it's a case of Permanent Change of Station. I'll take care of that right away."

"How soon will we have to go?"

"I report on December first, so we have plenty of time." He sensed my dismay. "It'll be great, Gil," he said, reaching out and drawing me to him.

I was speechless. This assignment had come on the exact day that we were going to sign the papers on our first house. Somehow I regained my senses enough to say, "It sounds like a wonderful opportunity."

"It really is, Toots. We can always buy a house, but an assignment like this only comes along once in a lifetime."

So he left to cancel our contract for the new house, and I stood watching at the front door as his car pulled out of the carport. I understood that a young officer needed to take advantage of every opportunity to advance his career, and that his success would mean our success... the success of our whole family. But my excitement about the new house had suddenly come to an abrupt and unexpected end. The words I'd read in Nancy Shea's book, *The Air Force Wife*, came back to me:

> *According to the law of averages, desirable stations are bound to be interspersed among the poor ones, so make the best of whatever comes along without assuming a martyr-like attitude.*

I thought about other passages from her book. It was repeatedly pointed out that the wife, though vital to her husband's career, always took second place. I tried not to think about the lovely new house, how it would have been the first real home of our own. I remembered how I had resolved to be the perfect Air Force wife.

The disappointment that I felt was soon quelled by all the activities involved in preparing for the PCS move to Cherry Point—the sorting, packing, and cleaning, the paperwork and Joe's final clearance of Turner Air Force Base. His excitement and happiness over his new assignment was contagious, and I too became enthusiastic, convinced that this was a valuable career move.

The boys were seven months and twenty-seven months old when Joe reported to Cherry Point Marine Air Station, North Carolina, on December 1, 1956. This was Baby John's first move. It was Little Joe's fourth.

The name of Joe's Marine squadron was VMF(AW)-114. I learned that "VMF" meant "Heavier Than Air Fighter," the designation given to all Marine fighter aircraft. The "AW" stood for "All-Weather."

"Aren't all aircraft heavier than air?" I asked Joe.

"Military balloons and helicopters aren't considered 'heavier-than-air' aircraft," Joe explained. "It's a different way of naming flying squadrons than the Air Force uses."

Our base housing was a large, partially furnished upstairs apartment in an eight-unit brick building. It was an end unit, roomy, with plenty of extra space for the two boys to play indoors if the weather was bad. Our sectional rattan furniture adapted easily to the new surroundings. A spacious, grassy area surrounded the building, with swings for the children. The large parking lot accommodated the cars of all the residents. We settled in very quickly, and Joe started his new job at VMF-114 immediately.

We were warmly welcomed at Cherry Point. Because Joe was one of only two Air Force officers on the base he received a lot of attention, and, of course, much good-natured ribbing about being the only "blue-suiter" in the squadron. We didn't meet the other Air Force pilot, Norm Duquette, while we were at Cherry Point, because he was in a different squadron with a different mission. However, by coincidence, he and Joe would be assigned to the same base following Cherry Point, and we would become close friends with him and his family.

Joe quickly established himself as a respected pilot and leader, and as a guy everyone liked for his fun-loving, outgoing personality. His flying career seemed to be thriving, as he checked out in the F-9F8 Cougar jet and began training to fly off carriers. It was a sleek, high-performance aircraft. It had swept-back wings that folded up, as most carrier-base aircraft did, allowing the planes to be parked very closely together on the carrier.

Within a very short time, we were absorbed into the social life of Cherry Point Marine Air Station, and making many new friends. The wives of the pilots were a close-knit group, and included me in their circle right away. I was beginning to feel at home again. And it made me happy to see how enthusiastic Joe was about his flying assignment.

A couple of months after our arrival at Cherry Point, our friend Al Schneider called with devastating news. Bob Willerford, our good friend and neighbor from our days in Japan, had been killed in a crash in Florida. Bob had been flying in the All-Weather School at Tyndall Air

JOE PRACTICES FOR CARRIER LANDINGS IN THE F-9F8 COUGAR WHILE WITH THE MARINES.

Force Base in Panama City. His plane, a T-33 trainer, had flown into a thunderstorm, and he had been unable to pull out of it. After Al's call I couldn't get Mary Willerford out of my thoughts. I remembered how she and Bob had so happily celebrated our marriage with us that week in Las Vegas, and how we became neighbors and close friends in Japan.

I remembered how Bob used to call us and say, "Let's get together. We'll get a babysitter for the house apes," or "Come on over to our place. Mary's cooking her New England special."

Lying in bed that night, Joe and I clung to each other. We didn't talk much. I knew he was thinking about Bob and about the crash. I thought again about Mary, of how she had helped me so much in those early days after the arrival of our first baby. I tried to imagine her shock and anguish upon learning that her husband had died in his plane as a result of violent weather. I wondered how she was coping, where she would go to live, how she would go on, raising her three children alone.

I was too afraid to allow myself to imagine what I would do if I were in her situation.

Some months later the phone rang one evening, just after we had finished our after-dinner routine of baths for the two boys. Joe was holding the two of them, pajama-clad, on his lap, reading bedtime stories while I did the dinner dishes. I dried my hands and picked up the phone. I was startled to hear Mary Willerford's voice. I knew who it was the moment I heard that cultured New England accent of hers.

"Hi, Gil," Mary said. "I'm traveling with the three kids across the country visiting all Bob's and my friends. Are you and Joe doing anything a week from today?"

She sounded totally in charge and unperturbed, her usual, capable self. I assured her that we'd be delighted to see her and the children, and urged her to stay with us as long as she could.

"I'll just stay two nights," she said. "We'll have to get back on the road so we can cover all the people I want to see."

I told Joe about her call. "Wow," he said, shaking his head. "That's quite a trip for Mary to be making all alone with three little kids!"

Mary was again very much in my thoughts that night. I wondered if I would be brave enough to drive alone across the country with my small children. I got up and went into the boys' bedroom and stood looking at the two blond, innocent babies sleeping there. I bent to kiss each of them lightly on the cheek, and tiptoed out of the room.

Mary arrived with the three children as planned the following week. The eldest girl was now six, the second was four and a half, and the little boy, like our own little Joe, two and a half.

It was a full house with Mary's three children and our two. She was her competent self as she cared for her children, feeding them, bathing them, putting them to bed. She and Joe and I spent the evening talking about Japan, mutual friends, and about Bob.

"His plane was intact, but smashed," said Mary. "He just wasn't able to pull out of the thunderstorm." She spoke matter-of-factly, as though Bob was going to come walking in the door at any moment. She was controlled, in charge of her emotions as she spoke, never once giving in to tears. As we talked, I wondered if she ever just let down and cried.

"How are you doing, Mary?" Joe asked softly.

"I think I'm doing pretty well," she replied. "The doctor tells me that the full impact of this hasn't hit home yet... that it might take several more months. At this point I'm not sure what I want to do or where I want to live. That's why I'm making this trip, to try to get some perspective on my life and to feel the support of all our friends."

I looked at Mary and knew that this was an incredibly strong young woman sitting with us in our living room that night—a beautiful widow with three small children. She was twenty-five years old.

She left two days later, and as we stood waving goodbye to her and the children I wondered when we would see her again. We stayed in touch for several years, and then after a time she remarried, and our letters grew more infrequent. I still remember her porcelain-like beauty, her intelligence and her strength, and how much I learned from her. And how she was able to maintain that calm, reassuring demeanor, always completely in control of the situation. I wanted to be like her.

Soon it was time for Little Joe to attend preschool on the base. The bus would come by for him each morning and would bring him home at lunchtime.

One day I walked out to the bus stop to meet Little Joe as usual. To my astonishment, the bus didn't make its normal stop in front of our apartment. It whizzed by me as I stood there. I stared after it, not knowing what to make of it, with my thoughts racing as to what I must do next. I waited as the bus made its circle around the housing area, came back down our street and stopped at the corner where I was standing. The bus driver, smiling, went to the back and picked Little Joe up, sound asleep, in his arms.

"I'm sorry, Ma'am," he said. "He fell asleep in his seat back there and I didn't see him."

I felt very relieved and reassured by his kindness. After that day he always waved and smiled when he pulled the bus up to our stop.

By this time we had made many good friends at Cherry Point. A few of Joe's closest friends were Harry Pribble, Burley Daye, Jack

Gagan, and Bill Deinema, all young pilots in Joe's squadron. In addition to the men in VMF-114 and their wives, we became acquainted with another young couple in our building, Billye and Bob Jenkins. Bob was a pilot in one of the other squadrons, and they had four small children. He and Joe hit it off really well together, and Billye and I got together often during the day, sharing coffee or sandwiches, and watching our children play together. We attended many of the social events on the base together as a foursome. Billye and I spent a lot of time talking about our families, our husbands, military life, and the latest social events. A small, dark-haired woman, Billye had a wonderful laugh and smile, and our friendship grew as we shared the daily experiences of our lives as mothers of small children and wives of jet pilots.

Billye and Bob joined us in celebrating my twenty-seventh birthday. The four of us went out to dinner, and then back to their place for after dinner drinks and a surprise birthday cake. We were becoming very close friends.

Early that fall, Joe and Burley Daye, his fellow pilot from Squadron VMF-114, put together a bus trip to Raleigh, North Carolina, to see the football game between the arch rivals Duke and North Carolina. The bus was filled with our Marine friends in VMF-114 as well as our neighbors, Billye and Bob Jenkins. It was a high-spirited, fun-filled group. At a stop sign in a small North Carolina town, we were all looking out the window, only to see, at that very moment, a transient man in dirty brown trousers and dusty, untied shoes wearing, of all things, an official Air Force blue jacket he had picked up somewhere. In his hand was a brown bag from which he kept taking long sips of the bottle inside the bag. All the Marines on the bus grabbed the opportunity to give Joe one of the biggest ribbings of his life.

"Hey, Joe! There's one of your fellow Air Force officers!"

"Boy, Joe, the Air Force only chooses the best, don't they!"

They showed no mercy and kept it up until the bus had passed through the town and was once again on the highway toward Raleigh.

For one of the few times in his life, Joe was speechless.

One day several weeks later, right after I had put the two babies down for their afternoon naps, Joe came home. When he walked in the door he had that look on his face that I had seen before. I stood looking at him, dreading to hear what I knew was awful news.

"It's Bob," he said. "Bob Jenkins has been killed."

I couldn't believe it. I had just spent the morning at Billye's. We'd made soup and sandwiches for the children together, and had been talking about the dinner dance that was coming up soon.

"Oh, no!" I cried. "Not Bob! Oh, my God! My poor darling Billye!"

Joe put his arms around me. I started to cry, and we just stood holding each other for a moment. Then Joe said softly, "Bob's commanding officer and the chaplain are there now. You should go over as soon as you can."

Shaken, I went to the bedroom and fell to my knees, praying for the strength to be of help to Billye at this terrible time. I stood up, attempting to pull myself together. I dried my tears, brushed my hair, and left Joe with the two babies.

There was no sound coming from Billye's apartment as I knocked on the door. The CO of Bob's squadron came to the door, and I told him, "I'm Billye's friend... her neighbor, Gilberta Guth."

"Come in," he said. "Billye's in the living room, with the chaplain."

I stood in the doorway of the living room. She and the chaplain were standing by the fireplace. Looking up and seeing me, Billye cried, "Gil... Bob!"

I will never forget the anguish in her voice, or her look of utter desolation as I went to her and took her in my arms. Wordlessly, we held each other tightly, her sobs coming up from her soul. The two men asked if I could stay with her, and I assured them that I would. I called Joe and asked him to bring our two babies to Billye's. I didn't want to leave her alone at all. Joe brought them over, and, going to Billye, he put his arms around her without a word. I could see his face, filled with anguish. Then he kissed me goodbye and left to go back to his squadron.

That afternoon Billye's phone started to ring, and I found myself fielding her calls. Some people she wanted to talk to, others she didn't. I held her hand as she called Bob's parents and her parents. People were calling to offer help, to bring food, to take care of the children. I suddenly was in the position of being Billye's spokesperson. It all seemed like a bad dream, unreal. I thought of the good example set by Bonnie Bower in Japan, when Pete Petersen was killed, how she gathered all of the wives together to help in any way we could. I remember thinking, "God must be answering my prayer. He's giving me the strength to do this." That's the only way I could explain to myself where my resources were coming from.

Over the next few days, until Billy's and Bob's parents arrived, I stayed with her constantly, making calls for her, helping her to arrange the funeral at Arlington National Cemetery. She asked Joe to be one of the six pallbearers. Another friend took her to buy a black dress and hat while I watched and fed the children... her four and my two. Her living room was the scene of somber comings and goings, and quiet conversations. Friends brought food and flowers, and went to Billye to hug her and murmur words of condolence. Even the children, young as they were, seemed caught up in the prevailing somber mood and played together quietly, not misbehaving nor causing any loud interruptions.

The morning of the funeral, preparing for the flight to Washington, D.C., Billye asked me, "Gil, will you see that the two boys are properly dressed, with white shirts and ties, and jackets, please." I helped her two little boys get dressed, washed their faces and hands, combed their hair. Looking back, I think it was adrenaline that helped keep me going. I felt devastated and heartbroken for Billye, but somehow I was able to maintain an inner calm through these incredibly sorrowful duties. Billye's mother had dressed the two little girls, the youngest of them not even walking yet. Billye and the children were ready. The doorbell rang. The military vehicles had arrived to take the family and the military escort of pallbearers to the flightline to leave for the one-hour flight to Washington.

The six men, all grim-faced, were in uniform, all wearing white gloves. Joe was the only man in the Air Force blue uniform. The five others were in their handsome Marine "dress blues"... teal blue trousers with a red stripe down the sides, dark blue jacket with brass buttons, and white cap.

I stayed in Billye's apartment that day with our two little sons, taking messages and accepting the many offerings of help which were pouring into Billye's home.

When they all returned early that evening our little boys and I went home with Joe. He described the heartrending burial ceremony with full military honors at Arlington: the horse-drawn caisson transporting Bob's flag-draped casket; the riderless horse with the boots turned backwards; the six pallbearers carrying the casket to the gravesite; the graveside service; the volley of rifle shots firing the twenty-one-gun salute; the "missing man" formation of jets flying overhead; and then the handing of the folded flag to Billye by Bob's commanding officer and, finally, the bugle sounding out the notes of "Taps."

"It's something I'll never forget," Joe said quietly. "I hope I never have to do that again."

I told Joe of the role I had played as Billy's spokesperson. We were both exhausted, physically and emotionally.

A few days later the moving van was at Billye's home. I helped take care of her children while she prepared to leave Cherry Point. People continued to bring food and other offers of help. By the end of the week Joe and I were saying goodbye to Billye, promising to visit her in Odessa, Texas, where she was temporarily going to live with her parents. A few tearful hugs, and then she and the four children were gone. It would be several months before we could visit her out in Odessa.

A cloud of sadness settled over the community at Cherry Point. However, the men returned to their regular flying schedules immediately and all of us began trying to resume our normal activities. Everyone was attempting to regain their spirits and cope with this sudden and unexpected disaster. It was as though the pilots, who faced the possibility of such losses daily, were forcing themselves to shake off the hurt, not allowing themselves to be vulnerable, pressing on with the challenge of maintaining their high level of flying proficiency. I tried to follow Joe's example, to not dwell on the emotional toll of such a tragedy. But it was not easy to do. I missed Billye's friendship, her laugh and the daily sharing of our lives that we had become accustomed to. Joe and I missed them both and the fun we'd had as a foursome for so many months. Besides the emotion, the facts of life about the dangers of flying were in front of us, and could not be ignored.

Shortly after Bob's death, VMF-114 received a new operational airplane—the F-4D Skyray. It was another sleek, high performance plane that Joe loved as much as he loved the Cougar. His skill and passion for flying seemed to be boundless as he continued to excel at everything he undertook, including daytime and nighttime carrier landings. I knew that this was a particularly hazardous type of flying, but I tried not to think about the danger. Instead, I focused heavily on the fact that Joe was an excellent pilot... one of the best. If he weren't, I told myself, he wouldn't be on this assignment.

It was at this time that I began my daily ritual of saying the Rosary. I recalled the image of my grandmother praying her daily Rosary each afternoon or evening during World War II. Each day, while our two little boys were down for their naps I would lie on the sofa, eyes closed, Rosary in hand, and pray the prayers I had been taught by her so many years before. I always felt refreshed, rested and calm afterwards, ready to face the rest of the day caring for our sons and greeting Joe when he came home.

Several weeks later Squadron VMF-114 left TDY for Roosevelt Roads Naval Air Station in Puerto Rico. The men were to perfect their skills as fighter interceptors in the F-4D. Joe's three tentmates were Harry Pribble, Bill Deinema, and Burley Daye. Burley, who today remains a good friend to the family, still talks about what he remembers most about "Rosie Roads"—the mud: "I hated that mud, and couldn't wait to get out of there!"

However, the fact that the four of them were such good friends helped make the Spartan life they were leading more bearable. According to Joe, when they weren't flying, things were even laughable and fun.

While the men were in Puerto Rico the Squadron VMF-114 wives got together frequently. We made a tape full of messages for them, containing mostly funny vignettes about our lives at Cherry Point without them. I saw quite a bit of Sue Deinema, Claire Pribble, and Irma Daye. Since our husbands were sharing their Puerto Rican assignment as tentmates, we had a lot to talk about when we received letters or calls from them. We talked about surface things, our children, and base activities. We never talked about anything deeper, such as our worries about our husbands; the unwritten protocol told us that such things were never discussed.

When Joe was away I always felt secure on the base, but I always performed what I called my "security check" at night after putting the boys to bed. Check all doors and windows to be sure they're locked; turn off stove and all appliances; turn out all lights; look out the window to see if car windows are closed. One night I had completed all the steps up to the last one. When I looked out the window to where I had parked the car, no car was there. I went out to the parking lot, thinking I'd parked it in some spot where it wasn't visible from the apartment. Our '55 Chevy was nowhere to be seen. I stood there in disbelief for a few moments. Running back into the apartment, I called the Military Police to tell them I thought my car had been stolen. Two MP's were at my door in minutes.

"Ma'am," one of them told me, "in all probability your car was taken by a prisoner who escaped from the brig this evening. We are out in full force looking for him, so I'm sure your car will be found."

They took down all the necessary information, and kept assuring me that the car would be found and returned. It gave me a very spooky feeling to know that I'd been the victim of a car theft.

The next morning I had a call from Harry Pribble, one of Joe's tentmates in Roosevelt Roads, who had flown back to Cherry Point on squadron business for a few days.

"Gil," he told me, "if you need transportation or anything, just call the squadron. Someone will always be here. Or you can call Claire at home. She'll be glad to drive you anywhere you need to go."

I knew I would need transportation before my car was returned, and I thanked him for all his help.

"Not at all, Gil," he reassured me. "That's what we're here for. I'll see that Joe knows what's happening."

Over the next few days the MP's were in close touch with me, and Claire Pribble and the other wives called often to offer to drive me or help with the children. Joe called in frequently also, to ask if I was okay and if there was any news about our car.

Finally, the car was found. The culprit had sped through the main gate the night he escaped and had driven it wildly until it ran out of gas and came to a stop a couple of hundred miles away, where he dumped it and ran. He was captured, thrown back in the brig, the car was towed back and repaired, and by the time Joe returned from Puerto Rico all was well.

Throughout this entire crisis I had felt uneasy, but also comforted by the closeness and support of our friends and the security of the base. The Military Police had acted promptly and reassuringly, and when it was all over I felt proud of myself for having maintained my calm.

When he returned from Roosevelt Roads, Joe brought home some beautiful gifts. One was a pair of alligator high-heeled shoes with a matching bag.

"They're beautiful!" I exclaimed as I opened the gifts. They were very elegant, and I wore them proudly for many years. Joe also brought some brightly colored toys for the two boys. They climbed all over him as they opened their presents, very happy that their father was home again.

Joe's brother, Jack, had been assigned to a ship in Norfolk, Virginia, which was not far from Cherry Point. One day Jack, his wife Joanie, and their baby girl Jamie arrived for a weekend visit. Joe had told me to send Jack to the Officers Club when they arrived. Since it was Friday, he would be celebrating the end of the week with his fellow pilots at Happy Hour. Joanie and I visited together until later that evening, when Joe and Jack came through the door, singing, and obviously in a very happy mood.

"Do you know what my big brother did tonight?" Jack asked us.

"Hell, Jack, it was no big deal," said Joe.

Jack then proceeded to tell us that when he, dressed in his Naval officer's uniform, walked into the Officers Club bar, he spotted Joe, in his Air Force flight suit, seated at the head of a long table filled on both sides with his Marine pilot comrades. They were all engaged in a martini chug-a-lug drinking contest.

"When I was observed standing in the doorway I received a bunch of loud boos from all those Marines," Jack went on.

Spotting his brother, Joe jumped up on his chair and shouted, "Listen up, all you Marines! This guy in the Navy uniform is my little brother, Jack Guth!"

All the Marines in the room shouted, hooted, and jeered at the two of them. But Joe had continued, "I want all you Marines to know that my little brother and I can outdrink, outfight, and outf--- all of you Marines put together!"

"I thought we were both gonna be dead," Jack told us. But all that happened was that the two of them were subjected to a lot of jeering during the chug-a-lugging, until finally, fortunately, everyone decided it was time to go home.

The next morning both Joe and Jack were feeling the effects of the previous night's festivities. They were both sitting in the kitchen in their bathing suits, debating if a swim at the base pool might help them feel better.

"Jack, I have the perfect remedy for a hangover," Joe said.

He took a cold watermelon out of the refrigerator, cut it in half crossways and gave one half to his brother, saying, "Now, do as I do, Jack."

He set his half on the table, pulled out the heart of the watermelon with both hands and pushed the cold, dripping fruit into his mouth and face, eating and slurping the cold, juicy, sweet watermelon. Jack followed suit. Then Joe placed the empty half-melon on top of his head like a helmet and let the cold juices drip down his face and over his chest.

"Oh, boy, does that feel wonderful!" Jack said from under his watermelon helmet. They both then took a quick shower and headed for the pool for a brief swim to complete their recovery.

We got a babysitter that night and the four of us went out for dinner. Joe and Jack regaled Joanie and me with tales of their antics as they were growing up in St. Louis. Jack told us that, as the older brother, Joe often instructed him "in intelligent behavior."

Jack and his family left the next day. Over the years our two families got together many times as our paths crossed due to the military assignments of the two brothers.

A few weeks later on November 10, the elegant Marine Corps Birthday Ball was held. The women were all in long, frothy formals. Mine was a rose-colored strapless gown with a tight bodice and layers of net in the skirt. The Marines were resplendent in either their dress blues or their black "mess dress" formal uniforms. The Air Force dress uniform at that time was simply the regular blue uniform worn with a white shirt and black bow tie. Joe took a lot of ribbing that night about "not even changing out of his everyday uniform."

With his usual aplomb, Joe told his Marine pals, "It's not the uniform that counts. It's what's inside the uniform!"

A short time later the Air Force came out with a new "tropical" uniform: khaki bush jacket, walking shorts, tan knee socks, worn with the usual black Air Force oxfords. Topping the whole thing off was a tan pith helmet. Joe immediately ordered the new uniform for himself.

That summer there was a parade celebrating a special Marine event. All the Marine pilots were in their summer khakis, carrying under their right arms their cherry wood "swagger sticks," a traditional accessory to the Marine officer's uniform. Their leather gloves were gripped in their right hands, in the Marine tradition. Joe Guth was in the formation wearing his new Air Force tropical uniform, complete with tan knee socks, black shoes, and tan pith helmet. Under his right arm he carried a wooden dowel which he had painted Air Force blue. His right hand was gripping a pair of yellow garden gloves.

The reviewing general stopped short in front of Joe.

"Who the hell are you?" the general snapped

"Captain Joe Guth, U.S. Air Force, Sir!" answered Joe.

"You're the damnedest thing I've ever seen. I don't ever want to see you wearing that uniform again, do you understand!?" barked the general.

"Yes, Sir!" Joe answered.

The men in formation were beside themselves trying not to laugh. It was a moment that they all, including Joe, never tired of describing.

There were many parties and dinner dances at Cherry Point. It seemed like we were always among the last to leave one of these social events. I told Joe one day that I was looking forward to the next big event, but I dreaded having to get up with our two babies early the following morning.

"I know what!" Joe said. "Let's get a babysitter for the evening, and then another to come in early the next morning, before the boys wake up, so we can sleep late. That way we can stay up as late as we want!"

That's exactly what we did. It was wonderful being able to sleep in after a late party, knowing that the two boys were fed, dressed, and well cared for. I told Joe it was one of the best ideas he ever had, and it worked so well we continued that routine every time we went to a late-night event. We were the only couple I ever knew who would employ two babysitters for one event—one for the evening, and one to come in early the following morning.

Joe always had an affinity for looking after the bachelor pilots. One of these at Cherry Point was his good friend, Jack Gagan. He was a short, stocky pilot of twenty-four who, at the time, was interested in meeting eligible young ladies. Joe mentioned to Jack that my half-sister, Donna, was coming from New York to visit us. Donna was a renowned doctor of chemistry who had received many national awards for her outstanding achievements in research.

Jack immediately asked Joe, "Is Gil's sister single?"

"Yes, she is, Jack," Joe replied.

"How old is she?"

"Thirty-eight, Jack," said Joe.

"Oh. Well, I like older women. How tall is she?"

"She's five feet ten, Jack," Joe answered.

"Well, I like tall women. What does she do?"

"She's a doctor of chemistry, Jack," answered Joe.

"That does it! Forget it. She sounds too smart for me!" exclaimed Jack. However, we did invite Jack for dinner when Donna was with us, and the four of us spent a very enjoyable evening together. Jack was surprised to find that in fact, Donna was not at all intimidating, but was a fun, delightful dinner partner.

After we had been at Cherry Point for several months, it was announced that an aerial gunnery competition would be held at the Naval Air Station in Guantanamo Bay, Cuba, during March and April of 1957.

True to his love of competition, Joe eagerly trained for the event. The pilots were to fly the F-9F8 Cougar, the swept-back wing, high performance aircraft being used in the Marine Wing at that time.

The time to fly to Guantanamo finally came. The winning pilot was, to no one's great surprise, Joe Guth. Later that year an impressive ceremony was held on the parade grounds of Cherry Point, with all the Marine pilots in the Wing standing at attention. The Marine Wing Commanding General presented the "Top Gun" trophy for the best aerial gunner in the Wing for 1957 to the grinning Joe Guth. Only Joe could hear the general mutter good-naturedly, "I can't believe I'm hand-

AIRFORCE EXCHANGE PILOT CAPT. JOE GUTH CAPTURES THE MARINE "TOP GUN" TROPHY.

ing this to an Air Force poag!" It was one of the proudest moments of Joe's flying career. And my pride in his ability to excel at everything he undertook was continuing to grow.

While we were at Cherry Point, our fourteen-year-old dog Judy died. After a few days little Joey, now four, noticed that she was gone. I felt that he was still too young to understand the concept of death, so I told him she had run away. It broke my heart when he would look out the window and ask me when she was going to come home.

Soon our eighteen-month tour with the Marines was drawing to a close, and the time was approaching, again, to pack up and move on. The Marines gave a huge farewell party in our honor and a "This is Your Life, Joe Guth," program, parodying Joe's flying career and his tour with the Marines. Harry Pribble acted as Master of Ceremonies at the party, with several of the other squadron members performing.

One vignette portrayed Joe on one of his first night flights at Cherry Point. As he was preparing to land in the F-9F8 Cougar he had radioed the tower and asked, "Where is the switch for the landing lights on this aircraft?"

He then heard raucous laughter over the radio coming from the control tower. "Captain Guth, Marine aircraft do not have landing lights!"

He had continued to take a lot of ribbing about this and other incidents from his exchange tour at Cherry Point. Many of them were portrayed at the farewell party, including his appearance at the parade wearing the new Air Force tropical uniform, and his winning of the "Top Gun" trophy.

There were cards and gifts for both of us at the party. The most memorable and treasured gift for Joe was an Air Force blue "swagger stick." He had always kidded the Marines about carrying their cherry-wood swagger sticks. Burley Daye explained to us that its purpose was to keep their hands out of their pockets. Harry Pribble had designed and had one especially made for Joe, with a pair of silver Air Force pilot's wings and Joe's name fused to the tip. Harry had taken it to the auto body shop on base and had the blue color glazed on, giving it an intense, glossy finish. It was, and is, one-of-a-kind, a tribute to Joe's exchange duty with the Marines.

That night at the party, Joe leaned over and whispered to me, "This is one of the high points, Gilberta!" All the adulation of Joe and the acknowledgments of me were very heartwarming, and I agreed. Yes, indeed, this was a high point.

Orders soon came, assigning Joe back to the Air Force from the Marine Corps. He was to report to Shaw Air Force Base, near Sumter, South Carolina, following a month's leave.

We packed up our belongings, said our goodbyes, and started out on our thirty-day leave. We headed west to Tucson, for a visit to my family.

On our way through Texas we stopped in Odessa to see Billye Jenkins. Odessa seemed to me a very dry, bleak and barren sort of place. Billye and her children were still living in her parents' home.

"I haven't made any decision about getting my own place, or even where I want to live," she told us. She was concerned about her children. "They are really feeling the loss of Bob, particularly the two boys. Thank goodness for my Dad... they listen to him far better than they do to me." My heart went out to her, alone now, with concerns about the effects of Bob's death on her children.

We left Odessa after a short visit. Billye, her parents, and her four children stood in the driveway and waved goodbye to us as we drove away. I looked back, waving, and wondering what would happen to Billye and her family. We stayed in touch for a few years, but we never saw Billye again. I still think of her, remembering how close we had become at Cherry Point, and how she was left a widow so suddenly, with four small children.

On the way to Tucson we stopped in El Paso for a brief visit to Joe's old friend, Howard Pierson, who was married and had a son who was our John's age. Our little boys played together while we caught up on news of mutual interest. Then, it was time to leave and continue on to Tucson.

We stayed in the family home in Tucson for a week, visiting with my grandfather, Pop, and my aunts and uncles. My mother was still living and working in Paris.

"Those are golden kids," my grandfather said about our towheaded boys. He seemed impressed that, at ages four and two, Joey and John were well behaved and well mannered. They loved it when he showed them his memorabilia from his years as a policeman, and they followed him everywhere he went.

One day Joe and I were planning to drive down to Nogales, the Mexican border town sixty miles south of Tucson. We were leaving the boys with my aunt Catherine for the day. My Pop stood on the front porch with Catherine and the children, seeing us off. Pop looked like he was trying to smile.

"Why don't we invite Pop to go along?" Joe asked me. I loved the idea. Joe jumped out of the car, bounded up the front steps and asked, "Hey, Pop, would you like to go to Nogales with us?"

"Would I!" Pop declared. He grabbed his hat, rushed down the steps with Joe, and piled into the backseat.

Pop enjoyed every minute of that trip to Nogales. It had been several years since his last visit there. He and Joe got along famously, and he loved the sights of the drive along the way, and walking the exotic streets of the border town. We took him to The Cave, a famous restaurant built into the cave of one of the Nogales mountains. We were serenaded by mariachis, drank Mexican beer, and ate the tasty native food—tacos, enchiladas, chili rellenos, and Mexican refried beans. We had our picture taken at our table, with Pop grinning broadly as the mariachis serenaded us. It was a memorable day with Pop, one that all three of us never forgot. Pop kept a print of that photograph on his dresser for the rest of his life.

After a few days it was time to leave for the East. Following the goodbyes and good wishes, we pulled away from the house—we were bound for St. Louis to visit Joe's parents before reporting to Shaw Air Force Base, South Carolina.

We were becoming seasoned at traveling with small children. The two boys were by this time beginning to be curious and excited about the sights we visited along the way. I learned to pack what I called a "fun bag" for each of them, containing plenty of snacks, games, toys, and books, so except when they were sleeping, they stayed well occupied in the car. Sitting next to Joe in the front seat, I studied the maps as we went along and served as navigator.

Joe's parents had recently sold their house in St. Louis and moved to an apartment. We found their new place, and after a warm and hearty welcome, we sat down in the living room for a glass of iced tea.

A few minutes later, the phone rang. Since I was closest to the phone, I answered. It was Burley Daye, calling from Cherry Point.

"Gil," he said, his voice breaking. "I've got terrible news."

"Burley, tell me," I said.

"Harry Pribble was killed this morning."

I called Joe to the phone. He knew from my stricken look that something awful had happened. "It's Burley," I said, handing him the phone. I went to the kitchen and picked up the extension phone.

"Burley, what happened?" Joe was asking, almost in a whisper.

"I was leading the two-ship flight. Harry was my wingman. I took off, became airborne and radioed the tower. They told me that I might want to come back... that my wingman had just crashed."

"Have they found out what happened?" Joe's voice was hoarse.

"We're not sure exactly what happened," Burley said. "However, the wreckage indicates that he might have lost his hydraulic power on take off. There's nothing that points to pilot error. They've concluded that the exact cause of the crash may never be known."

Joe was silent as Burley continued, "Harry's wife, Claire, saw the smoke from her house. Knowing that Harry and I were flying together that morning, she jumped in her car and drove to the flightline. When I returned and landed I saw her standing there. As I climbed out of the plane and took off my helmet, I knew that she didn't want it to be me."

Burley's voice cracked with anguish. He and Joe talked for a few brief minutes, and then hung up. I returned to the living room, where Joe was standing, staring at the phone. Joey and John's grandparents had taken them outside. Joe turned to me, his pain visible in his face.

Harry had been one of Joe's tentmates at Roosevelt Roads in Puerto Rico. It had been Harry who designed and made the special "swagger stick" for Joe. It had been Harry who was the Master of Ceremonies at Joe's farewell party. It had been Harry who was so supportive when my car was stolen, who offered help and told me, "That's what we're here for, Gil." We held each other for a few moments, not saying anything. There was nothing to say.

We clung to each other that night, each of us with our own thoughts. I knew that Joe must be going over what Burley had told him, trying to figure out in his own mind what might have happened with Harry's plane. I kept thinking of Claire, with her four young children. I imagined what must have been her thoughts that morning when she saw that column of black smoke from her kitchen window, what she must have felt when she saw Burley, instead of Harry, climb out of the cockpit and take off his helmet. I thought about what she must be feeling at this moment.

* * * *

Chapter Sixteen

VOODOO

Joe was quiet on the drive from St. Louis to Shaw Air Force Base, South Carolina. I knew he must be thinking of Harry, trying to shake off the hurt, not be vulnerable, trying to prepare his frame of mind for a new airplane at a new location. We didn't make many sightseeing stops on the way. It was as though he was eager just to get there, get us settled, and throw himself into the new challenges he would be facing. I, too, was quiet, lost in my own thoughts of Claire, and also trying to be supportive of Joe as he dealt with the loss in his own way.

Arriving at Shaw, we drove through the main gate and down the main street toward the housing office. Like all military bases I had seen, it was well-maintained and neatly laid out with all the necessary public buildings: post office, library, theater, gas station, hospital, family housing. Except for the ubiquitous Air Force blue uniforms and dark green flight suits, it could have been any small town in the U.S. The children and I waited in the car while Joe got our assignment to temporary visitor's quarters. Coming out of the housing office, he looked upset and angry.

"There's been some mix-up with my orders—they haven't arrived yet. They weren't going to assign us to guest quarters. I told them, 'What do you mean we don't have guest quarters? We've just traveled across the continent twice. I've got kids, a wife, laundry. Here's my copy of my orders! You've got to accommodate us!'"

THE RF-101 VOODOO.

He was at the end of his rope—after the long drive with the kids, and dealing with Harry's death besides. His show of frustration convinced the clerk that we should have guest quarters, and we stayed there a week or so until our furniture arrived and we were assigned to a comfortable duplex just outside the base.

Joe's new assignment was with the 17th Tactical Reconnaissance Squadron. The 17th was one of two squadrons flying the RF-101 Voodoo, a sleek, high-performance, two-engine jet. The mission of the 17th and 18th Tactical Reconnaissance Squadrons was to be combat-ready; should war break out, they would do photoreconnaissance flights over enemy territory. Joe loved the 101 Voodoo. He said many times over the years that it was his favorite airplane. There was a welcoming party for us at the home of Colonel Bill Laseter, the CO, and a wives' gathering hostessed by Janie Laseter at the Officers Club. Shortly after that a big dinner-dance was held at the club. We were quickly becoming assimilated into the social life at Shaw.

Among the families we were getting to know were Norm Duquette and his wife Louise, who had been at Cherry Point at the same time we were. We didn't meet them, however, until we arrived at Shaw. Norm Duquette had flown reconnaissance missions in the RF-80A Shooting Star in North Korea. He had been shot down on his eighty-seventh combat mission. Since the RF-80A had no ejection seat at that time, he was severely injured in the crash and then captured immediately. Over the nineteen months of his imprisonment he was horribly beaten, starved, and forced to endure incredible physical and mental abuse. Their third child was born shortly after he was shot down. He didn't see her until he was finally released, when she was eighteen months old.

When I met his wife Louise there at Shaw, I was struck by her gentle, quiet, and caring manner. It wasn't until later that I learned how much she and "Duke" and their family had endured. She was an inspiration to me as she quietly cared for her growing family and her pilot husband, and dealt with all the challenges of military life.

The two 101 Voodoo squadrons at Shaw Air Force Base were made up mostly of pilots who had been in operational photoreconnaissance most of their flying careers. This was a new direction in Joe's career, but after mastering the 101, he had no problem becoming proficient in the reconnaissance aspect of their mission. The motto of the photoreconnaissance squadrons was "Alone, Unarmed and Unafraid." The people in the 101 squadrons were an outgoing, friendly group, and most of them had known each other for years. Joe was soon named operations officer of the 17th, and we began to feel quite at home at Shaw.

I wrote a column in the base newspaper, featuring the wives' activities and other articles of family interest, such as teas, family gatherings and events, dinner-dances, and new arrivals at the base.

Our duplex was comfortable, with two bedrooms, and a screened-in back porch. Joe closed in the porch and insulated it so we would have a family room for watching TV and extra space for Joey and John to play in.

The boys' favorite TV program was *Zorro*. Joey had a Zorro Halloween costume that year—black cape, hat and mask, fake sword, and a stick horse to ride. John, in a cowboy outfit, would follow his brother, riding his stick horse as fast as his little legs could carry him. Every day Zorro and his cowboy sidekick would don their outfits for the day, to ride once again to conquer the forces of evil.

A few months after our arrival at Shaw, our Marine friends, Burley Daye and Bill Deinema and their wives came to visit us, with all the news from Cherry Point. VMF-114 was preparing for a nine-month Mediterranean cruise, known as a "Med cruise," to practice flying off the carrier USS *Roosevelt*. It was fun seeing our close friends again, but we felt a void without Harry and Claire Pribble.

The Air Force came out that year with a handsome mess dress uniform: black trousers, short "Eisenhower" jacket (white for summer, black for winter) with silver epaulets and buttons, and silver braid on the cap. Joe couldn't wait to buy the new uniform, complete with both the winter and summer jackets.

"Let's go to the Marine Corps Birthday Ball at Cherry Point in November," he said. "I want to wear it and show those Marines they aren't the only ones who have fancy dress uniforms! Wear your long black evening gown. We'll show 'em!"

The Marines always wore their resplendent dress uniforms to special occasions, while Joe previously had only the regular Air Force blues worn with white shirt and black tie. Not many people had seen the new Air Force dress uniform. He loved surprising everyone at the Marine Ball when we walked in with him wearing the handsome new Air Force mess dress. He didn't mind the kidding and playful comments his Marine pals tossed his way that night, introducing him as the "Commandant of the Argentine Air Force." He confidently whirled me around the dance floor, and loved it when his friends asked him, "Hey, Joe! What's that snazzy uniform you're wearing?"

Shortly after that, there were two more fatal accidents involving our Marine friends. Burley Daye called to tell us what had happened. Ken Baublitz was killed at Cherry Point, and Bob Minnick while practicing carrier landings on the USS *Roosevelt* off Mayport Beach, Florida.

Award-Winning Pilot Returns From Tour With Marines

An award-winning Air Force pilot who made an enviable record with the Marines will be assigned here tomorrow.

He is Capt. Joseph R. Guth, an Air Force exchange pilot, who has received transfer orders after completing 18 months' duty with Marine All-Weather Fighter Squadron—114, a unit of the Second Marine Aircraft Wing.

"I've enjoyed my tour with the Marines," he said, "and feel sure that many of my experiences with them will be of great value when I return to duty with the Air Force."

Last August, as a result of Captain Guth's winning two Navy "E" awards for aerial gunnery excellence, he was awarded the Second Wing Commanding General's Aerial Gunnery Trophy.

A competitive evaluation gunnery exercise of Marine Fighter Squadron-114 was held at the Naval Air Station, Guantanamo Bay, Cuba, during March and April, 1957. It was during this event that Guth obtained outstanding scores in air-to-air gunnery at 15,000 feet by scoring 74 hits out of a possible 140, and at 25,000 feet, 36 hits out of a possible 140, thus winning the two Navy "E" awards.

Guth's duties with the Marines consisted of piloting F4D "Skyray" jet aircraft and assistant operations officer. The captain will report to Shaw tomorrow, where he will pilot RF-101 Voodoos.

Captain Guth is married to the former Miss Roberta Cosulich of 901 N. Third Ave., Tucson, Ariz. He is the son of Mr. and Mrs. Joseph T. Guth of 5900 Devonshire Ave., St. Louis, Mo.

Two AF Pilots Qualify Aboard The Saratoga

Two Air Force pilots serving with the Wing as exchange flyers will tell sea stories with authority when they return to their branch of service.

Capt. Norman E. Duquette and Capt. Joseph R. Guth recently became carrier qualified with VMCJ-2 aboard the USS SARATOGA. Capt. Guth who normally flies with VMF (AW)-114 was ordered to VMCJ on temporary orders to receive the carrier training. He was awarded the Commanding General's trophy last week for the best aerial gunner in the wing for 1957.

The two Air Force men completed the training usually reserved for Navy and Marine pilots flying F9F-8-T Cougar jets.

The officers proved adept in utilizing mirrors for landings, along with the Marine pilots of VMCJ.

Capt. Duquette who is assigned to VMCJ has planned eight squadron photo missions and briefed the Marine pilots concerned with those missions.

Capt. Guth is now flying an F4-D Skyray only recently received by VMF(AW)-114.

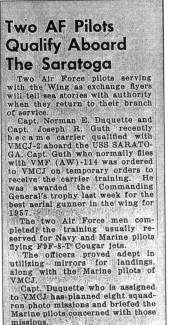

JOE AND FELLOW AIR FORCE EXCHANGE PILOT ARE ASSIGNED TO FLY THE RF-101 VOODOO.

Burley had been preparing to land on the carrier right behind Bob. "As Bob landed," Burley told us, "the arresting wire broke. He was going too fast to stop and too slow to take off, and he went over the side and into the water. The canopy blew underwater, and he was killed instantly. His parachute deployed and pulled him under. They knew he was dead. They didn't retrieve his body, because they didn't want to risk any additional lives."

We were deeply shaken by these disasters hitting our Marine friends. With his usual strong powers of concentration and determination, Joe returned to the task in front of him—to continue mastering the 101 Voodoo and the necessary photoreconnaissance skills, plus tending to his duties as the squadron's operations officer. I was busy caring for the two boys and keeping up with life at Shaw, but underneath it all I was thinking very much about the grieving wives, families, and friends back at Cherry Point.

A big New Year's Eve formal ball was held at the Shaw Air Force Base Officers Club to ring in the year 1959. Joe again wore his new mess dress uniform. My dress had a deep green, velvet strapless top and layers of green net skirt. Joe called it my "Scarlett O'Hara dress." It was a festive, romantic evening. He held me tight as he swung me around the dance floor, humming along with the music. He seemed to be "at the top of his game." In spite of the repeated tragedies and losses of our friends, we personally had a lot to be joyful about. We were very much in love, happy and healthy; we had two beautiful little boys; and his Air Force flying career was going great.

We had been at Shaw ten months when Joe came home from work one evening and told me that the two squadrons would be flying to France for a three-year tour of duty.

"Families will be allowed to follow as each man finds appropriate housing," Joe said with excitement.

I was overjoyed by the news. Living in France... what a dream assignment!

"It'll be great, Toots. Just think of all the traveling around Europe we'll get to do!" Joe said.

"I'm so excited!" I exclaimed. "When will we go?"

"The pilots will fly the planes over in six weeks. So we'll have to make plans to move you and all our stuff off the base before I leave."

It didn't seem like much time to prepare for such a major change. Everyone in the two squadrons had scores of questions. A detailed briefing was held for the men of the two squadrons and their wives one evening. It was conducted by Captain John Pennekamp, who, with his family, was already at Laon Air Base, France, where we would be going. He was sent back to Shaw to tell us all about the advantages, disadvantages, pluses and minuses of living in France. We wanted to know what was and what was not available, how to get a car over there, and most importantly, about housing. He was well prepared to answer our questions that evening. It was clear that one of the biggest challenges would be finding a place to live, especially for those who were not eligible for base housing, which was quite small and limited to families with no more than two children. We had already started hoping to add a girl to our family, so we knew that base housing would likely be either inadequate or unavailable.

The pilots started preparing to fly the 101's to France, and their families began readying to leave the base. We were not allowed to remain in base housing once our military sponsors were no longer assigned there. We decided that the two boys and I would go to my grandfather's house in Tucson to wait until we could join Joe in France. Before packing up for the move, a party with a French theme was held at the club, with the wives performing song-and-dance routines for the men. I was in a chorus line of five, wearing cancan costumes, singing,

> *How ya gonna keep 'em down on the farm*
> *After they've seen Paree?*

It was a fun and memorable show, and our husbands enjoyed it immensely, cheering us on and shouting, "More, more!"

Shortly before we left Shaw, Burley Daye called again from Cherry Point. The minute I heard his voice, I knew he had more bad news. Bill Deinema had been killed flying off the carrier USS *Roosevelt* during the Med cruise. Burley's voice quavered as he told us, "He took off, and about a mile from the ship he flew into the water. No one can figure out what happened or why he went in." Bill Deinema had been one of Burley's closest friends. He had been the fourth tentmate when Joe, Burley and Harry Pribble were in Puerto Rico with VMF-114. "Bill and I had been planning to meet our wives in Palma, Majorca, off the coast of Spain, for a vacation," Burley continued. "The skipper and flight surgeon went with me to meet the wives' plane. The three of us were standing there as the women's plane landed. I was the one who had to tell Sue Deinema that Bill had been killed. I was released early from the Med cruise to escort my wife and Sue back to the States." And after Burley left the Med cruise, still another Marine pilot, Dave Scofield, was killed flying off the USS *Roosevelt*.

"My God," I thought. "How many more of these disasters can Marine squadron VMF-114 take? How much more can any of us take, with all our Marine friends 'going in,' as the pilots called it?" I wondered how the wives of VMF-114 felt, with their husbands flying off the carrier—an assignment which had taken so many lives, in addition to the two lives lost recently at Cherry Point.

Once again I wanted to talk about my feelings, but I didn't feel I could talk about it to Joe, because I knew he was striving to maintain that sense of self-confidence and invincibility that was so vital. My new friends at Shaw had their own challenges, getting ready to leave for France. Again I turned to my faith to seek the strength I needed to cope with all the terrible news.

Burley left the Marine Corps shortly after that to pursue his own business career, but continued to fly with the Marine reserves for ten years. It was apparent that, once flying got under the skin of these men, it became such a part of them they hated to give it up. Burley settled in the San Francisco Bay Area and still remains a good family friend.

It was clear that Joe needed to prepare himself for leading some of the 101 Voodoos to France. He threw himself into the preparations, flying and studying his instrument books and maps. He and I spent time talking about the adventure of living and traveling in Europe—what we would do, what we would see. The excitement of both the pilots and the wives was building as we all got ready for this new adventure. Our household belongings were packed up and shipped out; we cleaned out the duplex for the inspection; and Joe put the two boys and me on a plane to Tucson. I was to wait there for him to find a house in France and send for us.

Right after the children and I left, Joe and the other pilots in the 17th Squadron left Shaw Air Force Base on May 3, 1959, to fly the RF-101 Voodoos to Laon Air Base, France. After in-flight refueling with KB-50's near Bermuda, Joe's plane developed problems. He and his wingman, Bill Talley, landed and spent the night there while Joe's plane was being worked on. During the night Joe was bitten by a centipede.

"You'll either recover quickly, or, if you're allergic to it, you'll die," the doctor told him, not very reassuringly. Joe didn't have an allergic reaction, but there was a knot on his leg that remained for several months. Fortunately it did not affect his flying, and they continued their flight on May 6. On the way to the Azores, Joe and Bill had another in-flight refueling, after which Joe's plane developed another mechanical problem. While they were in the Azores, they got a message saying that all the RF-101's required "Tech Order Compliance Inspection." They would have to wait for a maintenance crew to come to the Azores to inspect their planes. Finally, on May 14 they were able to take off and complete their flight to Laon Air Base France. They were the last pilots in the 17th Squadron to arrive at Laon. Lieutenant Colonel Bill Laseter, the squadron's commanding officer, and the other pilots met them joyfully. All had arrived safely, with no major mishaps. The 18th Squadron, also flying the 101 Voodoos, left Shaw a few days after the 17th, but didn't fare quite as well.

Two of their pilots had a midair collision over the water near the Azores, but luckily both of the pilots escaped and were picked up. Needless to say, there was much celebrating after all the pilots of both squadrons had finally arrived safely.

Years later, Bill Talley wrote to Joe about their flight:

"When we deployed to Laon, France, you selected me to fly on your wing. I felt honored. Your plane developed problems, and we aborted into Bermuda. You again had problems over the Azores, and we aborted again. You told me to land first in case your landing closed the runway. After I cleared the runway, you told me you were having problems and to take off and rejoin, so that I could fly on your wing to observe possible leaks or damage to your airplane. I jettisoned my drag chute and was prepared to take off downwind when you called again and told me you could land without assistance. I have thought about that several times and know it would not have been a good idea to take off downwind, but I would have done it for you."

Bill's letter expressed the affection and high respect which he and the other pilots in the squadron felt for Joe.

The boys and I were in Tucson, at my grandfather's house, for three and a half months. I was oblivious to all that had happened on the flight of the Voodoos to France. While I took private French lessons, learning the basic phrases and becoming comfortable with the pronunciation, our two little boys grew well acquainted with their great-grandfather. He taught them to help him in his garden, and they followed him around the yard and in the house, everywhere he went, like two little ducklings.

"They sure are golden kids," my grandfather said proudly about his great-grandsons.

Joe called me when he had found a house for us on the "French economy," as off-base housing was called. He sounded like he was close by, and it was wonderful to hear his voice. He told me that the house was located in the small village of St. Gobain, about twelve miles from Laon Air Base. John Pennekamp, who had come from France to Shaw to brief all of us, lived right next door with his family, so we had American neighbors as well as French ones.

I happily started preparing us for the flight to New York, with reservations on a military transport plane that would then take us to Paris. The day before we were to leave Tucson, I borrowed my uncle's car and took the boys for haircuts and to buy some small toys for the flight. They were both riding in the backseat as they always did. As cars were not equipped with seatbelts in 1959, Little John was standing behind me on the floor of the backseat, admiring his new toy car and saying, "This sure is nice..." But then, as I rounded a corner, the car door flew open and he tumbled out of the car. I quickly pulled over and jumped out, my heart in my throat. John was lying on the street, surprised, but not hurt. A kind motorist stopped and ran over to where I was bending over John, and a policeman arrived within moments. I was more shaken up than John was.

"Ma'am," the policeman said. "I think you should have a doctor check him out, just to be sure, and you might ask the doctor if you're okay yourself."

I held John in my arms for a moment, and then lifted him back into the car, his toy car still in his hand. He wasn't crying, so I was pretty sure he wasn't hurt. But knowing that we were leaving the next day on our way to France, I wasn't taking any chances, so I took him to the family doctor that afternoon. He was checked over, and found to be perfectly okay. I told my grandfather what had happened. He shook his head and said, "You were damned lucky!"

The next day, except for lingering thoughts about what could have happened, I managed to remain calm enough to get the two boys and myself ready to leave. Pop bent to hug his two great-grandsons, and in return they each grabbed him hard around the neck. Catherine and Manny stood with Pop on the porch as we got into the taxi bound for the airport. We all knew it would be at least three years before we saw each other again. I looked back to see them all returning our waves as we drove away.

"Bye! Have a good trip! Write!" they called. I didn't know that the next time I saw Pop, he'd be in a nursing home.

Joey and John, now five and three, were excited about this new trip, eager to be with their father again. They were good company for each other, and were good little travelers. They looked at their picture books together, John asking his big brother questions about the stories pictured, and Joey always responding with strong assurance, ready to demonstrate his advanced knowledge. They would also draw or color together, and John would ask, "Is this good, Joe?" His brother would look at John's work thoughtfully, and say, "Yeah, John, that's pretty good," or "You should make some clouds in that sky, John."

My half-sister, Donna, met us in New York at La Guardia for a two-day visit with her. She told me that she had asked a friend how to prepare her apartment for two young children, and what things we could do to entertain them. She hadn't seen them since she visited us at Cherry

Point three years before. They were excited about being with her, and captivated by the sights of New York. In between excursions, the impending flight to France to be with their father was their main topic of conversation. I was proud to have such well-behaved kids.

When it came time to leave, Donna drove us to McGuire Air Force Base, New Jersey. We all hugged goodbye, and boarded a Military Air Transport C-124 for the long trip to Paris. It was a cargo plane that had been converted to accommodate families going to and from overseas locations. After several hours we stopped in Iceland for an hour to refuel, and then continued on the remaining five-hour flight over the Atlantic Ocean. I had packed a lot of toys, books, and games in the "fun bags" so the boys were happily occupied when they weren't eating meals or napping. The seats on the plane were not luxurious, but we were comfortable enough to relax and get some sleep during the long journey.

As we landed at Orly International Airport in Paris, my excitement grew. I knew Joe would be waiting at the terminal. The children and I disembarked and entered the greeting lounge.

They both spotted their father at the same time. "Daddy! Daddy!" they shouted, running to him and jumping into his arms. He lifted them both and held them close. After the joyful hugs and kisses, he put them down and walked toward me smiling, his arms outstretched. The three months of separation melted away as we wrapped our arms around each other. I felt his strength, and looking into his clear blue eyes, I felt like I was home again.

"I've really missed you, Toots," Joe murmured.

"I'm so glad we're together again," I answered.

We stood kissing and hugging, oblivious to our surroundings. Our two sons tugged at their father, talking excitedly about their trip, their new toys, John falling out of the car. Our station wagon had arrived in France before we did, so it was waiting for us after we got our baggage. We loaded everything into the car, climbed in, and left Orly Field.

My mother, who was living and working in Paris at the time, had agreed to keep the two boys for a few days while Joe and I spent some time alone in Paris. Joe had already visited her and familiarized himself with driving in Paris. He drove us directly to her tiny apartment on the

Left Bank. She had a job as the secretary to the principal of Paris American High School, and had taken a few days off to care for her grandsons, whom she hadn't seen for two years.

"Mimi," as we all called her, had a way of entertaining the children and a sense of fun that told us they would be just fine with her while we enjoyed Paris together. She had two small air mattresses, and she told them they could help pump them up to use as their beds—the boys thought this sounded like great fun. We hugged Joey and John, told them to be good and mind their Mimi, kissed Mimi goodbye, and left.

We stayed at the luxurious George V hotel, ecstatically happy to be together again. We dined out at the charming restaurants, walked arm-in-arm up the Champs-Elysée, sat at sidewalk cafes to people-watch. We took a grand tour of Paris and the Marseilles. It felt like we were living a fairy tale existence, together and in love in the most romantic city in the world.

Soon it was time to pick up our sons and head for Laon Air Base, near the tiny village of Couvron, just under sixty miles from Paris. We were happy to see our boys again, and they were filled with tales about the good times they'd had with their Mimi.

One day Mimi had taken them to the park to feed the pigeons. John told her he was going to catch one, and she had replied, "Oh, John, I don't think you can catch that pigeon!"

And he promptly proceeded to do so, she told us, entertaining everyone nearby in the park. "All the Frenchmen wanted to rub their little blond crewcuts," she recounted. "French kids don't have crewcuts. Everywhere we went, people were smiling at them, and reaching to rub their little blond heads."

We said our goodbyes to Mimi, who promised to come visit us at Laon by train. Driving through the beautiful French countryside in our station wagon, I marveled at the turn of events which had brought us to France. We would be living here for three years.

As we drove through the main gate of Laon Air Base I felt like we really had arrived home. Though smaller than any of the stateside bases I had seen, it had the usual style of low buildings, landscaped grounds, and everywhere, people dressed in Air Force blue uniforms or green flight suits. The familiar sound of jets taking off and landing greeted us as we drove first to the base visitors' quarters, and then to the Officers Club for some lunch. A few people that we knew from Shaw Air Force Base had already arrived, and it felt good to be welcomed by old friends.

After lunch, Joe said to his sons, "Do you want to take a drive to St. Gobain and see where we're going to live?"

"Yeah!" said Joey excitedly.

"Yeah!" said John, always ready to follow whatever his big brother did or said.

* * * *

Chapter Seventeen

ST. GOBAIN

The French countryside was filled with beautiful, bucolic scenes that resembled the French landscape paintings that are so well-known around the world. The air and everything about the hills and the fields seemed to be engulfed by a soft blue haze. The occasional farmhouse was badly in need of paint and repair, and we saw a few country folk driving their sheep or their horse-drawn wagons along the narrow country roads. It felt like we had been transported into the previous century.

As we drove through the narrow main street of St. Gobain in our big station wagon I was acutely aware of the reactions we were getting from the villagers. Some stopped on the street and watched curiously as we drove by. A few of them, I thought, did not appear to be very friendly. Our new home, Number 5 Rue de Laon, was at the far end of the tiny town. Joe opened the door and we entered the house we would live in for the next three years.

It was a house that had been built specifically for American tenants, with indoor bathroom facilities, central furnace heating, and hookups for a washer in the basement. There were two bedrooms, plus space for a third bedroom in the attic and a fourth in the basement. Some of the features of the house were distinctly European, and though unusual in many respects, it was quite comfortable. The yard was large, but in a neglected, overgrown condition. To us the house looked heavenly, because we were all together.

Joe pointed out the house next door where our neighbors, the Pennekamps, lived. Owned by the same landlord as our house, it was an old, historic-looking home which had been renovated especially for renting to American families. I felt a surge of gratitude that we would have American neighbors close by, especially after the rather curious glances directed at us in the village. While we were looking over our house, our landlord, Monsieur Vuerings, who lived two doors away, came over carrying a bottle of red wine, a welcoming gift for us. He was a Belgique, with a jovial, mustachioed face and a hearty laugh. He spoke English with a charming Maurice Chevalier accent. He and Joe had already established a friendly, easygoing rapport, and he was immediately taken with our two little boys.

Our next few days were spent in the base visitors' quarters as we awaited the delivery of our household belongings. We quickly learned that the center of our social activity was the Officers Club. We had our meals there, and were gradually becoming reunited there with our friends from Shaw. I was overjoyed to see Louise, Martha, Patti, Betty, Sylvia, Ebba, Janie, and all the other friends from the 17th and 18th Squadrons.

After what seemed like a long wait, we met the moving van at the house in St. Gobain. The two movers stayed to help Joe carry our belongings into the rooms, and by late afternoon all our possessions, most of them still in boxes and packing crates, were in the house—all except the giant refrigerator we had bought in Albany, Georgia.

The task of getting the huge fridge into the house proved to be a daunting one. It was too tall to get in the front door, and there was no back entrance into the house. The only other entrance was from the small deck outside the living room, overlooking the rose garden. There was a sloped driveway which led down into the basement garage, but even if they could get it into the basement, the indoor staircase leading up into the main floor was too narrow for it to be brought up that way.

But there was also a large double window in the kitchen right over the sloped driveway into the garage. There was only one thing to do: the men tied cables and ropes around the fridge at the bottom of the sloping driveway, and Joe and Monsieur Vuerings stood in the driveway, pushing and steering the fridge upward as the two movers pulled on the cables from the kitchen window. They were attempting to lift the fridge up over the windowsill and into the kitchen. However, there was a point of its elevation at which it left Joe's and Monsieur's hands and hung mid-air.

"*Whoa! Alors!*" the two men yelled. Joe ran up into the kitchen as the two movers strained to hang onto the cables to keep from being pulled out the window by the weight of the fridge. Joe grabbed onto the cables with the movers, and the three of them continued to pull, straining and groaning with the weight of the task. Our neighbors had gathered to watch the operation, shaking their heads, waiting for the giant fridge to pull the men over the windowsill and down to the driveway, or for the cables to break and send the fridge crashing down onto the concrete. I couldn't bear to watch this impossible task. Joey and John stood outside, enthralled by the site of their father and the three men struggling with the problem. Finally, the refrigerator was pulled into the kitchen, moved into place and plugged in. Instantly, its familiar low humming sound started up. The men, including Joe, were exhausted. Monsieur Vuerings brought over one of his best bottles of wine, and the four of them proudly sat and decompressed, relishing the successful completion of their task, with Monsieur Vuerings providing the translation between Joe and the two French movers. They all were obviously very pleased with themselves, and I was relieved that no disaster had befallen any of them, nor our fridge.

Unpacking everything and putting it in place was always pleasurable for me. Joe took a few days off to do the heavy tasks and make a few repairs. The two boys had fun finding their toys and books, and putting them in their shared basement room. We began to feel settled again, but there would be much to learn about living in a European country.

On weekends when he wasn't flying Joe spent a lot of time cleaning up the big yard around the house. Working in the yard was relaxing and enjoyable for him, and he was a talented gardener. Using our power mower, he attacked the overgrown grass and weeds at the side and in the back of the house. Some of our neighbors stood in the street near the house, watching Joe as he shoved the roaring mower through the overgrowth, trimmed around the trees, and planted flowers along the low fence in the front.

Joe succeeded in transforming the area around our house into a beautifully landscaped, well-kept yard, complete with healthy lawn, flower gardens, and neatly pruned fruit trees.

Our French neighbors were fascinated by our ways of doing things. However, they stayed to themselves most of the time. I would attempt to greet them, always in their language, but the usual response was just a brief *"Bonjour, Madame."*

During the time we lived in France, 1959 to 1962, President Charles De Gaulle was pushing to get NATO and all the American forces out of France. Occasionally we would see graffiti scrawled on the walls of buildings in the small surrounding villages, saying "Americans, Go Home!" It was disconcerting, feeling largely unwelcome in our host country. It made us cling to our friends, each other, and the base even more.

We were in the middle of the Cold War. The threat of nuclear war was real. The 101 Voodoo pilots were on continuous assignments and ongoing readiness training to fly reconnaissance missions over the Soviet Union.

An orientation meeting was held for the wives of all the pilots, crews, administrative personnel, officers, and enlisted men on the base. Some 200 of us filed into the base theater on the appointed day, and none of us had any idea about what we would be hearing.

The meeting was opened by a high-ranking officer who, in calm, reassuring tones, told us that what we were going to hear was simply a precaution, and not meant in any way to alarm or frighten us.

We were told that we should all prepare an emergency evacuation kit. It should include food, blankets, baby supplies, clothing for ourselves and our children, and water for several days. We were to have our passports, and for each child over a certain age, we would have a *"Carte de Seizure."* In the event that an evacuation of the base and surrounding areas should be ordered, we were to pack our supplies and our children into our cars, meet at the appointed location, form a convoy, and start driving toward Spain.

We all sat there in silence, trying to grasp the full meaning of what we were hearing. I realized that if such an order did come down, our men would immediately be deployed to perform the reconnaissance missions they were preparing for. We, the wives, would be on our own to evacuate ourselves and our children to safety.

I envisioned a convoy of women in cars filled with children, driving across miles of hazardous roads, flat tires, car breakdowns, sick children, fearful days and nights, worries about our husbands.

As we left the theater, I knew that the question on everyone's mind was, "Could this really happen?"

When I talked to Joe about it that evening, he said, "Toots, it's only meant to help you prepare for a possible problem, like insurance. In all likelihood, nothing like that will happen. It's just good to be prepared. So just make the preparations and go about things like always. There's no need to worry about it."

I resolved to do as he suggested, and set about preparing our emergency evacuation kit. That part was easy. It was more of a challenge to "go about things as always." But gradually, as we fell into the new routine of living in France, the social life and the traveling, the memory of the orientation meeting was pushed into the back of my mind. I rarely gave it much thought, except when the occasional "alert" was called, or when Joe and the others had to suddenly leave in response to what was going on in the world.

One concern was that Algeria was in the middle of a civil war. The French Algerians objected to Algeria being given its independence from France. It was feared that these French Algerians would send paratroops into France to voice their objection to the pending independence. The pilots at all the U.S. bases in France were grounded for a week out of concern for a possible eruption that could bring danger to the American forces, which had no involvement in the situation.

We were told to close our shutters at night. There were nights when the French tanks went rumbling right past our house. We could hear their roaring and feel the ground shaking as they approached and drove through our little village.

Eventually, De Gaulle had his way about Algeria's independence and things seemed to return to normal as far as our bases were concerned. It wasn't until two years after we left France that De Gaulle succeeded in getting NATO and the American forces out of France. NATO was transferred to Brussels, Belgium, and all U.S. bases in France were closed in 1964.

Although there were many sights to see during our time in France, Laon Air Base was the center of all activity for our American families as well as for the pilots. There we found friendship, shopping, social events, and medical care. We attended church there, and movies. There was a party, dinner, dance, or informal get-together almost every weekend. I drove to the base almost every day. It was like a refuge where I could find friends and the familiar, secure feeling of being on an American airbase. I was also very grateful to have Dee and John Pennekamp as neighbors. They were warm, gregarious, and fun. They had four young children with whom our two boys quickly became playmates. Nearly every day, all of the children gathered either at my house or Dee's to play.

One rainy weekend night here was nothing going on at the club, so we settled in for a quiet evening at home. After the boys were in bed Joe went into the kitchen to make us a cocktail before our candlelit dinner for two. But he came back out and said, "There isn't a thing to drink in the house. We're out of everything." We both sat there a moment, contemplating our plight. Suddenly Joe jumped up and said, "I know! Let's open that bottle of red wine that Monsieur Vuerings gave us for a welcoming gift."

The label read *"Banyuls, Produciado en España."* It was a deep red Spanish port. We were doubtful as Joe poured the two glasses, but our eyes widened as we savored the first taste—it was delicious. Ever afterward we picked up a bottle whenever we could find it. It was rather hard to find, but through the years we never forgot our first, delectable taste of Banyuls that rainy night in France.

We hired a household helper, Monique, a bright and pretty young woman, so we could start doing some traveling. She was dark-eyed, with beautiful long, black wavy hair. She loved Joey and John, and played with them, and taught them French words and songs. She made them laugh, and they grew to love her.

The two of us made a trip to London, leaving the boys with Monique. The trip was an exciting experience, seeing the House of Parliament, London Bridge, the Tower of London, many other historical sights, and the musical *My Fair Lady*, on the London stage.

Shortly after the London trip the boys and I went with Joe to Garmisch, Germany, where he was assigned for a special training. Although it was still fall, snow had already fallen in Germany. The snow-covered villages and the surrounding mountains looked like scenes from beautiful picture postcards. While Joe was in class I took Joey and John on the cable tram ride up the Zugspitz Mountain. We strolled in the little village of Oberamergau, where the Passion Play takes place every ten years. We were thrilled by the European countryside during the car trip to Germany and back home. And soon after the trip Joe and I learned, much to our joy, that a baby was on the way. We were both hoping very much for a girl.

Mimi and our family were invited to Paris for Thanksgiving to join the family of my youngest uncle, Philip. A gifted artist, he had remained there at the end of his U.S. Army service in World War II. It was a grand opportunity for him to study art in Paris while working for NATO as a Department of the Army Civilian. Just five years older than I, he was like a brother to me. He had married a French lady named Janine, and they lived near the Bois du Bologne with their two children.

An hour or so after our arrival at their home, I was helping Janine in the kitchen. She said to me, "I must tell you, I was dreading meeting you and Joe, and your children. Most Americans I have met are loud, rude, and their children are little monsters."

I was shocked. Somehow it seemed like an unfair assessment of Americans, but I was learning that hers was a very common impression among French people about Americans and their children. We had quite a pleasant visit with Philip and his family. I was pleased that our two little boys had probably improved Janine's opinion of American kids.

The rainy season in France started in full force during the holidays. Endless weeks of grey, cold rainy days were upon us. The pilots often had to go to "sun bases" throughout Europe and North Africa to get their flying and training requirements accomplished. I became increasingly thankful for the Pennekamps next door, for the friends at the base, and for the base itself. We had no telephones and no TV, so we had to learn to rely on our own resources to stay connected and in touch. Monsieur Vuerings had one of the few phones in the village, and he told us to always feel free to use it should the need arise.

I learned to fill the furnace in the basement with coal each night when Joe was away. First, I shook all the "clinkers" out, so that air could flow freely up through the bottom. Then I poured buckets of coal into the furnace, filling it to the top, so that we would have heat through the night and hot water the next morning. Then in the morning I repeated the process so that we had heat and plenty of hot water for the day. I felt a little like a pioneer woman, capable of taking on many of her husband's chores during his absence.

Mimi came from Paris on the train to Laon occasionally. The Pennekamps and their children became very fond of her, and we often got together when she visited. Their children and ours loved the entertaining way Mimi told stories to them. She had a bright green net "fairy godmother" costume, which she kept at our house, and when she came to visit she would don her costume and entertain all the children for hours at a time. They would sit wide-eyed and fascinated as she dramatized some of the children's fairy tales, changing voices for the different characters in the stories.

Several months after our arrival, the runway at Laon Air Base had to be repaired, so the planes and a few pilots at a time were sent TDY (Temporary Duty) to Toul-Rosiere, a base west of the town of Nancy, to continue getting in their flying requirements. The arrival of our new baby was a few weeks away when Joe left on one of these TDY's to Toul-Rosiere. Patti Davey, whose husband Tom was in Joe's squadron, came out to St. Gobain to stay with me in case the baby arrived before Joe's return. One evening one of the other pilots in the 17th came to the door with a gift from Joe. It was a very large, gorgeous copper urn Joe had bought while on a flying assignment to a "sun base" in Morocco a few days before. He had put it in his friend's cockpit and asked him to deliver it to me for our seventh wedding anniversary, April 19, 1960. It was a beautiful surprise, and it touched my heart very deeply. It remains a striking piece in the entryway of our home.

The next evening after we had put Joey and John to bed, Patti and I were sitting in the living room when I said, "Patti, I think it's time to go to the base hospital."

Patti, not yet a mother herself, became quite anxious, but I was sure we had plenty of time. My suitcase had been packed, and our helper Monique was prepared to stay with the two boys on short notice. She was a very calm, capable young woman, and I knew that Joey and John would be fine with her.

Patti drove me to Laon Air Base Hospital, and I checked in. She asked the doctor if she should call my husband at Toul-Rosiere.

"You can call him," Doctor Nielson said. "But tell him not to get excited. We've got plenty of time."

Patti called Joe and told him exactly what the doctor had said. Joe later said that he went to bed after the call, but was lying there with his eyes wide open until, finally, at 1:00 a.m., unable to stand it any longer, got up, threw on his clothes, tossed a few things in a bag and jumped in his car. He drove all night in his Volkswagen back to Laon, arriving just half an hour before I was wheeled into the delivery room. I was overjoyed to see him when he walked into the labor room. Exhausted, he sat in the chair by my bed, trying not to doze off, until I told him, "Go get the nurse, Joe."

It was time. Dr. Nielson was head of the OB-GYN department at Laon. He was a big, handsome, kindly young doctor whom I had not met previously. The delivery of our beautiful daughter, Lesley, went well. I was overjoyed that we now had the girl we'd hoped for... Lesley Augusta Guth, born at 6:26 a.m., April 21, 1960. She was given my grandparents' last name, Lesley, and Joe's mother's name, Augusta.

One of the nurses was taking care of the baby when I became aware that something was wrong. It was a familiar scene as the other nurses and the doctor had suddenly become very intense. Dr. Nielson was kneading my abdomen and issuing brisk orders to the others in the room. I felt someone give me a shot. I began to feel weaker, and I felt like I was getting sleepy. Dr. Nielson's big hands continued to knead my abdomen, harder and harder it seemed, until finally I drifted off.

I was in the hospital room when I awoke. Joe was standing there holding my hand, his face filled with anxiety. Dr. Nielson said, "You really scared me in there. You started bleeding so fast... no matter what I did I couldn't get it to stop."

It was uterine atony again—the same thing that had occurred at John's birth. For some reason my uterus just didn't "clamp" after giving birth. With the injection of the medication and the kneading, the situation had again been brought under control. The doctor stayed a little longer, and then he shook Joe's hand, said he'd be back, and left the room. Joe sat in the chair by the bed, holding both my hands. The nurse brought Lesley in and placed her in the bassinet by my bed. Joe and I looked at our beautiful little daughter with pride and happiness.

"She's really cute," Joe commented, touching her dark hair. "I'm really glad we got a little girl like we wanted." But then his voice softened, "Dr. Nielson really scared me when he told me what had happened to you, Gil."

"I'm fine now. He said everything will be fine," I assured him.

After a while he stood up, kissed our baby girl gently and turned to me, "Get some rest now, Toots. I'll be back later. I love you." He leaned over, kissed me, and quietly left the room.

The baby and I were kept in the hospital for a week, until the doctor felt certain that everything was okay. We had the "rooming in" routine which meant Baby Lesley was kept in a crib by my side during the day, and taken to the nursery at night. It was wonderful to be able to touch her and feed her, and a nurse was always available to lend a helping hand. Joe brought Joey and John to the window of my room the next day so they could see their little sister, since children were not allowed in the hospital. They gazed at her as I held her up to the window, showed them her tiny hands, her little feet. They thought it was funny when she yawned or made little baby faces.

She's beautiful, I thought. "You're going to grow up to be a beautiful woman, sweetheart," I whispered to her as I held her.

Dr. Nielson dropped in several times a day. He admitted, "I've been having nightmares about a woman giving birth, and then starting to bleed so fast, and I'm unable to do anything to stop it. I don't think I'll ever forget how frightening that was."

Finally the day arrived for Joe to take Lesley and me home. While I had been gone the first bursts of spring and regrowth had arrived in the French countryside. The apple trees in our front yard were bursting with glorious blossoms. Dee Pennekamp had cut some of the branches and put them in vases all over our house. I felt that I was being welcomed home by the joy of nature, friendship, and love.

Monique ran out to the car to greet us as Joe helped the baby and me out of the car. Joey and John were jumping up and down with excitement and delight. I handed the baby to Monique, and it was obvious that it was love at first sight.

"Leslee," she said softly. From that moment on, Lesley became Monique's baby… nurtured, played with, showered with the love and care that Monique would have given a child of her own.

A few weeks after Lesley's birth we gave a big party to celebrate her christening. In addition to our friends from the 17th Squadron, the Pennekamps were there, and Philip, Janine, and Mimi came from Paris. Mimi's gift to Lesley was a beautiful handmade christening dress and cap, made in Paris. The French spring weather brought everything into bloom, and the joy of the occasion filled the little house at Number 5 Rue de Laon.

The tranquility didn't last long. The following week, one of the pilots in the 18th Squadron, Park Baker, was killed on a midnight flight at Toul-Rosiere. His wife, Martha, was eight months pregnant with their third child. Dr. Nielson went to her home to check on her, and commented that he couldn't hear the baby's heartbeat. He was concerned, but told Martha that it was not unusual for a baby sometimes to be positioned in a way that the heartbeat was not audible. Martha's household belongings were packed up two days later, and she and her two little boys, ages seven and four and a half, started their trip back to the States. A squadron wife named Terry Snell, who was a nurse and midwife, was sent along to accompany Martha and monitor her condition. They stopped at Ramstein Air Base, Germany, where she was checked over again before continuing on to the States.

Upon her arrival in the U.S. she was sent directly to Walter Reed Army Hospital. It was determined that her baby was dead, and they recommended that she remain in the hospital there. However, she was determined to attend Park's funeral in Youngstown, Ohio, and insisted on continuing, promising to enter the hospital immediately following the funeral, which she did. Their baby was buried next to Park a few days later. We were all shaken when we got the news of these events. First, a young mother of two children losing her pilot husband, followed by the loss of her baby immediately afterwards. It was yet another reminder of how fragile the life was that we were leading, and how disaster could overtake our idyllic lives at any time.

We coped by not allowing ourselves to dwell on the specter of possible death that hung over our lives. If we had not been able to block it out, I wonder if any of us could have endured the uncertainty and the fear. That unwritten protocol kept the wives from even hinting about our anxieties to each other.

A few months later Joe was assigned to lead the American 66th Tactical Reconnaissance Wing's team in the Royal Flush VI competition, to be held at Beauvechain, Belgium. It was a NATO competition, and involved British, German, Norwegian, French, Belgian, and American flying teams, one group from the north of Europe, the other from the south. Known as "The Olympics of Photoreconnaissance," the competition was scheduled for May 15 to 17, 1961. But Joe, the other four pilots, the support staff, and the maintenance crews assigned to Royal Flush began training months before. It was necessary for every one of the thirty-four individuals on the American team to train and increase the speed and efficiency in the delivery of his part in the total effort.

And then we had some more happy news: right after Joe was assigned to Royal Flush VI we learned that our fourth child was on the way. We were told early on that, because of my history of uterine atony, I would be sent to the large Air Force hospital at Chateauroux when it came time for the baby's arrival. By plane, Chateauroux was several hours away from Laon Air Base. I would be flown there by an Air Evacuation plane about a week before the baby was due, and would remain there at least a week after the baby arrived, since there was only one Air Evac flight each week. It was a policy at smaller base hospitals throughout France that first-time mothers and women who had had complications of any kind with previous births would be Air Evacuated to Chateauroux.

We thought it would be nice to have a second girl, so "Lesley would have a playmate," as Joe said. However, in 1961 there was no way to pre-

A CARTOON OF JOE AS LEADER OF ROYAL FLUSH VI TEAM STATIONED IN FRANCE.

dict the sex of an expected child, so we knew that, boy or girl, this baby would complete our family, and we were delighted.

So Joe and his Royal Flush VI team started their intensive training and preparation for NATO's "Olympics of Photoreconnaissance." Joe was full of enthusiasm and pride in his team. A born competitor and leader, he seemed energized by the prospect of meeting the best of the best from the other nations of Europe. I was engrossed in my role of Air Force wife and mother, as well as in the social life of Laon Air Base, which was continuing at full speed in spite of the frequent absences of the pilots. Joey was now in first grade, John was happily playing with his little Pennekamp friends, and baby Lesley was thriving.

Since the village of St. Gobain was only twelve miles from Laon Air Base, the 101 Voodoos frequently flew over our house. When we heard a plane's roar that was louder than usual, we knew it was Joe flying over. The kids and I would run outside, look up, and very quickly the plane would return, fly right over us and dip its wings as it roared by. We always knew that it was Joe flying by to say hello.

"It's Dad, there's Daddy!" the two boys would shout, waving and pointing up to show their little sister, "Lesley! That's Daddy that flew by!" In reply, little Lesley would point up and shout, "Daddy!"

It was always a thrill, and Joe took some reconnaissance photos of our house from his plane.

Most of the school teachers at Laon were single young women. They reminded me of Joan and me and how our lives had been at Williams Air Force Base, just eight years before. Joey's teacher was Miss Shirley Metzger, a lovely young woman, well liked by everyone. She and John Stavast, one of the pilots in the 18th Squadron became an item, and all of us were delighted about their romance.

One day we learned that the Pennekamps would be leaving France. John Pennekamp had been assigned to Germany to become a general's aide-de-camp. I was devastated upon hearing the news. Dee and I had become very good friends, and our children had grown to love playing together. Dee and John, and Joe and I had spent many happy hours enjoying each other's company out in our isolated little French village. But this was a great career move for John, so Joe and I decided that the gracious thing to do would be to celebrate their good news with them and throw a big farewell party in their honor. They were a very popular couple, and had many, many friends. We had a black satin flight jacket especially decorated for John with mementos of his career at Laon emblazoned on the front, back, and sleeves. We gave Dee a beautiful piece of Steuben glassware to add to her collection. The evening of the party came, and our house was packed with well-wishers, pilots and their wives, the base priests, Monsieur and Madame Vuerings, and a few other French friends of the Pennekamps. It was a grand party, but the downside of course was that they would soon be leaving.

The question of what our new neighbors would be like frequently entered my mind. I prayed that they would be compatible, since living in such isolated conditions made it vital that neighbors help and support each other. My hope also was that they would have young children for our kids to play with.

My prayers were answered by the arrival of Connie and Garland Page and their four sons. The three eldest were all older than our boys, but their youngest was just John's age. So John had a newfound playmate, and Joe and I quickly discovered that Connie and Garland were, like the Pennekamps, warm, friendly, and outgoing, always willing to be of help, and always ready to socialize.

With Joe often gone with the Royal Flush team, I was relieved that Connie and Garland were nearby. Connie and I visited often, and occasionally went to the base or to the surrounding villages together.

After months of preparation, the Royal Flush VI teams were finally ready for the competition in Beauvechain, Belgium. Joe was excited about the readiness of his team. He felt that they were well prepared, and was confident that they would do well.

But unfortunately, the Americans suffered a heartbreaking, very narrow defeat. "Extenuating circumstances" were described as a factor. This was of little consolation to Joe, as he was not accustomed to defeat. In fact, he was so accustomed to being a winner in everything he undertook, he handled losing very poorly. He had wanted this victory with all of his being. Now back home, he was trying to cope with the disappointment.

"We should have won. We were so close!" he exclaimed. I knew that there was little I could say to console him. He was very quiet for several days after they returned. I understood from past experiences that he was trying to reconcile in his own mind what had happened, trying to recover his sense of confidence and move on from the crushing disappointment of having been so close to victory. His way of doing it was to quietly work through it on his own, drawing on his own resources to help him return to his usual, ebullient self. All I could do was love him, and leave him alone.

A month later, the time for the arrival of our new baby was approaching. I was told to get ready for my Air Evac flight to Chateauroux. Monique would be staying in the house, since Joe still came and went frequently. So I packed my bag, talked with my boys about "being nice to their little sister Lesley," shopped at the commissary for an ample supply of food, and got ready to go. The morning of my flight, Joe drove me in to the base, took me to the flightline, and we stood saying goodbye. There were two other women there, both great with child as I was, waiting to board the plane, saying goodbye to their husbands. I tried to smile, and told Joe, "Next time you see me I'll be skinny again, and we'll have a new baby!"

His face serious, Joe said, "I'll be worried about you. I'll call you every evening to see how you're doing." And then it was time for me to board the plane. Joe put his arms around me, pulling me as close as he could, and kissed me goodbye. "Take care of yourself, Toots. I'll call you tonight."

Upon our arrival at Chateauroux several hours later, we were taken to our ward in the hospital where several of us shared a very large room, completely surrounded by windows. It was bright and airy, and we each had our own bed, dresser, and privacy curtain. The Base Exchange was just across the street from the hospital, so during the day we were free to go there, to the library, or to walk about the base. We were expected to return to the hospital for meals and for doctor appointments, which were frequent. The nurses kept pretty close watch over us, and we knew that they would be there for us should we need help at any moment.

Joe called every evening before he left Laon Air Base to go home to St. Gobain. After I had been there exactly a week, with still no sign of the new baby, I worried that I might have to miss the following week's Air Evac flight back to Laon. Joe called that evening, and I could tell that he was getting concerned about my length of time there as well.

However, as luck would have it, the time for the baby's arrival came right after Joe's call. I checked myself into the maternity ward that evening, and our third son, Daniel Raymond Guth arrived at 9:30 p.m., June 28, 1961.

I touched his soft cheek and kissed him. He was a beautiful, dark-haired, chubby baby, the picture of health.

"Lesley and I will have to hold our own, Dan, with you three boys plus your Dad," I told him. Daniel was a name Joe and I both liked, and the middle name, Raymond, was after Joe's father's brother, Uncle Ray. The uterine atony had occurred again, but they were ready for me, and the problem was quickly brought under control. I was wheeled into a semi-private room, and the baby was taken to the nursery for the night. The hospital used the same "rooming in" routine that I had experienced before, allowing the new baby to be kept with the mother during the day and returned to the nursery at night. It was wonderful to get a sound, uninterrupted sleep every night.

Joe called the next morning, and was astonished when the nurse told him that his son had arrived the night before. He was connected to my room, and said, "I just had a feeling I should call this morning. What a surprise! How are you? How do you feel?"

"I feel fine, Joe. It happened again, though."

I heard him gasp slightly over the phone, and for a moment he didn't say anything. "I wish I could see you. Are you sure you're all right?"

"Yes, I am," I assured him. "They really take good care of us here. The doctors and nurses are great. It's very comfortable, and even the food is good! And you should see little Daniel. He's so cute! He looks like the Gerber baby in the ads for baby food."

"I can't wait until you get back. I'll call you this evening. Give him a kiss for me. And take care of yourself."

We promised to talk every evening, and then he hung up. It was going to be a full week before I could get the Air Evac flight home. Daniel was a very healthy, happy baby. He seldom cried, and got a lot of attention from the nurses, who thought he was so cute. I was up and around in a few days, anxious to get back home. But I had to wait the full week, until finally it was time for little Dan and me to board that Air Evac flight back to Laon. I was pleased that I was able to wear one of my favorite cotton dresses home.

One of the nurses told me as I was leaving the hospital, "If it weren't for the baby in your arms, no one would ever know that you had just given birth!" I beamed at her, very happy that I could keep my promise to Joe that I'd be "skinny again."

The Air Force vehicle was waiting outside the hospital to drive us to the flightline. After the flight of several hours, we finally landed at Laon Air Base. Gathering up the diaper bag, Baby Daniel, and my purse, I left the plane and walked into the boarding lounge where Joe was standing, smiling. He came toward me, grinning broadly, his arms outstretched. He took the baby from me, and holding Daniel in one arm, he put the other arm around me and pulled me close to him.

"I'm really glad to see you, Toots," he said softly. We stood holding each other, our little son between us. Then Joe took us out to the car.

We hugged again, and I murmured, "I'm so happy to be with you again!"

He held the baby and helped me into the car, and then gently handed the tiny bundle to me. I was so glad, so relieved to be back.

When we arrived home, Joey and John ran out to meet us. We went inside to the living room, and I sat on the couch, holding Daniel for his brothers to see. Monique brought Lesley in, who was just beginning to walk by herself. She ran on her tiptoes over to me, and I showed her our family's latest addition, her baby brother, Daniel. She touched his little feet, his hands, and tried to pat his head. Joe and I told the three children how Daniel must be treated very gently. Monique stood nearby, smiling.

"Oh, *Daniel*, what a nice boy." She took him under her wing at that moment just as she had taken Lesley fourteen months before.

Monique had placed flowers all over the house. Connie Page from next door came over bringing food, and stayed for a moment to admire our new little son.

"He is so sweet, Gil!" she exclaimed. "I think he looks like you!" I was pleased by her words. Our other children had a very strong resemblance to their father. It was nice to hear that one of the four might look a little like me. I put the baby down in his bassinet and Joe escorted me into the bedroom to rest. I was very, very tired. And I was very, very happy.

A few weeks later, Joe was away on an overnight training mission. I was in the kitchen warming the baby's bottle, when the doorbell rang. Monique went to answer it. She came to the kitchen and said, *"Madame, Il y a deux père à la porte."*

"Madam, there are two priests at the door."

* * * *

Chapter Eighteen

AU REVOIR

My heart was pounding as I walked slowly out of the kitchen toward the front door. A dozen memories flashed through my mind: Pat Petersen being escorted into the chapel at Komaki, pale, and all in black; Billye Jenkins turning to me in the living room of her house and crying out in anguish, "Gil... Bob!"; Mary Willerford traveling across the country with her three small children, alone, a widow at age twenty-five; Claire Pribble looking out the kitchen window of her home at Cherry Point and seeing that column of black smoke. By the time I got to the door I was shaking. I saw Father O'Neil, the base chaplain, standing there with a visiting priest at his side.

"Hi, Gil. We're looking for the Pages' house. We're invited there for dinner."

I felt my knees go weak as I leaned against the wall. "Oh, Father," I murmured, and slid to the floor.

"Oh, my God, her husband's a pilot!" Father O'Neil exclaimed. "I'm so sorry, Gil. I forgot. I'm so very sorry!"

The two of them helped me to my feet. Attempting to regain my composure, I pointed out the Pages' house next door, and assured them that I was all right. Still apologizing, they turned to leave. I returned to the kitchen, still trembling. Monique had poured me a cup of tea. Without saying anything, I sat down at the table, and with a shaking hand, took the cup from her. She didn't say a word, but bent to kiss me on the forehead.

She took the warmed baby bottle and went to the baby's room to feed Daniel. I sat there for a few minutes, staring out the window.

"I can't let this get to me," I thought. I knew that if I dwelled on it and let myself think about all the dangers and all the possibilities I would fall apart. I had learned how not to imagine an airplane disaster happening to us. I had no plan for such an event, because I just didn't let myself think about it. I had almost convinced myself that Joe was as invincible as he believed himself to be. I told myself that Father O'Neil's mistake was nothing more... just a mistake. I wasn't going to tell Joe about it when he returned from his flight the next day. But when he got home that evening he told me that Father O'Neil had gone to see him right after he landed that day. Father told him what had happened, and apologized profusely for the scare they had given me. I've never forgotten that cold fear that I felt that day as I walked from the kitchen to the front door of our house in St. Gobain.

Joe's parents came to France to visit when Daniel was six weeks old. They hadn't seen their two new grandchildren, and they were thrilled to meet Lesley and tiny Daniel for the first time. We had a christening party for the new baby, and introduced Joe's folks to all our friends. Joe's dad played with Joey and John every day, had "jumping contests" with them, and took them for walks in the village. His mother loved helping take care of her little granddaughter Lesley and new baby Daniel. We took the folks to Switzerland and to Holland with the two older boys, leaving Lesley and Daniel with Monique.

We had many good times traveling with Joe's parents, and we wanted them to stay longer so we could take them to see more of the sights in Europe. But after three weeks they said they needed to get back. There was a house they wanted to buy in Florida, and they didn't want to lose out on the opportunity to get it.

I had to fight back tears as I hugged them and said, "I wish you didn't have to leave!" Having them with us in St. Gobain as our extended family had been so comforting and helpful. They were such warm, loving people. Now we would, once again, be on our own in this isolated French village, relying on our own resources to maintain family stability. Joe took Joey and John with him to drive his parents into Paris for their flight home from Orly Field. I stood at the door, watching as they pulled out of the driveway. Little Dan was in my arms and Lesley was standing close to me, waving and calling, "Bye, Grandma and Grandpa!"

A couple of months later Joe and I left the four children with Monique and Julie, a close friend of my mother. We went to the Oktoberfest in Munich. It was our first time alone in quite some time, and we enjoyed the time away and the robust, upbeat atmosphere of Oktoberfest.

Joe still left sometimes with the other pilots to fly at "sun bases," but Laon Air Base continued to be the center for our connection with our friends. As the holiday season approached, there were fashion shows, dinners, festive parties, and dances. Christmas of 1961 was our last Christmas in France.

We had adjusted to life in Europe pretty well, and thanks to Monique, I had become fairly fluent in French. She loved our children, and they loved her. She and I had become fast friends, and she and Joe got along very well. She tried to help him with his French, and the two of them would usually end up laughing at his attempts. Since his daily routine kept him at either Laon Air Base or some other American Air Force Base most of the time, he didn't have the exposure to the language that I had—living out "on the economy" in the French village and having Monique with us to help me rapidly improve my French. I knew that my life would have been very difficult without her.

For New Year's Eve we invited Philip and Janine for a quiet, at-home dinner, just the four of us. After the kids were in bed, the four of us got very dressed up—Philip and Joe in tuxedos, Janine and me in formal dresses. We had cocktails and hors d'oeuvres, and an elegant, candlelit dinner. It was a very special evening, and Joe and I followed that tradition for many New Year's Eves to come—usually with just the two us, dressed to the nines, celebrating at home alone.

Several weeks later Joe was studying to take the Graduate Record Examination, in preparation for applying to graduate school. He felt that it was time to start preparing for the day when his career would require a higher level of academic study.

The exam was to be held all over the world on the same date, including Paris. Philip and Janine invited us to stay with them in Paris, and to go as their guests to the ballet after Joe had taken the exam. We drove to Paris the day before the test, and the next morning Joe left very early for the all-day exam, which was being given in the center of the city. It was late afternoon when he returned, very tired after the long day. That night we went to dinner and the late performance of the world-famous Paris Ballet. Rudolf Nureyev had just defected to the West, and he was appearing that night to dance *Sleeping Beauty* with Dame Margot Fonteyn at the Paris Opera House. She was noted for her role as Aurora in *Sleeping Beauty*, and I was thrilled at the prospect of seeing these two great ballet stars perform. The Opera House was a beautiful, ornate, and elegant structure. The rows of seats, arranged circularly in front of the stage, were steeply tiered, so that sitting at a fairly high level, we found ourselves looking almost straight down at the stage.

I was absolutely spellbound during the performance. Glancing over at Joe, I saw Philip hanging onto him to keep him from tumbling out of his seat and down to the stage. He was so exhausted after the all-day exam, that he couldn't stay awake. Philip was trying hard not to laugh. Janine, like myself, was enthralled with the performance.

We left the next day to return to Laon, thanking Philip and Janine for their hospitality, urging them to come to see us soon in St. Gobain.

"I know the ballet must have been spectacular," Joe said. "Too bad I couldn't stay awake to see it!"

Several weeks later Joe came home with a letter from "USAFIT," the United State Air Force Institute of Technology. He had passed the GRE with flying colors, and had been selected to study for a master of business administration. He would be attending George Washington University, in Washington, D.C. It was a two-year program, but it would be completed in twelve months.

"It's a good opportunity to prepare myself for the remaining years in the Air Force," he said. "And it will be a plus for my career after I retire from the military." He was happy and excited about being selected for the program.

So in May of 1962, with our three-year tour in France drawing to an end, we started preparing to return to the States. Many of our friends were leaving also, so there were a lot of get-togethers and farewell parties. The day came when the moving van pulled up in front of the house, and the movers started packing up our belongings. The next day they returned to begin loading the van. It looked like the nightmare with the fridge was going to have to be repeated, but fortunately getting it down from the kitchen turned out to be easier than getting it up through the kitchen window had been, three years before. Some of our French neighbors again stood in the street watching the movers carrying out our belongings. Monsieur Vuerings came over with a lovely bottle of our favorite, Banyuls port, and told us, "One of your neighbors just said to me, 'Too bad they're leaving—such nice people!'"

I looked at Monsieur with amazement. Never, in the three years we lived there, had any of the neighbors stopped by to say hello, or chat, other than to respond to my greeting with, *"Bonjour, Madame."*

The task of loading the van was completed. Monique and I had done the necessary cleaning of the house, and it was time to go.

Monique said to me, in French, "Madame, if we never see each other again on this earth, we will meet again in Heaven."

Her words brought tears to my eyes, and we hugged each other tightly. We were both fighting back the tears. Joe hugged her goodbye, and she knelt to hug Joey, John, and Lesley one last time. I was holding baby Daniel, now one year old, and she reached out her arms to him to hold him once again. The station wagon had been sent on ahead. The six of us piled into the Volkswagen, with Joe in the driver's seat and me sitting beside him, holding little Daniel. Joey, John, and Lesley were in the back.

Monique stood there as we slowly drove away. I looked back and saw her running after the car, waving, trying to smile, calling out, *"Au Revoir! Au Revoir!"*

"Monique!" John cried, looking out the back window. She kept running, waving, until we turned the corner and she was out of sight. I have thought of her last words to me many times through the years. Just eight years before, we had said a similar goodbye to Mitsuko as we left Japan. We were now leaving another dear, devoted friend in France—a friend whom we probably would never see again.

* * * *

Chapter Nineteen

THE ENDURANCE TEST

None of us said much on the drive from St. Gobain to Laon Air Base. I knew that Joey and John were thinking about Monique, as I was. She had been like an older sister to them. She had treated Lesley and Dan like they were her own babies. She had been a wonderful friend to me, and Joe had become very fond of her as well. We would all miss her sense of humor and her lighthearted, cheerful ways. I hoped that the excitement of returning to the States would ease the pain of saying goodbye to her. Before we left I had written her a long letter, telling her how much we all loved and appreciated her, and had it translated into French.

Joe was intent on the long trip facing us, traveling with four young children from Paris to New York, picking up the station wagon, and driving to Washington, D.C. to begin his course of studies at the George Washington University School of Business.

We arrived at the base and pulled up to the Officers Club. Joe left the children and me, with all our luggage, in the lobby. As usual there were friends sitting in the comfortable, familiar surroundings. Pilots in their flight suits were in the nearby dining area having a quick lunch before going to the flightline for their afternoon take offs.

The kids and I waited there for Joe while he took the Volkswagen to the base auto shipping center, from where it would be sent to the States. He got a ride back to the club and joined us for our last lunch there.

Most of our friends at the club that day were, like us, preparing to depart for the States. It was good to see some of them one last time before leaving. Many of them were assigned to the same bases, to continue flying in photoreconnaissance squadrons. We were the only ones going to Washington for the MBA program. As we sat chatting about our various assignments, the realization hit me that we were not going to be stationed at an Air Force base—this would be a first. The familiar and secure surroundings of a base which we had grown accustomed to were to be exchanged for a year in a huge metropolitan area, living in a suburb, with no base connection. I tried to reassure myself about it: it would only be for a year, and really, our address didn't matter. What mattered was that we loved each other and that our family was together. I didn't know that we were facing a very stressful year, full of new and very different challenges.

I watched the two older boys visiting with some of their school friends after we had finished lunch. I reminded myself that children make new friends very quickly. But when the Air Force bus arrived to take us to Paris, I felt the sadness that always came when it was time to say goodbye. There were hugs, well wishes, and tears. Once again I was wondering if we would ever see these friends again. We left the club, piled into the waiting bus, and pulled away. Some of our friends were standing out front, waving to us.

We drove through the base, past the familiar spots that had been like part of home for three years, and went out the front gate.

It was a rough, bumpy ride to Paris. It seemed like the French bus driver was taking the turns on the small country roads on two wheels, and we felt like we had to hang on for dear life. Throughout the ride I was thinking of all the last-minute planning and preparations I had made for the kids, hoping I hadn't forgotten anything. I had resolved to make the trip go as smoothly as possible. We'd be traveling with four children under the age of eight, including an infant who was not yet walking. I had told the two older boys to pack their own "fun bags," with only as much as they could carry themselves. I'd packed a little bag of toys and books for Lesley, now two, and had assigned John, now six, to help her keep track of it and to entertain her throughout the trip.

Joey, not quite eight, was to be on hand to help his father with luggage and any unforeseen events, and to assist me with baby Dan when necessary. We had plenty of snacks, milk, food, and other baby equipment for Dan, and a change of clothes for everyone.

We arrived at the Orly International Airport terminal, checked in, and boarded a 707, the first of the huge passenger jet aircraft. We were all seated together, six across, Joe at one end, Joey next to his father, then John, then Lesley, with me in between her and Baby Dan. The baby was in my arms, or in Joe's, for most of the trip, but the seat assigned to him was handy for holding all his baby equipment and serving as a changing table for him. John helped entertain his little sister during the flight, and when she was napping, he and his brother Joey would read or play games together. Sometimes Joe or I would read to the kids, and sometimes all of us would doze off. Logistically, the long overnight flight went quite well, and Joe and I were both relieved and pleasantly surprised that there were no major difficulties.

Arriving at McGuire Air Force Base in New Jersey, the first order of business was to pick up the station wagon. The children and I waited at the terminal while Joe went to pick it up.

"I couldn't believe it!" he told us when he came back to get us. "I got into the car, turned the key in the ignition, and it started up! After being in storage all these weeks!"

We drove through Manhattan, amazed at all the sights: the towering buildings, the traffic, the noise, the hustle and bustle of American life. It was an overwhelming sight to us after our three-year stay in a tiny French village, with no American connections except at the fighter base near Laon. But it was good to be back in the States.

We stayed in New York overnight. We were all starving when we arrived at the hotel. The kids and I waited in our hotel room for Joe to go out and get hamburgers for all of us.

"This hamburger is the best thing I've ever tasted!" Joey exclaimed.

We rousted everyone early the next morning and started out on the drive to Washington, D.C. We went directly to the temporary apartment reserved for us in Springfield, Virginia, just outside Washington, and, exhausted, carried in our belongings. The long trip home was over.

Our friends the Pennekamps were living close by, and they saved the day with an invitation to a wonderful meal that night at their home. Their children and ours were overjoyed to see each other again, and it was comforting and fun to be with our good friends. They told us all about what it was like to live in the nation's capital. It was 1962, and the Kennedy administration was at its peak. It was an exciting time to be in Washington, D.C.

Joe's classes started two days later. Our "hold baggage" containing the minimal household necessities and a few clothes arrived, and we settled in as best we could in the sparsely furnished apartment. We were awaiting the arrival of our household belongings and the move into more permanent housing. There was no phone or TV, but fortunately we were used to being without these extras.

One day toward the end of Joe's first week of classes, a telegram came before he had arrived home. It was from his brother, Jack, in St. Petersburg, Florida. Joe's and Jack's parents had moved there right after retirement, just two years before. Jack was stationed near there at the time, with his wife and three children.

His telegram informed us that their dad had been taken to the hospital in St. Petersburg that day. He had been experiencing chest pains, but it appeared that he was resting comfortably. Since we had no phone in our temporary apartment, Jack's telegram suggested that Joe call him that evening for an update. I handed Joe the telegram when he walked in early that evening, and after reading it he said, "I've got to call Jack right away. I'll go down the street to the public phone."

He was gone just a few minutes. I was feeding the kids when he walked in. One look at his stricken face told me that something had happened. I stood up and went to him.

"Dad is gone. He died two hours ago." I put my arms around him, and felt him sob softly.

"I've gotta go there. I'll have to take a whole week to help Jack with Mother. I'll fly down tomorrow after I tell the dean I have to go."

That night we couldn't bring ourselves to tell Joey and John that their grandpa had died. We told them that he was very sick and that their daddy had to go to see him. We decided to wait until Joe got back to tell them, thinking it might be easier that way.

Joe left for the university early the next morning, and an hour later came back to get ready for his flight to Florida. He looked flushed and stressed when he walked in.

"The dean told me that I'll never be able to catch up if I'm gone a whole week, and that I might as well drop out of the MBA program right now. But I told him I have no intention of doing that. All he had to say to me then was 'Suit yourself.' He really pissed me off."

I watched him pack his bag, the stress of his grief and frustration lining his face. He shoved his clothes into the suitcase, tossed his shaving kit on top, and closed the lid.

"I'm ready. Let's go," he said. I drove him to Washington National Airport, and the kids and I watched him board the plane for Florida.

Driving home, I thought about his father, how much Joe had loved and admired him, how Joe used to love to tell us funny stories about growing up in his father's house. I thought about how his dad had played with Joey and John, had jumping contests with them, took them for pony rides. The last time we had seen his parents was a year before, when they had come to France for a visit. Joe's dad was only sixty-seven years old. The more I thought about it the more I realized what a major loss for our family this was. Joe had hoped to see his parents once we got settled and could invite them for a visit to Washington.

I stopped at a pay phone to call Dee Pennekamp, and told her what had happened. That afternoon, she drove up in her station wagon, her four children in the back.

"Come on over for dinner," she said. "The kids can play, and you can relax and have a drink and eat with us."

I was profoundly grateful for her thoughtful gesture, and was comforted by the Pennekamps' company that evening. Looking back, I realize what another strong demonstration of support within the Air Force family this was, totally unsolicited and unexpected.

While Joe was gone I tried to take the children to the pool in the apartment complex almost every day to escape the hot, humid days of Washington. Sometimes Dee brought her children over to swim, or we would go to her house for all of them to play together. As I watched them happily playing, I thought of how innocent and protected they were from the tragic side of life.

Joe returned after a week. He told me about his father's funeral, about his mother being in a state of shock and grief, how he and Jack did everything they could to help her settle her affairs in St. Petersburg. She had made the decision to move back to St. Louis where she had relatives and lifelong friends. Jack would be helping her with that, though he was facing a PCS move from the St. Petersburg area himself in the very near future.

We took Joey and John aside the next day, and Joe told them gently that their grandpa had died and had gone to Heaven. Joey's lip trembled as he absorbed the news. John looked at us intensely as he tried to understand the full meaning of what they'd just been told.

"Does that mean we won't see Grandpa anymore?" John asked, looking up at Joe and then at me. His question tore at my heart as I tried, as gently as I could, to explain that it meant that Grandpa was gone, and we would see him when we got up to Heaven ourselves. Joe appeared overwhelmed with emotion. He stood up, hugged each of the boys, and left to go start studying.

"Grandma is just fine, and she'll come to see us again soon," I told the boys. They both stood looking at me for a moment, and then turned to go outside to play. I realized that the concept of death was still beyond their comprehension.

Joe threw himself into making up the coursework he had missed. His class was made up of thirty-two Air Force officers, who met regularly as a group to discuss the program. They were to be responsible for passing the entire two-year course of study by taking the comprehensive examinations at the end of one year. They knew it would be impossible for them to attend all of the required classes. They divided themselves into eight study groups. Each study group was responsible for attending certain classes, taking notes and doing research on one-eighth of the one-year program. Periodically all thirty-two men would meet, and the leader of each study group would "brief" the others on the coursework and assignments of the class attended. Each man would meet individually with any member who was in need of extra assistance with a specific class. It was to be a totally joint effort. Their goal was for each of them to be awarded an MBA at the end of the one-year program.

We found a house to rent for the year in North Springfield, Virginia. It was on a quiet residential street which was inhabited mostly by military families—Army, Air Force, Marines, and across the street lived the commander of a Navy nuclear submarine and his family. Our house had a huge window in the second floor bedroom which we fixed up for Joe to use as his study room. The window overlooked the entire street, and Joe's desk faced out the window. Joe often studied well into the early morning hours. He became known as "the man in the window," since he was visible from anywhere on the block, almost any time of the day or night.

Joey was in third grade that year, and John was in first. I could watch them walk across the grassy field behind our house to the school, which was visible from my kitchen window and from the back porch. While they were at school I was busy with Baby Dan and little Lesley. When the older boys came home I tried to maintain a reasonably quiet atmosphere for Joe, who by late afternoon would have returned home from classes and gone into his study room, closed the door, and began studying until dinnertime. After dinner he was back to studying. I would clean up the dinner dishes, get the kids ready for bed, with baths, stories, and prayers. Joe would come out of his study to kiss each one goodnight, only to return to it again, studying until the wee hours of the morning.

As the weeks progressed, Joe's work became more and more demanding. He was getting less and less sleep, and in fact, he said later that he was surprised to learn that he could survive on less than three hours of sleep per night. In order to remain on flying status he got the required hours of flying time each month from Andrews Air Force Base, and kept up with the prescribed periodic check flights. He thus maintained the "minimums" required of all military pilots.

All this pressure began to manifest itself in Joe through a lack of patience, especially with the kids. I tried in every way I could to keep them under control and to maintain an even keel in the household. But the pressure began to wear on me, too, and at times I felt like I was hanging on by my fingernails, wondering if we could make it through the whole year.

One day while Joe was studying, Joey got in a big argument with John about something, and they each were insisting on having their own way.

I tried to get them to negotiate, but they started yelling at each other.

Joe came bursting out of his study room and down the stairs, shouting, "What's going on!?" Joey started telling him, in a high-pitched voice, what the argument was about. Joe grabbed him by the shoulders and pushed him up against the refrigerator and roared, "Let it go, Joe! Just let it go!" I hated the whole scenario. Everyone got very quiet. Then suddenly Joey was crying, John was crying, Lesley was crying, and Daniel started to wail.

Joe stalked out of the kitchen, saying, "I don't want to hear another sound out of any of you!"

I stood there with the four crying children, attempting to console them, telling them that their daddy was just tired and working hard at his studies. They were all very quiet as I put them to bed that evening after their prayers.

"I wonder if we'll make it through this year," I thought wearily as I lay in bed that night. I knew that Joe would be studying well into the morning. When he finally did come to bed, neither of us said anything about what had happened. But through the years Joe recalled that scene in our North Springfield kitchen, and said many times, "I'll never forget the look on Joe's face when I pushed him up again the fridge. I wish I hadn't done that."

Saturday evening was the one evening that Joe would knock off the studies and watch TV with the family until time for the kids to be read to and put to bed. Then he and I would have some time to relax with a drink, have dinner and talk, or watch a TV program together. One Saturday evening after the children had gone to bed, I told him, "Gee it's good to talk to someone over four feet tall!" We'd all go to church together Sunday morning, and then after lunch it was back to the books for Joe. I remember feeling at times that this was an endurance test, not only for Joe, but for me as well.

To compound the stress, it seemed like one or the other of the kids was always sick that year in Washington. I would take them to Ft. Belvoir Hospital and Dispensary a few miles away. In answer to my question about why they were getting sick so much the doctor told me, "You've just returned from France after three years of living in a totally different climate. We have different "bugs" here. It takes a while for kids, and adults too, to get used to the new surroundings and build up their immunities."

What he said made sense to me, so I continued taking whichever one of the kids had an ear infection, strep throat, or bronchitis for treatment at Ft. Belvoir, and was very glad we had a military hospital close by.

One rainy day the kids were all playing indoors, and Lesley fell on the coffee table and split open her bottom lip. Joe was home that day, and he rushed her to Ft. Belvoir, her lip bleeding profusely, while I stayed home with the three boys. He told me later that he held the poor little thing's feet down and a corpsman held her arms down while the doctor sewed up her lip.

"She was screaming at the top of her lungs. I'm sure he started stitching before the Novocain had taken complete effect!" he said, shaking his head. Little Lesley got a lot of comforting and attention from all of us that evening after her terrible ordeal.

That fall Catherine wrote me that Pop had gone into a nursing home. He had suffered a debilitating heart problem, and she knew he shouldn't be left alone while she was at work during the day. Something told me that I should try to get to Tucson to see him. I called Joe's mother in St. Louis, and asked her if she might like to come for a visit so I could fly out to Tucson for a week to visit my grandfather. I would take Baby Dan with me, so she would only have Lesley to look after during the day, until Joey and John came home from school. Gussie seemed grateful for the invitation. She was still grieving for the loss of her husband, Joe's dad. She said she would love to come and help out. She stayed for three weeks, and told us many times how glad she was to be needed again. While I was in Tucson, she cooked wonderful meals for the family every night, got Joey and John off to school in the morning, and took care of Lesley. She taught Joey and John some card games, and was always calm and loving to the kids. Joe and his mother had a good rapport, and the whole family loved having her there.

During the week I was in Tucson I went to the nursing home every day to visit Pop. Catherine also stopped in to see him every day on her way home from work, as did my other aunt, Carmel.

While I was in Tucson I also went to visit the mother of my childhood friend, Becky Jones Graves. Much to my surprise and delight, her mother told me Becky and her husband, Charlie Graves, were living in Annandale, Virginia, just a few miles from where we were living. Becky and I had been friends since I was nine and she was ten, and had been very close as children, like Joan and I had been. We used to tell everyone we were sisters. Becky's mother made us identical dresses, and we loved wearing them to school and trying to make everyone believe we were sisters. A lot of our friends were convinced that we were, even though she was short and blond and I was tall and dark-haired. I promised her mother I would contact Becky as soon as I returned to Washington.

One day in Tucson, Carmel mentioned how "Pop loves to be read to," so I started reading some of his favorite books to him: sea stories, fishing stories, *The Phantom Bull,* Sherlock Holmes, and others. While I was in college he had enjoyed reading some of my textbooks, especially my Humanities textbook. There were still a few of my books around the house in Tucson, so I took some of them to the nursing home and read those to him also. He loved seeing Baby Dan, and made him laugh with funny faces and noises. I was sorry that he couldn't see little Lesley, but I promised him I would bring her next time.

The last day I visited him before returning to Washington, I turned to leave his room, and looking back, I waved to him, and showed Little Dan how to wave to his great- grandpa. From his hospital bed Pop raised his hand in salute, and at that moment I knew that I would never see him again.

When I got back to Washington, Gussie stayed for another week. One evening I heard her crying in her room. I tapped on her door and asked, "Mom, are you all right?"

She stopped crying and said, "Yes, I'm fine, Gil. Thank you. Goodnight." It was obvious that she wanted to be alone. I knew she was grieving for her Joe, my Joe's father, who had died just four months before. During the day she was an inspiration to watch, always pleasant, always smiling, always ready to play with the kids and help with cooking or household chores. We all were sorry when it came time for her to return to St. Louis. We promised her that we would visit her as soon as the year in Washington was completed.

One day the following spring, I had put Lesley and Dan down for their naps. Joey and John were in school. Joe was home studying that day. Exhausted from the morning, I lay down and promptly fell asleep. A short time later Joe came into the room, and woke me gently by touching my shoulder.

"Gil, Catherine just called from Tucson. Pop died this morning." It took me a few moments to absorb what he had just told me. I couldn't believe that my Pop was really gone. Joe sat on the edge of the bed, holding my hand. "Are you all right?" he asked.

He held me for a few minutes, and then I said, "I'm okay Joe. I'll just lie here for a few minutes and then I'll call Catherine back."

He kissed my cheek and said, "Call me if you want me, Toots."

Getting up a couple of minutes later, I called Catherine, and she told me that the funeral would be held in two days. There would be full police honors, including a hundred-man police motorcycle escort through Tucson and out to the cemetery. It grieved me, knowing I couldn't go to Tucson for my grandfather's funeral.

"Don't worry, honey," said Catherine. "We'll take care of everything. Pop would understand that you can't be here."

After we hung up I put my head down on the kitchen table and cried, overcome with grief and loneliness. Joe came to the kitchen and put his arms around me. Neither of us said anything. We had both suffered heavy family losses within a few months of each other. I knew he was still grieving the loss of his father. We wordlessly comforted each other for a few minutes, and then he went back to his studies.

I talked with Catherine and Manny several times over the next few days. They described the honors paid to Pop by the Tucson police department. My grandfather was quite well-known in Tucson. He had played a role in the capture of mobster John Dillinger in the 1930s. Children growing up in Tucson during his years as a beat cop remembered how he escorted them across the street on their way to school.

I imagined the procession of police officers on motorcycles escorting the hearse through Tucson. Then the graveside ceremonies, very similar to military burials, including the twenty-one-gun salute and the playing of "Taps," with all the police officers standing at attention and saluting. Pop was laid to rest next to his wife, my grandmother, who had died eighteen years before.

Soon after returning from my visit to see Pop in Tucson I contacted my friend, Becky. A year after high school graduation she had married her high school sweetheart, Charlie Graves. He had gone into the Army as an enlisted man, gone through Officer Candidate School, picked up two master's degrees along the way, and was now about to be promoted to Lieutenant Colonel. He would retire some years later as a Brigadier General. He and Joe hit it off famously. Charlie, like Joe, was an avid handball player. Joe took a break from studies occasionally to play handball with Charlie, and we got together with them once in a while on Joe's night off on Saturdays. They had two children, a girl the same age as Joey, and a little boy Lesley's age. Our children played together when Becky and I got together during the day to renew our lifelong friendship, talk about our childhood, our high school days and some of the struggles and joys of growing up.

"Remember when we decided to be crime fighters, and put together costumes, complete with capes?" Becky laughed. "We used to put them on whenever we thought there was a crime to be solved and we had to look for clues."

We shared much laughter about this and many other youthful foibles, including our early adolescent crushes. It was wonderful having such long-time friends close by, and it helped me to fill the void caused by Joe's total immersion in his study program. To celebrate Charlie's promotion, they hosted an elegant party at their home. It was a happy, beautiful event—a lovely break in Joe's demanding schedule. And they helped us celebrate my thirty-third birthday on March 28, 1963, with a little party at their home.

I decided to take the children to see as many of Washington's points of interest as possible. Joey was now going on nine, John almost seven. I reasoned that the two older boys were old enough, hopefully, to appreciate and remember some of the nation's historical spots. So I'd pack up the car with snacks and baby supplies, drive the four of them into D.C., and, with Lesley and Dan both in the stroller, take them to the major spots: the Washington and Lincoln monuments, the Reflecting Pool, the Capitol, the White House and the other famous parts of the beautiful capital city.

After what seemed like an eternity, the graduate program was, at last, drawing to a close. Joe was working intensely on his thesis, attending classes, meeting with his study group, or with the entire class, for briefings on the courses required for graduation. I helped by proofreading and typing some of his papers. The day of the comprehensive exams came, and a few days later the scores were posted. To everyone's great relief and joy all thirty-two of the men in the class passed and would receive their graduate degrees.

One day shortly before graduation, Joe came home and said, "Toots, let's give a party for the whole class. It will really be a cause for celebration. Let's really do it up."

I agreed heartily, and a few evenings later our house was the scene of the joyful celebration of all thirty-two officers and their spouses. Everyone was in great spirits—the grueling year was ending, and they were to be awarded their MBA's.

The graduation ceremony was held outdoors, on a beautiful Virginia spring day. The bleak winter landscape had been transformed into lush green, with blooming fruit trees and bright flowers everywhere. The families and friends of the men were all seated near the outdoor stage. There were all ages—babies, children, spouses, parents, and even some grandparents of the graduates. Each of the thirty-two officers, in uniform, proudly received their diplomas. After each man's name was called, there were yells, whistles, and cheers. When their father's name was called Joey and John jumped up and shouted "Hooray for Dad! Yay Dad!" Lesley, following suit, jumped up and down and joined her brothers in shouting "Daddy! Hooray Daddy!" Even little Daniel, now two, joined his siblings and, trying to jump up and down, yelled "Daddy, Daddy!" The air was filled with the happiness and pride of that day.

Right after graduation all thirty-two men and their families prepared to scatter to the four winds to their new Air Force assignments. For us it was to be Hanscom Air Force Base, near Bedford, Massachusetts, in the Boston area. We packed up, cleaned the house, said goodbye to neighbors and friends, and left for Hanscom.

* * * *

Chapter Twenty

THE HUB OF THE UNIVERSE

Laurence G. Hanscom Field lies between Bedford, Lexington, and Concord, Massachusetts, near the very spot where the Revolutionary War of 1776 began. I learned that within walking distance of our house, the area was packed with sites of famous events of great historical significance.

On one of the local radio stations that I tuned into every morning, the announcer always began each broadcast by saying, "You are listening to station KBIX in Boston, the Hub of the Universe!"

It was June 1963 when we arrived there. American forces were being sent to South Vietnam as "advisors" to help stem the advance of the communist takeover from North Vietnam to the South.

After spending a week in base visitors' quarters, the moving van arrived and we were moving into what seemed like wonderful housing, with all the facilities and security of the base close by. Our apartment was a two-story end unit in a four-unit building. The buildings were pretty close together, but in the back was a large grassy area with playground equipment for the residents' children. The three bedrooms were upstairs, and we situated the three boys in the largest one, with Lesley in the tiniest of the rooms facing the front of the house. Joe built a divider between the living room and dining room. It was a solid wood screen on which we hung some of the artwork we had collected in our travels. There was a full basement in the house, which Joe divided into a woodworking shop for himself and a play area for the kids. In the third section of the basement he insulated the walls, installed wood paneling and carpeting, and added comfortable furniture. This served as our family TV room.

For the first time in his Air Force flying career Joe's primary assignment was not as a jet pilot, except for the year in Washington. He maintained his flying status at Hanscom by getting his required time and check rides accomplished, but his assignment, in "materiel procurement," was based on the fact that he had just completed the master of business administration program. He enthusiastically delved into his new duties, eager to use the new skills which he had just acquired at George Washington University. However, he looked forward every month to his time spent flying, taking check rides, or engaging in other aviation-related duties.

"I know I won't be a jet pilot for the rest of my life," he said, "but I'm going to keep flying as long as I can."

He was beginning to prepare himself for his entry into civilian life, which at this point was six years away. He was now thirty-nine.

Our neighbors all had children close to the ages of ours. The kids quickly found new friends to play with, either indoors during bad weather or in the grassy area behind the house, where they could be watched from the kitchen window.

Soon it was time for school to start. Young Joe was going into fourth grade, John into second. Lesley was now three, and Daniel was a chubby, happy two-year-old. The base school was just two short blocks from our home, and we soon found out that academically the school had a more challenging curriculum than the boys were used to. Joey especially seemed anxious about how far behind he was in his classes. In the evening Joe would help him with his math, and I would assist both boys with their spelling and English homework. Young Joe was becoming a very good student, and was quite serious about his schoolwork. Though the school was close by, John's grade had to be bussed to another location on the base, due to overcrowding at the main school. John was always the first one up in the morning, because his bus came by for him very early. Though he was only seven years old, he would make his own sandwich for lunch and get himself out the door in time to catch his

JOE RECEIVES AIR FORCE COMMENDATION MEDAL; GILBERTA AND SONS ATTEND CEREMONY.

bus. We were proud that at such a young age John was demonstrating such independence and resourcefulness.

In our building lived two little girls who became Lesley's and Danny's playmates. Their mother, Mary Margaret, and I had what we called our "playschool." They would play at our house, or Lesley and Dan would go to their house to play almost every morning. The four of them would have lunch together, and then would go to their own home for their afternoon naps.

I became active in the Hanscom Wives' Club and in the Women's Sodality at Church. Young Joe was now old enough to go into training to become an altar boy. The base chaplain was a very popular, well-known priest, and he was a wonderful trainer in teaching the kids how to serve at Mass. Every Sunday morning would find the six of us getting ready to leave for church. Later on, when winter set in, the parkas, snowboots and warm caps added to the complexity of the operation.

"It was easier to move a whole squadron of jets to Europe than it is to get this family out the door in time for church," Joe commented.

Since Dan was only two, we left him at the base nursery during Mass that first year. After church, when we went to pick him up, he would be standing at the nursery window looking for us. He didn't like being left behind, and would let us know it by saying as he got into the car, "Leave me alone—I'm crabby!" He was much happier when, the following year, he was allowed to join us at church.

Danny gave us quite a scare one sunny day. I had been watching him play from the kitchen window with his little friend from across the courtyard, also two and a half. I turned for a moment to tend to something on the stove, and when I went back to the window he was nowhere in sight. I ran outside, looked all over the playground, and went to my neighbor's house. Neither of them could be found. The neighbors started to help look for the two little boys. I kept calling Dan's name. I was beginning to feel frantic. I called Joe at work. "I'd better call the AP's," Joe said, referring to the Air Police. "I'll be right home."

Joe and I and the parents of the other little boy went up and down the street, calling their names. The neighbors were looking everywhere. The AP's asked us what the two children had been wearing and began searching, going into the woods near our home, calling for them.

After an hour of growing panic, Joe and I spotted two little figures several blocks from our home. They were sitting in the middle of a mud hole close to the edge of the woods, happily making mud pies. They were covered from their hair to their feet with the gooey mess.

"Dan!" Joe cried when we saw them. We were so relieved we had trouble hiding our smiles as we both ran over to them. Joe then yelled, "Get out of that mud! We've been looking all over for you! We even called the AP's to help look for you!" When Dan and his friend saw the uniformed Air Police getting out of their truck, their eyes widened, and they scrambled out of the mud hole, almost ready to cry. It was hard to be angry, but Joe said, "You ought to get a good spanking, young man! You're coming home with us right now!"

The AP's came over to express their relief that we'd found the children, and one of them said, "Don't you two ever wander off like that again!" The two little boys could only nod vigorously, murmur "Yessir!" and toddle toward home as fast as their little legs could carry them.

We took many excursions in the New England area. The Lexington Green, where the "Shot Heard Round the World" was fired, was located a short ride from our home. We took the kids there, and to a reenactment of the beginning of the Revolutionary War on the Old North Bridge in Concord. It is held every year on April 19, Patriot's Day, which was also the anniversary of our marriage. The participants were all in Minuteman and British "Redcoats" uniforms. The kids were awed by the marching and the exchanges of gunfire, which very realistically portrayed the drama of that historical event. Nearby Concord was filled with historical homes which had been occupied by Louisa Mae Alcott, Nathaniel Hawthorne, and other famous literary figures. And just blocks from our home was an ice cream stand which, it was claimed, was on the exact spot where Paul Revere had begun his midnight ride. During the summer months we walked there almost every evening for ice cream treats. It was an area rich in American history and literature— a wonderful learning spot for our school-age kids.

Driving up the New England coast to Maine on vacation, we became familiar with "rough and ready" lobster stands. The fresh-cooked lobsters cost $1.00 apiece, and there were always picnic tables available for sitting and enjoying the delectable lobster, fresh French bread, and coleslaw. The first time young Joe saw a red, cooked lobster, he said. "Ooh, I don't want to eat that big bug!" But his dad convinced him to try one bite, covered with melted butter. The moment he bit into it, his eyes grew large, and after savoring it, he said, "I'd like a whole one, please!"

Soon it was fall, and everything I had ever heard about the turning of the leaves in New England proved to be true. Near the base was Henry Thoreau's famous Walden Pond, and surrounding the pond were beautiful woods, which in the fall took on the glorious varicolored hues I had only seen in pictures. On Sundays we would pack a brunch of boiled eggs, cooked sausage, coffeecake, orange juice, and milk, with a thermos of coffee for Joe and me. After Mass we would drive to Walden Pond, choose a picnic table with the best view, and savor the spectacular beauty of the spot while we ate our breakfast. We cut some of the branches of gorgeous leaves, brought them home and brushed them with a mixture of glycerine and water to preserve them. I placed them in vases throughout the house, and they never lost their bright colors.

There were swimming lessons taught every summer at Walden Pond. Joey and John were both taught to swim there, and in future years would get a kick out of telling their friends that they learned to swim in Thoreau's Walden Pond.

On November 22, 1963, I had just risen from my afternoon rest and Rosary. Lesley and Dan were still taking their afternoon naps. Suddenly Joey and John came bursting through the front door.

"Mom!" cried Joey. "The President was shot! He's in the hospital! They told us about it at school!" "

Shocked, I rushed downstairs to the TV room and turned on the news. President Kennedy had just been pronounced dead at Parkland Hospital in Dallas. Joe came home a short time later. We hugged each other wordlessly. In disbelief, we watched the developments on the television. Like most Americans that dark November weekend, we sat glued to the TV, trying to absorb the enormity of what we were seeing and hearing. Joey and John sat beside us most of the time, asking for explanations as events unfolded. Lesley and Dan, still too young to fully grasp what was happening, quietly played at our feet.

The base appeared to be totally shut down that weekend. Everyone was in their homes, watching in horror the replaying, over and over, of what had happened in Dallas, the sorrowful hours of the procession through Washington, and the burial of our young president at Arlington National Cemetery.

By Monday morning we felt numbed by the intensity of the weekend events. Everyone was intent on trying to return to some semblance of normalcy. Joe returned to work, and I turned to my tasks of caring for our four children and providing for the family's needs.

My neighbors had schooled me in preparing for the New England winter. When the first snowfall came we were equipped with snow boots, hats, gloves, parkas, and, for the two youngest children, snowsuits. As winter set in, the snow began to pile up, and every night we heard the snowplows coming to clear the streets for the next morning.

"Please remove all vehicles from the street!" the drivers would announce over their bullhorns. Since little Lesley's room overlooked the street, she would hear the snowplows roaring toward our house in the middle of the night. The first few times she heard the sound, she was very frightened and woke up crying. Joe went to her and showed her out her window how the snowplow was clearing the snow away so that the cars could drive down the street the next morning. She gradually became accustomed to it. She always drew laughter from all of us when, in her deepest voice, she would imitate that voice on the bullhorn.

One week Joe was away and I forgot that he had left the Volkswagen parked on the street in front of the house. Remembering it the next morning, I went out front to move it, and it wasn't there. Looking closely, I saw a huge mound of snow right in front of our house. It was the Volkswagen, completely covered with snow, with not one corner of its bright orange color visible. The snowplow had done its job well the night before, clearing the snow from the street, but totally covering our orange Volkswagen. I had to wait for Joe's return for him to help me rescue our car from beneath that mound of snow.

As winter went on, it became more and more blustery. From the downstairs TV room we would watch as the ground-level windows became immersed in snow, and we could hear the wind and force of the blizzard outside.

The following year, 1964, the clouds of the war in Vietnam hung heavily over the U.S. Then the Gulf of Tonkin incident that year drew us further into the conflict, and the Vietnam War began to escalate. American forces were beginning to be deployed in larger and larger numbers. We started to hear of pilot friends who were being assigned there. By 1965, more and more pilots were being sent, and we began hearing about friends of ours who had been shot down, killed, or taken as prisoners of war. One of these was John Stavast, the 101 Voodoo pilot who had married our son Joe's first grade teacher, Shirley Metzger. He was shot down and taken prisoner just six months after their marriage. He was one of many who would be prisoners of war for close to six years. Others we knew were POW's for varying lengths of time. One of these was Bill Talley, who had been Joe's wingman on the flight of the

101 Voodoos to France. Another was Leo Thorsness, who had flown with Joe in Albany, Georgia and Puerto Rico. He had helped celebrate the night Joe walked away from the serious accident in 1956 while they were flying out of Ramey Air Force Base in Puerto Rico. All of their imprisonments were unbearably long and terrible. We learned that another pilot we had known in France, Ed Atterberry, attempted to escape from the prison camp, was caught, and was beaten to death.

It was beginning to look like every available U.S. pilot was being sent into combat in Vietnam, regardless of their current duty assignment. Everyone was anxious about the direction the war was taking. Joe was ripe for reassignment as a jet combat pilot, even though we had only been at Hanscom less than a year. I began to live in dread of him being sent to Vietnam. While I had full confidence in his flying ability, at age forty he was several years older than the average pilot and had not been "combat ready" for three years. I was haunted by terrible thoughts about his luck running out, of his being shot down, killed, or taken prisoner for an unknown number of years, maybe forever. I wondered if any of these thoughts were plaguing him, too.

I remembered what he had written to me just after he had been transferred from Korea to Japan:

> Believe me if I ever have the feeling that I'm not coming back I've taken my last airplane ride. I don't think there's enough rank in the Air Force nor enough money to get me into the plane when I didn't have the utmost confidence.

Our son Joe, now in fifth grade, was beginning to learn of world events in school and on the TV news. I'm sure he, and to some extent our other children, were aware of my great anxiety about their father. But young Joe was the one who began to exhibit signs of emotional stress. He became very quiet, and showed no interest in playing with his friends or his siblings. He spent a lot of time reading alone in his room. The level of anxiety I was experiencing must have been affecting my health, because I started having physical problems which I had never experienced before. That spring, my doctor told me that the only way to stop my physical symptoms was with a hysterectomy. I didn't want to schedule it because I didn't know what was going to happen—whether Joe would be assigned to fly in Vietnam or kept at Hanscom Field.

One day Joe came home and said, "I'm going to take a couple days off. I've got to think things through. I just want to sit quietly, and maybe read, and think about things."

He would get up at his usual time in the morning, shower and dress, eat breakfast, and sit in his lounge chair in the living room, reading, or just sitting quietly with his eyes closed. Sometimes he would go for long walks. He didn't want to talk, and I knew from past experience that when he was this preoccupied, the best way I could help him was to let him be, and not try to make conversation or ask questions.

I had no desire to visit with my neighbors or even go outside. It was as though we went into total seclusion for those next several days. Young Joe was very aware that something was wrong, and we learned later that he was beginning to imagine that one of us, Joe or I, had a terminal illness and didn't want to tell them. It was a terribly difficult time for all of us. I was ill with worry and anxiety, unable to eat, sleep, or think clearly.

Finally, one day Joe said to me, "I've decided what I'm going to do. I'm going to remove myself from flying status. Flying pay will stop, so I'll take a cut. But it's the only way to handle this. I want you to go ahead and schedule your surgery, and I'll take some time off to help you while you recover."

I was stunned by what he said. I knew of his love for flying—it had been his Air Force career and his whole life. I knew that in giving it up he would be letting go of that pride in being a military pilot that he had always treasured... the dream which he had accomplished with such great success.

In thinking about it later I realized that this decision of Joe's, which had been reached at such a high emotional cost to himself, demonstrated his deep love for me and for our children, probably more than anything else he had ever said or done.

I underwent the recommended surgery a few weeks later, and gradually my strength returned.

The war news was not good. We continued to learn of friends being assigned to Vietnam, of fatalities, of prisoners being taken. I knew that Joe's heart was heavy during those months, and that he was fighting mixed feelings about his decision. But he never whined or complained about it. The three-year tour at Hanscom was drawing to a close, and we were awaiting word of our next assignment, possibly our last, since Joe would become eligible for retirement in 1969.

And then orders came. It was to be Norton Air Force Base in San Bernardino, California. This would be Joe's first assignment as a non-flying officer. He still wore his pilot's wings, and did so until the end of his Air Force career.

*   *   *   *

Chapter Twenty-One

THE FINAL ASSIGNMENT

Before leaving Hanscom Field we bought a Starcraft camper trailer and a new Ford station wagon. We all spent the first evening we had the camper sitting in it, admiring it and talking about the fun we'd have traveling in it.

"Boy, Dad!" said Joey. "This is really neat!"

"This is going to be so much fun!" John declared enthusiastically.

Our plan was to take a month's leave and camp on the way west to Norton Air Force Base, visiting some of the national parks and interesting sights along the way.

The movers came and packed up everything except the clothes and other belongings we kept aside to go in the camper. We began cleaning up the apartment to pass the required base inspection. We'd been told about the tough inspection standards at Hanscom, and spent hours cleaning every nook and cranny, including the overhead lighting fixtures and the tops of the doorframes. After two days we'd finally finished the task and were sitting down to wait for the inspector.

"My God," Joe suddenly exclaimed. "Look at your hands!" I looked, and saw that they were red and wrinkled from the strong cleaning agents we'd been using. "Next time, we're getting a cleaning service!" he exclaimed. "Put some lotion or something on your hands. They're really wrecked!"

The inspector came, went through the apartment room by room, and signed off on the inspection report. Then there were the goodbyes to our neighbors and friends. This time our children were old enough to feel more of an impact in saying goodbye. They had known these playmates for three years. Some of the neighborhood kids watched as we pulled away in the new station wagon, towing the camper behind us.

Everyone was waving and calling "Bye! Have a good trip! Have fun!" I hoped that the excitement of camping and sightseeing across the country would help all of us be okay with yet another move; it was my eleventh.

Our first night out of Hanscom was the first night any of us, except Joe, had camped out. We stopped at a campground in New York State, all of us green and unschooled in the ways of camping with a family. In fact, it was almost like a comedy of errors as we bumbled through setting up the camper, cooking our first meal, and getting the kids into bed for the night. However, we quickly learned some of the do's and don'ts through trial and error, and after a few days we felt like we were getting pretty good at it. Everyone had their assigned duties when we would stop for the evening, always before dark. It was Joey's and John's job to open up the camper like their dad had shown them. Lesley and Danny gathered kindling for the campfire. I would get the supplies ready for the evening meal, and Joe would go about setting up our camp and starting our campfire. In the camper there was a small fridge for our perishables and a cupboard for non-perishable supplies. I cooked on the three-burner butane stove in the camper, and sometimes Joe grilled our meat or chicken on the portable barbecue outside.

The thing we liked most was the campfire that Joe would keep going during and after dinner. We'd all sit around it and sing, accompanied by Joe on his ukulele. We would roast marshmallows or tell stories until bedtime. We tried each day to stop at a campground that had shower facilities, laundromats, and nearby restrooms. Occasionally we would pull out to a roadside site just off the highway and settle in for the night.

Our first major stop was St. Louis, where we visited Joe's mother for a few days. We made her promise to visit us in California as soon as we got settled. Then on westward toward California, visiting points of interest along the way. It was a fun-filled adventure. Everyone was in good spirits as we traveled across the country.

One day we had just parked at one of the large campgrounds in beautiful Rocky Mountain National Park. Ten-year-old John left for the restroom while we were busy setting up.

After a while, noticing that he still hadn't returned, I asked, "Where's John?"

No one in the family had seen him since he left for the restroom. Joe and I looked at each other. We started searching for him, calling his name, asking people if they had seen a young boy in a blue shirt. Beginning to panic, Joe and I split up to go in opposite directions. I took Lesley and Dan with me. Joe took young Joey with him. After about an hour we found him, wandering through the campground, close to tears. He had taken one of the many turns in the area, and couldn't find his way back. When he caught sight of us he ran toward us, into our outstretched arms. We were so relieved to find him that we couldn't be angry with him. That evening all the kids listened with widened eyes as Joe gave them a lecture about not wandering off alone.

"You must keep Mom or me in sight at all times!" he told them firmly.

We stayed several days in Rocky Mountain National Park. I loved the clear air, the smell of the tall pines and the beautiful mountains. Young Joe was quite taken with the chipmunks which were everywhere. He took pictures of them, using up a full roll of film on nothing but chipmunks. Grand Canyon was our next important stop. The six of us stood taking in the grandeur of the world-famous place. Our PCS move had turned into a great travel adventure.

We went on to Tucson to visit my relatives. It was my first visit since Pop had died. The house felt very empty and different without his presence. I went into his room and saw on his dresser the picture of him with Joe and me being serenaded by mariachis in The Cave restaurant in Nogales. The memories of the fun we'd had that day flooded over me, and I knew I would always miss him.

It was good being in my hometown again, seeing my uncles, aunts, and lifelong friends.

It was mid-summer by then, and the Southwest was approaching its peak temperatures. Our first night out of Tucson we camped in Blythe, a border town between Arizona and California. It was so hot that sleep was impossible that night. After an entire night of tossing and turning, I woke Joe up before dawn and said, "It's so hot here! Let's get out of here!" We woke the kids, closed up the camper and got underway. Joe chuckled every time he told people how I rousted everyone before dawn and moved us on out of Blythe within minutes.

He seemed to relax on that trip west, and appeared to enjoy the interesting and picturesque sights we visited, and showing his children the many wonders of the outdoors. He spent a lot of time with the two older boys, teaching them the how-to's of camping, tending campfires, and barbecuing.

One evening as we were sitting around the campfire, Joe stood up and said, "I'm going to go look at the birds." Our son Joe got up and said, "I'm going to go look at the birds, too." John then said, "I'm going to go look at the birds too." Then little Dan jumped up and said, "I'm gonna go look at the birds, too!" Lesley stood up then and said, "I want to go look at the birds, too!" The boys all told her, "No, Lesley, you can't go—you're a girl!" It was obvious that her feelings were deeply hurt as she watched the four of them go off into the woods.

"They never let me do anything with them, Mommy," she said, her lip trembling.

"Les, honey, they don't mean to leave you out." I explained why she couldn't go with them "to look at the birds," telling her, "You and I can do a lot of things together that they can't or won't do." She seemed satisfied with the explanation. She gradually learned to hold her own very well with her three brothers.

Thirty days after leaving the Boston area we arrived at Norton Air Force Base. It was a blistering hot day. We parked the camper, checked into the visitors' quarters, changed into our bathing suits, and drove over to the Officers Club pool.

As we walked toward the beautiful, inviting pool, Lesley suddenly took off in a run and jumped into the deep end. Joe immediately went in after her. She had forgotten that she couldn't swim, and was so eager to cool off that she let her enthusiasm take over. Joe quickly pulled her out before she became frightened, however. She was always fearless in the water from that moment on. She became an excellent swimmer, and would eventually compete on her high school diving and swimming teams.

After the long hot trip across the desert, the Officers Club pool was a lifesaver that day. Our two eldest sons, having learned to swim at Walden Pond near Hanscom, took to the pool immediately. I took care of Danny in the shallow end of the pool and Joe looked after Lesley, teaching her the basics of swimming, or playing with the two older boys. As soon as possible after our arrival I signed all four of them up for swimming lessons at Norton for the rest of the summer. Joey and John were in the advanced classes, and by the end of that summer all four of them had become good swimmers.

Within a few days we found a house to rent for the three years we would be at Norton, and our household belongings were delivered. The house was in a suburb of San Bernardino called Highland, north of the base. It was 1966. Our son Joe was now twelve, John ten, Lesley six, and Dan five.

Joe's assignment was in materiel management and procurement. It was obvious that he missed flying very much. I began to notice that he occasionally was moody, or had sudden bursts of impatience, especially with the kids. The Vietnam War was continuing to escalate, and I knew that his thoughts were heavy as he watched the news. We continued to hear of friends who had been lost or taken prisoner. Also, since his resignation from flying status he had been losing his enthusiasm for the Air Force, and he was becoming more eager to retire and start over again in a civilian career.

"It doesn't have anything to do with you," he'd say after a mood or an outburst of impatience.

Even though I understood all the issues that were troubling him, I still found it hard sometimes not to take it personally. I reminded myself that our love for each other was the foundation of our life together. Fortunately, we were able to maintain a basic family stability in spite of his occasional moodiness and my sensitive nature.

The kids were all in school now—Dan in kindergarten, Lesley in first grade, John in fifth, and Joe in seventh, his first year in junior high.

John had started altar boy training our last year at Hanscom, and the two boys signed up to serve at Mass together at Norton. One day the base chaplain called and asked if the two boys could serve at a wedding Mass. They were both delighted, and very eager when that Saturday morning came and I drove them to the base chapel. They had a very nice surprise that day when the groom tipped each of them five dollars. Ever since then, they were always very willing to serve at weddings.

One particularly hot Saturday, however, young Joe fainted during the wedding—probably from the heat, combined with the lack of circulating air near the altar of the chapel. The priest had to stop the ceremony to carry him out, help him out of his altar boy garb, give him water and help him revive. Our son was very embarrassed, but Father Schreiter assured him, "Joe, just think how the bride and groom will have a special story to tell about their wedding—how the altar boy keeled over and had to be carried out."

Joe was promoted to Lieutenant Colonel while we were at Norton. He and a few other promotees gave a big promotion party at the club. I bought a special dress for the occasion: a short, shift style, with short sleeves, very pale pink cotton brocade, with a matching unlined coat. The evening event was grand, with cocktails, dinner, and dancing. We had a festive, memorable time. I sensed that to Joe it was also a celebration of the fact that he would soon be starting a new career as a civilian.

One day in early 1969, as the date of his decision whether to retire from the service drew near, Joe said, "Toots, I probably won't be promoted again. I'm thinking of putting in for retirement right away." He had never liked the politics and bureaucracy of military service, and we both knew that his voluntary removal from flying status had, in effect, finished his career as an Air Force officer.

"If I retire right away, I won't be quite forty-five yet, and I shouldn't have too much trouble going to work in some kind of business."

Without dwelling on what I knew must be his disappointment over the recent developments in his Air Force career, he put in for retirement at the earliest date of eligibility. With his usual indomitable spirit he set about making plans for his return to civilian life. We decided to settle somewhere in northern California. My mother was now living back in Tucson. She came to San Bernardino to take care of the kids while Joe and I took several trips to explore possible sites. We both loved the San Francisco Bay Area, and decided to build a house in the small city of Novato, north of San Francisco. Joe returned to Novato alone to find a lot, and selected one that was within walking distance of an elementary school, a junior high school, and a high school. Lesley and Dan would be in elementary school, John in junior high, and Joe would start his first year of high school, which was tenth grade.

"You won't have to be driving them every day from that location, Toots. They'll all be able to walk to school until all four of them graduate from high school," he said proudly as he described the new lot. "And I located our new church, Our Lady of Loretto Catholic Church. It's just a mile away," he added.

Joe decided that he wanted to build the house himself. He had always loved working with his hands, especially in carpentry. To build the house he would have to have a contractor's license, so he took two days off and studied from morning until night in the San Bernardino Public Library for the licensing exam. True to his usual ability to succeed at everything he undertook, he passed the examination and was issued his California Contractor's License.

He was becoming increasingly eager to leave the Air Force and begin building our house. It would be the first house we had ever owned. He gave the family a choice: stay in San Bernardino while he built the house, or live in the camper near the new location. Our unanimous choice, strongly supported by me, was to live in the camper while the house was being built.

We packed up our belongings, and this time we hired a service to clean the house we'd been renting. Joe took the remaining weeks of his accrued leave time and we left Norton, prior to the date of his official retirement. We drove the two cars to Novato, I in the station wagon towing the camper, and Joe leading the way in the Volkswagen. The kids took turns, one at a time, riding with Joe. They saw it as a real treat to be leading the way in the Volkswagen with their dad. After two and a half days we found a camper and trailer park in Petaluma, a few miles north of Novato. The park had showers, restrooms, and laundry facilities—just what we needed. There was also a pool, which I knew would be a godsend for the kids that summer. Joe hired a contractor to work with him and to help select the sub-contractors. Then construction on the new house began.

The date of the official retirement ceremony to be held back at Norton Air Force Base approached. The kids and I talked about what we could do for their father to recognize the significance of that day, since Joe had no intention of flying back to Norton for the ceremony. The four children composed, signed, and framed a Certificate of Merit. The certificate stated that it "Commends Lieutenant Colonel Joseph R. Guth for his Exceptional Performance as Father and Head of His Family." We surprised him by presenting it at a private "ceremony" in front of the camper. Joe was grinning from ear to ear as each of the four kids said a few words of congratulations to their dad. The date was July 6, 1969. This certificate still hangs in his home office today.

*   *   *   *

TOUCHDOWN:

THERE IS LIFE AFTER THE AIR FORCE

1969-1998

* * * *

Chapter Twenty-Two

CIVILIAN LIFE

The seventy-nine days we spent living in the camper while Joe built our house was another adventure in itself. Every morning bright and early before the kids were awake Joe would get up, go down to the community men's showers and get shaved, showered, and dressed. Each day he woke either young Joe or John to get up and go with him to help with the house-building. As the project progressed, he started taking both boys with him every day. Joey was now almost fifteen, John thirteen.

One day when they got back to the camper, John exclaimed, "Mom, Joe and I both got to hammer in the floors to our own rooms!" Our house plan was for each of the kids to have their own bedroom, which would double as their study rooms. The three boys would share a bathroom, and Lesley would have her own half-bathroom close to her bedroom. The master suite was on the opposite side of the house from the kids' wing. Though it would be a rather modest house on a quiet residential street close to the schools, it was a unique and innovative plan for a family with four kids.

The two older boys were getting acquainted with the contractors and construction workers of the building project, and often had funny stories to tell about their workday. I would pack a big lunch for them in the morning, with plenty of snacks and cold drinks for them to have during their day. One day while the roofers were at the site it came time for the lunch break. Joe and the two boys opened their lunch boxes and discovered that I'd forgotten to put forks in their lunch for the salads I had made for them. The construction workers and roofers, also on their lunch breaks, thought this was funny, and ribbed Joe about it.

"Now what are you gonna do, Joe?" one of them asked. Without saying a word, Joe took one of the roof shingles, and broke it into six long pieces. He then proceeded to cut and whittle each piece until he had six very narrow sticks. Giving a pair of the sticks to each of his sons and himself, he began to eat his salad, using the shingle sticks as chopsticks. Joey and John, though not very adept with chopsticks, proceeded to follow suit. The workers who had been watching looked at each other, then at Joe, then back at each other. "I've never seen anyone do that before!" one said. And the crew never said anything more about any missing forks in lunch boxes.

The lot which Joe had bought for the house was a third of an acre which had sat idle for several years, due to a working well which was right in the middle of it. Joe built the house right on top of the well, and hooked up the well's pump to the landscape watering system of the house. Access to the well pump was through a trap door inside the house under one of the built-in cabinets. It was this well water which in future years enabled us to maintain our landscaping during some of California's serious droughts. The majority of homeowners were on water rationing during those times. Joe connected up the city water for our personal use, saying, "I feel better using city water for drinking, bathing, and using inside the house. Guess I'm still a city boy at heart."

As we became acquainted with our new neighbors, several of them commented on Joe's resourcefulness in building the house right on top of the well. "I'll be damned, Joe," one of them said. "No one ever thought of doing that until you came along!"

Joe seemed happy while he was building the house. Having always enjoyed woodworking, gardening, and any activity using his hands, he seemed to be thriving. He became more physically fit, and appeared more relaxed than I had ever seen him, in spite of the hard physical work of construction.

Toward the end of the construction, I began to meet with the local businesses providing the carpeting, the interior painting, the fixtures,

THE GUTH FAMILY IN FRONT OF THE HOUSE THAT JOE BUILT.

and the floor covering for the new house. It was a new experience for me, and even though we were working within a fairly small budget, I loved doing it.

Finally, the house was completed. There wasn't a tree or bush growing anywhere on the lot, but to us the house was beautiful—the first home of our own. Moving day held a special excitement for all of us. The kids all unpacked their own things and proudly went about setting up their own rooms, hanging their own wall decorations and pictures, and placing their books, memorabilia, and treasures where they wanted them. My first chore, as usual, was to get the kitchen "operational" so we could start having regular family meals. The older boys were by this time beginning to be hearty eaters, just like their father. I went to the nearby Hamilton Air Force Base commissary regularly and filled the station wagon with groceries for the week. It took a lot of cooking to keep our growing children and their father filled up.

We were fairly settled in by the kids' first day of school. Before it was time for the kids to wake up that day, Joe went to the stereo and put on a recording of John Philip Sousa marches. He turned it up to full volume, and the sound of the lively martial music filled the entire house.

Moans came from the four kids' bedrooms, and young Joe shouted, "Dad! Knock it off!"

"Okay, guys!" their father called. "Up and at 'em! It's the first day of school!"

The four gradually got used to their father's way of announcing the beginning of every school year. However, many years later, Lesley was incredulous on her first day of classes at San Francisco State University. Joe dialed the phone number in her freshman girls' dorm room, and when Lesley answered the phone, he turned up the volume on the Sousa marches. "Dad! I can't believe you!" she groaned through the phone. Her roommate told her that her dad was crazy.

Soon after we moved into that house Joe decided to build a second house, using the same floor plan, for speculation. He set up an office for himself in the garage, and employed the same contractor to help him that had helped with our house. The two of them got along well, and as a long-term resident of Novato, the other contractor had a good knowledge of the best and most reasonable sub-contractors in the area. Joe's idea was that if his second attempt at home building was successful, he might go into the business on a permanent basis.

On weekends he worked on the landscaping of our own house, drafting all four kids to help him in every way they could, according to their age and size. What developed out of their efforts was a gorgeous landscape made up of shrubs, trees, hedges, fruit trees, flowerbeds, strawberry and blackberry patches, and a vegetable garden.

After the landscaping project came the bricklaying project. Lesley and Dan's job was to carry buckets of sand to Joe and the two boys to pour between the bricks. Mine was to drive out to the brickyard once a week while Joe was working on the other house and, with the help of the kids, load the back of the station wagon with bricks. Joe and his children laid a brick floor across the full width of our house in back. They then enclosed it with huge arched windows overlooking the gardens, creating a beautiful sunroom that stayed bright and sunny most of the time. These projects took every weekend of the first couple of years we lived there. But what we had when it was completed were a front and backyard that were the envy of the neighborhood, plus a beautiful sunroom across the entire back of the house.

Joe surprised young Joe and John by presenting them each with a $100 bill at the end of the project. They were both overwhelmed when they opened their envelopes, each with a crisp bill and a note of appreciation from their dad inside. Years later our boys were forced to admit, "I didn't realize how much I was learning about doing building and landscaping while Dad was making us do all that stuff!"

After several weeks the construction of the second house was completed. That house was slow to sell, and Joe began to realize that it was not a good time to go into the building business.

I started doing substitute teaching in the public schools in Novato. Although I was called into all grade levels to teach, most of the classes I substituted for were in junior high.

One day I came home from teaching and found a note on the kitchen table: "Gil: I've gone into San Francisco to talk to a headhunter. Back in time for dinner. Joe."

"A headhunter," I thought. "He must be thinking about going to work in the city."

When Joe returned home we sat down at the kitchen table and he said, "The construction business is just too uncertain right now. I've signed up with a couple of headhunters who both think that, with my MBA, I shouldn't have any trouble getting a job with some company as a controller or financial manager."

We sent Joe's resumes out in answer to countless newspaper ads. I typed his letters of response to attach to the resumes, and soon he was being called in for interviews.

One day he came home from an interview that he had been particularly excited about and said, "I can't believe that guy I met with. He read my resume, looked up at me and said, 'A retired Air Force officer, eh? I'm not interested in talking with you. You guys are all alike... think you own the world just because of the stuff you did while you were in the service.'"

Joe said he was stunned, but also angered by the man's remarks. That evening he told me, "I think it's really important for me to de-sanitize my image, so that I don't come across as some former Air Force hotshot who can't get over his military experiences."

I wasn't sure what he meant by "de-sanitizing," but I gradually came to understand that he was referring to his desire not to play up his accomplishments as a pilot and an officer, because he knew that they were irrelevant in terms of the business world. We redid his resume, emphasizing the training he had received in his MBA program and in the six years of service in the Air Force which had followed, maximizing those business skills. We also emphasized his more recent experience as a licensed California contractor. He also let his hair grow out from the military haircut he had always worn.

Soon Joe was hired as the controller of a construction and property management company, a job he threw himself into wholeheartedly.

In February of 1973 the Prisoners of War of the North Vietnamese were released and flown to the U.S. As we watched the event on the news, we recognized several of our jubilant friends as they celebrated on the C-141 transport planes bringing them home. One of them was John Stavast, who had married our son Joe's first grade teacher in France.

When Joe saw his friends' joyful faces on those planes he could hardly contain his happiness. "There's John!" he said, jumping up from his chair. John Stavast had been assigned to fly in Vietnam just six months after he and Shirley married. He was shot down and imprisoned by the North Vietnamese for almost six years. Several of the pilots who saw his aircraft go down had remarked to each other, "There's not a chance in hell that he survived." Shirley, his wife, told me she somehow knew he had not been killed. She waited for him those six long years, knowing in her heart that he had survived.

Another friend who returned was Bill Talley, who had been Joe's wingman on the 101 Voodoo deployment from Shaw Air Force Base, South Carolina, to France in 1959. He had been a POW in Hanoi for over a year. When Joe spotted him on the TV, he again leaped into the air saying, "It's Bill! There he is!"

We saw Leo Thorsness' return. "It's Leo!" Joe shouted. He had flown the F-84F Thunderstreak with Joe at Turner Air Force base in Albany, Georgia. I remembered Joe's letter from Ramey Air Force Base in Puerto Rico, describing Leo Thorsness and Harry Archuleta "dancing" in celebration at the pilots' party the night Joe walked away from what could have been a fatal accident. Upon his return from Hanoi, Leo Thorsness was to be awarded the Medal of Honor, the nation's highest military decoration. We would see him years later, and he still remembered "dancing" the samba with Harry that night in Puerto Rico in 1956.

We called each of the wives whose husbands we knew and recognized on TV and those whose names we recognized in the newspaper. The joy we shared during that time could only be dimmed by thoughts of those who didn't return. Some had died in prison, like our friend Ed Atterbury. Some were listed as Missing In Action (MIA), and some still remain so listed.

The return of the POW's was the answer to years of hopes and prayers, and was one of the most joyful times we ever shared.

Joe continued working as a controller in the construction and management field for several years, until he made a change to a large property management firm. He worked in that firm for twenty years, and was the executive vice president of the company.

The children began to excel, each in their own way. Young Joe continued to be an accomplished student. He was taught to play golf by his dad, and became very good at it. He made his first hole-in-one while on the high school golf team. John learned to play handball from his father and became an excellent player, later becoming a nationally rated handball player. Lesley, always an excellent swimmer, was on the high school diving team and the gymnastics team as well. Dan played Little League baseball, and junior high school football, and a little later he took up golf. His dad taught him the game's finer points, and he took to it enthusiastically and skillfully. Dan and John both ran with their dad in the "Bay to Breakers" race several times, a race held every year, and extending from the San Francisco Ferry Building, across the city out to the ocean. It soon appeared that all four of our children had inherited much of their father's competitive spirit.

In 1974 Joe's mother moved from St. Louis to a retirement center close to our home. We frequently brought her to our house for weekends, and were delighted as she became a real part of the family.

As Joe pursued his civilian career and the two older boys were leaving for college, I began to realize that I would soon be facing an empty nest.

JOE, AGE 61, IN THE SF BAY TO BREAKERS.

Lesley and Dan would be finishing high school in a few years and then they, too, would probably be leaving for college. I thought about what I would be doing with my time when that occurred, and realized that I had not really explored or pursued any of my own interests for many years. Lesley was now fourteen, and Dan was thirteen. I was forty-four.

Young Joe, the accomplished student, won many scholastic awards in high school and the University of California at Berkeley. He completed his BA in biochemistry there as a Phi Beta Kappa, went on for a PhD in biochemistry at the University of Wisconsin, and then to New York University Law School. John received an appointment to the Air Force Academy. We were very proud of both of them. Joe and I visited John at the Academy for "Parents' Weekend," and were very much impressed with the grandeur of the place and the academic and athletic programs there. John, always a sports enthusiast, was on the Academy handball team and the intramural cross-country team. The whole family attended his graduation from the Academy. My mother, whom the children still called Mimi, went also, along with my aunt Catherine. It was a proud moment for all of us.

One evening, I said to Joe, "Lesley and Dan are in junior high school now, and old enough that I can be gone sometimes during the day. I'm thinking about going back to school for my master's degree."

Joe looked up from his paper, grinning broadly, and responded, "Toots, I think that's a great idea! I know you've wanted to do that for a long time. Find out where you can go, and let's do it!"

I settled on a small private college not far from our town, called Dominican University. It had a beautiful, bucolic setting, and I could drive to it within a few minutes from our home. Since most graduate classes were in the evening, I spent most of the day in the college library doing my assigned reading and class projects, to avoid the distractions of being in my house where there were always chores to do. At first I was shy about speaking up in my classes, and my study habits were very rusty. But gradually I began to feel my confidence returning.

One of the most gratifying comments from one of my professors was the following message which he wrote on one of my term papers, which I have kept ever since: "The time is approaching when you no longer will feel it necessary to apologize for your own level of understanding."

My return home from classes was often not until ten at night or later. Joe was very supportive of my endeavor, and did all he could to make the two years pass smoothly for me.

After two years the comprehensive examination was to take place. I studied day and night in preparation for it. My close friend, Gail Laird, whom I had met in one of my classes, studied for hours with me in the college library. We quizzed each other on questions we knew would be asked. Happily, we both passed the comprehensives and were awarded a master's degree in education, a degree which had the potential of taking us in many directions. Joe and three of our four children proudly attended the graduation ceremony, held on the beautiful grounds of the college. The only one missing was John, who was still away at the Air Force Academy at the time. After the ceremony, Gail's family and ours met at our home to celebrate Gail's and my achievement. It was a proud moment. She and I remain close friends to this day.

The night after graduation, we had a little celebration dinner at home with just our family. There was a large envelope on my plate. To my great amazement and surprise, the envelope contained details about a luxurious cruise to Mexico... a graduation gift from Joe. I was speechless. It was a completely unexpected, wonderful gift. I was deeply touched, and I couldn't hold back the tears of happiness.

The direction of work I chose was the field of career counseling, which led to an unusual and very rewarding career. The Vietnam War had just ended around the time of my graduation, and the influx of Southeast Asian refugees was beginning. I was doing my master's degree internship at the nearby community college, and in January of 1976, large numbers of Southeast Asian refugees began enrolling there. They were among the first refugees to escape from Vietnam when Saigon fell, and they were eager to learn English as soon as possible. Many of them were highly educated in their own country: teachers, pharmacists, architects, and doctors. Many of them were "boat people."

One day in a counselors' meeting I asked, "What can we do to help all the refugees who are enrolling?"

The head counselor's reply was, "Gil, why don't you put together a program for them?"

The answer took me aback, but I dove into the assignment wholeheartedly and was soon meeting with the refugees several times a week, an endeavor which turned out to be one of the richest experiences of my life. My friend Gail soon joined me in the work and together we made some wonderful friends with this group of newcomers who had endured so much. Three years later I was hired to design and implement a complete employment services program for Southeast Asian refugees in San Francisco. We assisted refugees from Vietnam, Cambodia, and Laos to find work in their new home. I loved my job. I loved the Southeast Asian people. Some of the stories they told me of their escape to freedom were awe-inspiring, and I will never forget them.

In 1980 Joe's mother died. We all flew back to St. Louis to bury her next to Joe's father. It was the first time our children had seen their father cry. She had become such an integral part of the family, and there was a real void left after her passing.

That same year, Joe's pilot class of 52-Charlie held its first reunion. It was in Memphis, arranged by Joe's pal Howard. Since then, the pilots of 52-Charlie class have met every two years, and we attended almost all of them. I found it a wonderful opportunity to be with the wives of these men, many of whom had become some of my closest friends. Joe chaired the 1992 reunion of 52-Charlie in San Francisco. The 101 Voodoo pilots also began having reunions, and it is always good to be with the friends who were with us in France for three years.

I've attended U.S. Air Force, Marine, and Navy pilots' reunions. Watching the interaction between the pilots at these reunions has always touched me. I had become aware that military aviators exhibit an exclusivity and "esprit de corps" unlike any other organization or fraternity I had seen. When they first greet each other, sometimes after years, there are bear hugs, joyous laughter, and broad smiles, and much pounding on the back. The years fade away as they exchange tales of flying feats and near-misses.

Joe once said to me that "the bullets get closer and the stories get more spectacular every time we meet."

I was at a reunion of Air Force Forward Air Controllers, pilots who had flown some of the most hazardous missions of the Vietnam War. I sat facing one of them when he saw a fellow pilot walking toward the table. His face paled as he jumped up and rushed toward his comrade, his arms outstretched.

"I thought you'd been killed!" he cried, bursting into tears. The two men embraced emotionally. I'll always remember the look on that pilot's face as he held in his arms the friend he thought he had lost.

Years after we started attending these events, I would be at a reunion of Vietnamese fighter pilots. There were about 400 of them there, from all over the world. Some of them hadn't seen each other in thirty years, since their country of South Vietnam had fallen to Communist North Vietnam.

"This could be a reunion of American fighter pilots," I thought to myself as I sat at the banquet, watching them greet each other. They

DRAWN BY COL. LARRY GARDNER, CLASS OF 52-C, NOW DECEASED.

52 CHARLIE
C/O JOE GUTH
60 Corte Patencio
Greenbrae, California 94904
(415) 461-8660

Pilot Class 1952 Members, Relatives, Friends:

Welcome to the Reunion of the Pilot Class of 1952.

This is a memorable occasion and I hope each of you will join in the celebration of our graduation from pilot school 40 years ago. I know we will all celebrate with appropriate enthusiasm and vigor. This occasion is also a time for us to pause for a moment or two and reflect on our good fortune. We were fortunate to be given the opportunity to learn to fly and when we became pilots, we became members of a very select group. Not many are given that opportunity and fewer still earn those coveted wings. I know each of us wore those wings proudly and, as we did, they became a permanent part of what we were. They showed everyone who saw us our achievement and what we had become.

But more important than the symbol of what those wings meant to others, was what those wings meant to us. Those wings confirmed our belief in ourselves, reformed our self image and made us conscious of belonging to a select group. They changed us forever.

Pilot training was one of the most intense, unforgettable and influential experiences of our lives. And, a large part of that experience, the part that keeps coming back again and again, is the others we served with. The bonds that grew then were more than friendship, they were uncommon bonds forged under unusual conditions. Often, when you try to remember those experiences and the pilots you served with, there are some blank spots because no one is around to remember them with you and there is a lot you have forgotten. Friends and family may have long ago begun to yawn over old war stores, never realizing the subtle, yet profound, influence those experiences and bonds had on you. This reunion offers you a chance to remember, fill in the blanks, rediscover long-lost friends, compare experiences, be with those who understand and finally put in the proper perspective that most profound and powerful part of your life.

We're almost ready to celebrate. The last pause in our remembrance is for those comrades who have fallen along the way. We shall not forget any of them for they were part of the comraderie that grew in that favored group.

Now it's time to celebrate.

Let's do it!

Cheers,

Joe Guth

Joe Guth
San Francisco, California

May 28, 1992

THE LETTER JOE INCLUDED IN THE 52-CHARLIE REUNION PACKET.

exhibited the same camaraderie, pride, and enthusiasm that I'd seen at so many American pilots' reunions. I watched their wives, delicate, beautiful, exquisitely dressed, many of them in their traditional *ao dai,* or "long dress."

I realized that these wives endured many of the same anxieties of American pilots' wives. And these women had endured even more, watching their country fall, escaping with only their children and their lives. Some of these people, both men and women, endured years in the "re-education camps" of the Communist regime before finally getting to the United States. And then they had to start all over, in a new country, with a new language and culture, possibly never to return to their native land.

I was struck by the patriotism and pride exhibited as the program unfolded that evening. The flags of both countries were displayed as "The Star-Spangled Banner" was played, followed by the Vietnamese national anthem, its somber oriental tones filling the room, and then a military ceremony honoring fallen comrades. Looking around the room, I saw many of the Vietnamese men wiping their eyes with their handkerchiefs.

The evening proceeded on a happier note, with music, speeches, and squadrons standing up and shouting with pride when they were named, and the ongoing socializing, bear-hugging, and back-pounding as those Vietnamese fighter pilots circulated around the room.

Though I couldn't understand a word of the speeches, I understood every feeling and emotion that was expressed that evening.

The year that Joe Guth chaired the Class of 52-Charlie reunion in San Francisco, he placed a personal letter in each attendee's program packet, an example of the bond that exists between the men who wear the wings of the military pilot (see page 357).

In the early 1980s I was hired to develop an employment service program similar to the one in San Francisco. It was in the town of Novato, serving the entire community. I continued in that capacity for the next ten years, becoming a real part of the community and making many friends.

In 1992, soon after we hosted the 52-Charlie reunion in San Francisco, news came out about American soldiers and pilots being held in Russia, Korea, and Vietnam.

A list was released, naming 125 men previously declared killed in Korea. Two of those named were two of Joe's closest friends in pilot class 52-Charlie who were thought to have been killed. They were friends that Joe had written me about from Korea. He was extremely upset by this news.

Our journalist daughter, who at that time was a writer on a Bay Area newspaper called the *Vacaville Reporter*, wrote a Veteran's Day piece about her dad and his reaction to this news:

> *My dad is one of the strongest people I know. Over the years I've seen him cry once: at my grandmother's funeral. This year, I've seen tears come to his eyes a half-dozen times as he has contemplated the fate of his comrades and what might have been.*
>
> *Last year at this time, I called my dad to wish him a happy Veterans Day. He said it was the first time anyone had acknowledged his service in three wars. Today is Veterans Day. I'm going to call him again.*

Joe had no thoughts of total retirement from his job. He loved working, loved the challenge of handling the financial management of his company. As my retirement age approached, however, I decided that I would step down. I hoped that Joe would begin to take more time off and that perhaps he and I could do some traveling, since the children were now all grown, launched in their careers, and beginning to marry. Young Joe entered the field of patent law, combining his backgrounds in both science and law. John, after leaving the Air Force, completed his MBA at Pepperdine University and went into the field of business consulting. Lesley completed a BA in journalism and was becoming quite accomplished in that field. Dan was beginning a successful career in the field of telecommunications. We were very proud of the accomplishments of our four children.

For our fortieth anniversary in April of 1993, our four children surprised us with a portrait of Joe and me which they had asked Joe's brother Jack to paint for us. Without our knowing it, they sent some photos of us to Jack, and he combined two of them: one was the portrait of myself I had sent to Joe the Christmas he was in Korea. The other was

FAMILY CELEBRATES JOE AND GILBERTA'S 40TH ANNIVERSARY
(PAINTING BY JOE'S BROTHER, JACK GUTH).

of Joe climbing out of his plane. Jack superimposed one upon the other, and created a lovely and very unusual portrait of us. We all went to Lesley's house for a cookout on our anniversary, and the four kids presented us with the portrait painted by Jack. Joe and I were speechless and overcome with emotion when we saw it. It was a wonderful surprise.

On the New Year's Eve before my retirement in 1995, Joe took me to a lovely restaurant for dinner and dancing. On the table in front of me a card had been placed, and opening it, I read his note saying that he was planning to take me to Hawaii for two weeks following my retirement in March. I was overwhelmed by the wonderful surprise. On the dance floor, holding me tight, he said, "I'm proud of you, Gil, for all you've done and all you've accomplished." I remember it as one of the happiest evenings of my life.

The retirement party given for me at the agency where I worked was filled with good wishes, cards, and gifts. Our two younger children were there, and spoke a few words, and the two other children had written their comments to be read aloud at the occasion.

And then Joe rose to speak. His words were loving and full of fun and upbeat comments about the plans I had for my new life after retirement. He spoke of the traveling we were planning to do in the coming months, beginning with the two-week trip to Hawaii.

The two weeks in Hawaii that April were relaxing and breathtaking. I felt like Joe and I were beginning a wonderful new phase of our life together—with all the children married and involved in their careers, our financial future assured, and our health perfect.

We returned from Hawaii on our forty-second anniversary, April 19, 1995 to find three urgent phone messages from Joe's doctor. Joe had undergone a routine checkup just before our trip. His doctor was urging him to come back in as soon as possible.

* * * *

Chapter Twenty-Three

THE FINAL CHAPTER

The day of Joe's medical appointment came. He had left to see his doctor before going into work that morning, and I was doing the breakfast dishes when I heard his car roar back into the garage.

I held his hand and cried as he told me what the doctor had found. He would need to have prostate cancer surgery within the next couple of months. A few days later we went into San Francisco for a second opinion and the diagnosis was verified.

In the ensuing days I got ahold of every book about Joe's illness that I could get my hands on. Between us, we read them all and reported back to each other about what we learned; we were determined to learn as much about his illness as possible.

"I want to wait to tell the kids in person," he said. The family was planning a reunion at his brother Jack's home in Jerome, Arizona in May. "I'll tell each of them individually when we're at Jack's."

The family reunion was also the grand opening of Jack's new art gallery. A talented artist, Jack had turned to his art full time after his retirement from the U.S. Coast and Geodetic Survey. Our kids and Jack's all flew in, and many of Jack's college and service friends were there. It was a joyful, festive event. But for Joe and me there was a cloud of worry hanging over us. After the gallery opening, both families went together to a mountain retreat for a few days. It was there that Joe took his brother and each of his children aside individually and privately told them that he was facing prostate cancer surgery the following month.

The kids and Jack were all as stunned at the news as we had been. How could this be? Joe was the picture of good health. He still had the trim, firm build of a thirty-year-old. This news was totally sudden, unexpected and devastating.

The day of his surgery came, June 6, 1995. Joe said, "I want to do it on that date, just to prove I'm not superstitious."

June 6 was not only the anniversary of D-Day, but June 6, 1962 was also the date that his father had passed away. I waited outside the operating room during his surgery. His doctor emerged smiling, and said, "It went very well. He should be just fine now. He'll be ready to go home in a couple of days."

His "couple of days" never came. He developed complications which sent him into the Intensive Care Unit, onto a respirator and complete life support system.

"He's developed acute pancreatitis, a severe inflammation of the pancreas," we were told. "He is unable to breathe normally, so he has gone into pneumonia, and his kidneys have failed. So we'll have to keep him on life support until hopefully he can make it on his own."

"Doctor," I pleaded, "why has this happened?"

"We aren't sure. But an allergic reaction to either the anesthesia or the pain killer might have caused his pancreas to go crazy."

Our four children came in and out of the hospital constantly. The eldest, Joe, lived in New York City at the time, John in southern California. They were both flying in and out of San Francisco every few days. Lesley and her husband, Robert, and Dan, with his wife Joanne, were coming to the hospital every day after work. I was there from early morning until late at night.

After ten days the decision was made to transfer Joe by ambulance to the University of California at San Francisco Medical Center. There was a world-famous specialist there who might be able to save him.

On the day of the transfer we had a Mass said for Joe's recovery at the church across from the hospital. During the service the family all sat together, gripping hands, praying that his life would be spared. Then it was time for him to be transferred from the nearby hospital to San Francisco.

We all followed as he was being wheeled into the hospital elevator. Dan, walking beside the gurney, gave a thumbs-up to his father and said,

"You'll be okay, Top Gun! Way to go, Top Gun!" Because he was still hooked up to the respirator and other life support equipment, we didn't know if he could hear us or see us.

The four kids, their spouses, and I cried as the medics transferred Joe, still on life support, into the fully equipped ambulance for the ride into San Francisco. "We'll take care of him!" the driver assured us as they closed the ambulance door and pulled away. We all held hands and stood weeping as we watched the ambulance speed away from the hospital parking lot. Then we jumped in our cars and drove to San Francisco.

When we arrived at UC Medical Center in the city, Joe had already been connected to the life support system in the Intensive Care Unit. In the days following, the four kids and I were in and out of the hospital constantly. All of us camped in the visitor's lounge, trying to catch a couple of hours of sleep but not wanting to leave the hospital while Joe was in ICU. One or two of us at a time would sit in Joe's small area in the ICU, watching the gauges record his breathing and other vital signs, watching him and hoping for any sign of improvement.

After two days it was decided that he would undergo surgery to clear out the infection in his pancreas, which was still raging out of control. One of the residents spoke to us afterwards: "The next forty-eight hours should tell the story."

Joe's brother Jack and my half-sister Donna flew in. A few days later a second surgery was performed. Several more days passed before it looked like he was going to survive.

After four weeks in ICU at UCSF, he was transferred to a hospital room where he remained for two more weeks. Since the life support equipment had been disconnected, he could now talk to us. I stayed in his room constantly, every day—sometimes until late at night. Sometimes I stayed overnight, sleeping on the unbelievably uncomfortable guest bed beside him. I called it "the torture rack," too short for an adult, narrow, and hard as a rock. But it didn't matter, since I couldn't sleep anyway. I would get up and watch the night nurse or the aides when they came in throughout the night to tend to Joe. I needed to learn how to take care of him once we went home. The kids and I were in touch constantly. Young Joe and John continued to fly in often, and Lesley and Dan came in every day. Joe's Air Force friends and business associates were calling for the latest on his condition, and neighbors were leaving messages inquiring about him. Joe's body became totally decimated during those months. The way he looked reminded me of the terrible pictures of men walking out of the concentration camps after the end of World War II. He had a huge scar from his sternum down to several inches below his navel.

After weeks of not knowing what the outcome would be, the day of his release finally came. We were all beginning to feel the sense of relief that now, at last, we knew that he would be all right.

The day Joe was to be released, his doctor came into the room and told him, "It's okay for you to leave the hospital now. We'll send you to a rehabilitation hospital near your home for a week or two so you can regain some strength. Then you can go home. But there's another problem."

We sat stunned as he told us that during surgery to save Joe's life, a biopsy had been taken which revealed a very rare, slow-growing form of cancer, called a carcinoid.

"It's a very peculiar type of malignancy," the doctor confirmed. "It's an extremely slow-growing thing, and it's likely something else will get you before this does, Joe. I would expect you to live your normal life span. So just go home and start regaining your strength. We've shown Gilberta how to take care of you. You'll be fine."

I felt numb with shock and dismay. After all he had been through, after all the family had endured together, and just when we thought he was out of the woods, we now had to face this new, unknown future. It almost felt like we would be waiting for the other shoe to drop.

The ambulance then took Joe to the rehab hospital, where he was to have daily physical therapy. Driving from the city, all I could think of was the doctor's news.

Joe worked hard in the rehabilitation hospital. He did his exercises faithfully, and tried to eat, even though taking food remained difficult for him. I went there daily, with fresh clothes for him, and the "get well" cards which were pouring into the house. Friends were calling him every day, and a few came to visit him. He came home after about ten days. I had done some redecorating in the house, and had put flowers everywhere to welcome him home.

"The house looks beautiful!" Joe exclaimed as we walked in. The nurses had taught me how to care for him as his wounds healed and he began to regain his strength. Little by little he started to rebuild his body, at first just walking around inside the house and out onto the deck for a few minutes, until he would go back to his bed, exhausted.

Then we started taking walks in the nearby park. At first we would stop every few yards at one of the park benches so that Joe could rest. And then he became able to walk halfway through the park, rest, and then walk back out. Thanksgiving came, and he asked Dan and John to go with him to pick out a weight machine so he could start working out at home.

By the time the holidays were over Joe had started going in to work for a few hours every day. He still tired easily, but he was working out on the new equipment every morning. With his usual determination he began to regain his strength and stamina. Within a few months, though still quite thin, he had built himself up to the point that he was working full time. Shortly after that, he returned to his beloved game of golf. With his unflagging discipline and perseverance he soon was playing with his accustomed high level of skill. Soon afterwards he was named captain of his golf team. It appeared that the doctor's prediction was correct, that this newly discovered illness was not going to present an immediate health problem for him.

However, two years after his original surgery, his health suddenly took a turn for the worse. He couldn't maintain his weight. He started to have problems with pain. He began to grow weaker. It was like a downward spiral that he couldn't pull out of. Soon he could only work for a few hours each day. He wrote a letter to his golf club, and resigned as a member and as team captain. In response, he received a letter telling him that his resignation was not accepted, and that they would await his return to lead their team on to future victories.

Together we tried everything we could to keep his weight up, but nothing helped. I learned about a doctor in Albuquerque who specialized in Joe's illness. We flew there with high hopes that he might be accepted for clinical trials which were being conducted internationally under that specialist's leadership. We stayed there with our friends Becky and Charlie Graves. It was March 1998.

There were two days of tests before Joe's appointment to see the doctor. When we weren't at the hospital he was resting back at Becky and Charlie's house. Finally, we met with the doctor, with high hopes and expectations.

Our hopes were soon dashed to the ground when the doctor said to Joe, "Unfortunately you won't qualify to be in the clinical trials because certain conditions exist in your situation which disqualify you. There are a couple of treatments which you might try. They don't have a very high level of success, however, and they do have very severe side effects."

We then left Albuquerque and came home. With a heavy heart, I called the doctor back and asked him what his prognosis was. He replied, "Weeks, maybe months. Not years." I felt despondent, but did my best to keep up a strong, optimistic attitude. I was praying for a miracle, hoping against hope that Joe's condition wouldn't continue getting worse.

The forty-sixth reunion of his 52-Charlie pilot class was held that May at the Air Force Academy in Colorado Springs. Joe had never missed a reunion. I wasn't sure he was strong enough to make the trip this time.

"I'm goin'!" he said determinedly. It was apparent to everyone there that he was very, very ill, but he loved being there with buddies from his flying days. He rested in our hotel room between events, but always showed up, relishing the camaraderie and the friendly pilot banter.

He told me one day that he had driven to the little cemetery near our home, and liked the way it looked. "But I don't want one of those headstones that lie flat on the ground. And I want to be up on a hill, so I can have some perspective." He also told me that he wanted to be buried from our Catholic church.

I felt like my heart was broken "right down the middle," as our friend had said so many years before. Joe's words told me that he knew he didn't have much longer to live.

I called the church rectory the next day, and a voice answered, "This is Father William."

"Father," I said, "I'd like to come and talk to a priest about a family matter."

"How about right now?" he answered. I went over to the church immediately, and Father William Myers met me at the door.

"Come in and sit down," he said, shaking my hand. I immediately felt that I was talking to the person I needed. His warm smile and his kindness reassured me that he would understand as I started pouring out my heart to him.

"Would you like for me to come and visit Joe?" he asked.

"Yes, I would, Father," I responded. "Let me ask him and I'll call you back." Father William came to visit a few days later, and I sensed that Joe liked him and gained much comfort from him.

Joe went back to work each day for a few hours, still determined to keep going. He would come home and fall on the bed for the rest of the afternoon, exhausted. And then in mid-July the doctor prescribed morphine for his pain, and he knew that he could not go into work again.

Jack and his wife came, as did our sons and daughter. Dan went with me to talk with the people in the cemetery office, and to pick a gravesite. As we drove into the cemetery, Dan said, "Remember Mom, we have to 'move into a different zone' when we take care of these details."

When John arrived from southern California, he and Dan went with me to the funeral home across the street from the church. We made the necessary arrangements, not knowing exactly when we would need to carry out the plans. The kids stayed all day and all night for days, sleeping all over the house, in the guestroom, on couches, on the floor. Through it all Joe never lost his indomitable spirit.

Our sons Dan and John, and Joe and I were sitting in the patio one day. An unusual bird flew into the yard, and in an attempt at making conversation, Dan said, "I wonder what kind of bird that is."

Without missing a beat, and in all seriousness, Joe said, "That's a red-breasted mattress thrasher." Dan and John looked at each other and suddenly burst out laughing at their father's unexpected pun.

Another day, sitting outdoors with our daughter Lesley, Joe commented, "I'm ready to go, but nothing's happening!" A plane flew overhead just then. Joe leaned back in his chair, looking up at it, and watched it until it flew out of sight.

The nurse from Hospice came regularly to check on him. One day Joe said to her, "I feel like I'm dying."

"You are, Joe," she responded softly. He nodded, and said nothing.

My heart was breaking, but somehow I was able to keep going. Probably that adrenaline again, and fervent prayer.

A few days later he was growing so weak he was unable to leave his bed. Soon he drifted into a semi-coma. The Hospice nurses told us that we should keep talking to him, because he could probably hear us even though he was unable to respond. We were usually all in the room with him, but each one of us also spent time alone with him.

I was sitting at his bedside one day with Lesley standing nearby. Joe opened his eyes and reached up as if to put his arm around me.

"I love...," he said, unable to finish his thought. His arm dropped, and he closed his eyes. We never heard him speak again.

Father William came and gave Joe the Last Rites. He conducted a moving service at Joe's bedside. Then he asked each one of us to speak to Joe and to tell him how we felt about him.

"I love you, Joe," I told him through my tears.

Dan, our youngest, said, "Thanks, Dad, for teaching me how to be a man."

John said, "You weren't a perfect father, Dad, but I wasn't a perfect son."

Young Joe and Lesley could only say, "I love you, Dad."

Through my tears I murmured, "I love you, Joe. I'll always love you."

Then Father asked that each one of us spend five or ten minutes alone with Joe, speaking to him about anything that was in our hearts. Each one proceeded to do as he suggested.

In my private moment with him I told him how much I loved him. I said that even through the tough times I had always loved him. I told him that I would remember the good times, and love him forever.

Gradually, he drifted into a full coma.

We were all with him when he died in our home on August 6, 1998 at 2:14 in the morning. It was just three weeks short of his seventy-fourth birthday.

Joe Guth was buried with full military honors at the small cemetery near our house, following a funeral Mass at our nearby church, conducted by Father William. All of the men in the family wore one of Joe's dress ties in tribute and each of the four children spoke about their father. Our son Joe read the following quote which he and his brothers had found in a small wooden box in Joe's office:

The cockpit was my office. It was a place where I experienced many emotions and learned many lessons. It was a place of work, but also a keeper of dreams. It was a place of deadly serious encounters, yet there I discovered much about life. I learned about joy and sorrow, pride and humility, and fear, and overcoming fear. I saw much from that office that most people would never see. At times it terrified me, yet I could always feel at home there. It was my place at that time in space, and the jet was mine for those moments. Though it was a place where I could quickly die, the cockpit was a place where I truly lived.
(Author Unknown)

His tombstone was designed by his four children. On it is inscribed an image of the 101 Voodoo plane and the words "Top Gun," in honor of his great love of flying, and his love for his favorite airplane. We visit his gravesite frequently, and as we stand at that place there never fails to be a plane flying overhead, preparing to land at the small regional airfield nearby.

In the ensuing weeks and months our children and close friends rallied to help me deal with my loss. Each of the kids visited regularly, or invited me to their homes. Friends invited me to dinner or lunch. The first Christmas after Joe died John brought a bottle of Banyuls, the Spanish port that Joe and I had learned to enjoy in France. The love of our children and close friends, and my deep faith were what helped me survive the dark tunnel of grief that was engulfing me. I sought solace by trying to establish a new routine, attending daily Mass, going to the gym every day, seeing family and friends and regularly meeting with Father William, who continued to counsel and encourage me.

"Gilberta," he would say, "I don't know what is going to happen, but I just know there is something wonderful ahead for you." I didn't believe him, and kept telling him that I really thought my life was over. But he never stopped encouraging me and telling me to have faith and know that God's will would be done.

About a year after Joe's death the Veteran's Administration determined that his fatal illness could have been related to the nuclear radiation to which he was exposed during the atomic test he witnessed in the Nevada desert in April 1953.

I could never have dreamed that the event that brought about the beginning of this love story would also bring about the ending.

* * * *

EPILOGUE

Over the next few years following Joe's death I relied heavily upon the support of my family, my friends, and my faith, as I attempted to find a new way of being in the world without Joe. I felt as though I would never be really happy again.

Among the friends who wrote notes and called occasionally was Joe's old friend and pilot classmate, Howard Pierson. A week before he died, Joe had requested that Howard deliver the eulogy at his funeral. Howard spoke at the vigil service the evening before, and at Joe's funeral Mass. He presented me with the flag at Joe's military burial. He wrote to each of my four children and me after the funeral, and he called periodically to see how we were doing.

We saw each other occasionally at military reunions, which I attended in order to see old friends and stay connected to Joe. A highly decorated pilot, Howard had flown over 10,000 hours in many different types of military aircraft. He had retired after a distinguished Air Force career, having flown combat in Korea and Vietnam. Like Joe, he was a veteran of three wars, having served in World War II as a seventeen-year-old in the U.S. Navy.

I remembered that he was the first friend of Joe's that I met when I arrived in Japan as a young bride. It was he whose fiancée had fallen in love with and married the first mate on her way over to marry Howard in Japan. He was the guy who brought the frozen turkey to my first

Thanksgiving dinner. Joe had given him his first jet ride while we were all in Japan, during the time that Howard was flying the B-29 Superfortress in Korea.

As the correspondence and phone calls between Howard and me continued, they gradually began to take on a different tone. But there just seemed to be too many obstacles to a romance. He was living in Dallas, caring for his father, a lively, delightful gentleman who was over 100 years old. Howard's four children were also living in Texas. Mine were all in California. It could never work.

However, as time passed, I began to think that maybe I could learn to love again—perhaps the obstacles were not insurmountable. And then what I had thought was the impossible did happen. The obstacles were not insurmountable after all. I did learn to love again.

Howard Pierson and I were married at tiny Old St. Hilary's church in Tiburon, a small town on the San Francisco Bay, on February 16, 2002.

His dad, who was going to be Howard's best man and who was going to live with us, passed away just two months before our wedding at almost 104 years of age. But his gentle spirit was strongly felt by all those at our wedding who remembered him.

At the reception, Howard offered a toast to Joe, his friend, and to Bill, his father.

My daughter Lesley, who was my Matron of Honor, also gave a toast: "There were so many obstacles that Gilberta and Howard faced: the geographical distance between them; what would the kids say; what about Howard's beloved Pop—so many concerns. But Howard and Gilberta persevered, and brought us to this moment, and reminded us all, once again, of the Power of Love."

I have been and continue to be amazed at the events chronicled in this story. I could never, ever have foretold, as a young bride in Japan, what the years would bring. As I wrote in the Prologue, it has been a life of "decades marked by happiness, joy, fear, courage, tragedy, triumph... and love."

* * * *

AFTERWORD

Hundreds of military and civilian friends continue to maintain contact, keeping the bonds of friendship alive. Flying honors awarded to Joe by the Marines were on display at the Marines' Memorial Club in downtown San Francisco for a time, and a tree was planted and dedicated to his memory in the Presidio of San Francisco National Cemetery.

Four oak trees were planted in the yard of the family home and dedicated to him by his four children.

Each year Joe's three sons and son-in-law arrange and sponsor the "Joe Guth Memorial Golf Tournament." In honor of the tournament, his brother Jack painted a portrait of Joe, depicting him in his classic golf swing.

The main tournament award is the "Joe Guth Indomitable Spirit Award," which goes to the player who "makes the best, toughest save of the round. This prize requires overcoming adversity and is not to be awarded for lucky breaks or dumb luck."

Joe Guth is well remembered. He touched everyone who knew him... his family, his military comrades, and his civilian friends. He will never be forgotten.

* * * *

IN APPRECIATION

My first words of appreciation go to my family who, from the early days and weeks of working on this book, unfailingly have encouraged and cheered me on. My three sons, Joe, John, and Dan all helped stimulate the memories that became the framework for the story. Very special thanks must go to my daughter, Lesley, herself a talented journalist, who from the very beginning generously gave of her time, expertise, and love. She and I found a lovely new dimension to our relationship… two women working together for a common goal: to tell the story of our military family's life.

The countless friends that we gained over the years, both military and civilian, have offered their enthusiasm and encouragement upon hearing of this project. Dozens of those who had shared our military life offered invaluable technical advice in providing me with accurate details about the aircraft and the flying events that are chronicled here. Many of these friends have come forward and offered wonderful written words of support. For these I am most grateful and humbled.

The dedication and efforts of our friend and computer consultant, Dave Ganapoler, deserve grateful recognition. He patiently guided me through many computer frustrations and mechanical "glitches."

My lifelong friend and classmate, John C. Waugh, himself a noted Civil War historian, has written a beautiful Foreword for which I cannot find adequate words to express my thanks.

Kudos to Nita Ybarra, award-winning designer, for the book's beautiful cover. The experience of working with Simon and Kate Warwick-Smith and Cierra Trenery of Warwick Associates has been both rewarding and fun. I thank them for their expertise, creativity, and energy in helping to bring this book to publication.

Finally, my love and thanks go to Howard Pierson.